Litigation in the Netherlands

Dutch Business Law

The series Dutch Business Law is a continuous publication in loose-leaf form under the editorial supervision of Steven R. Schuit, a former partner of Allen & Overy and professor of law at Utrecht University and at Nyenrode Business Universiteit.

This current publication is a bound edition of the series previously published in loose-leaf form.

The purpose of Dutch Business Law is to provide a good understanding of the practical implications of the relevant areas in Dutch law under consideration. The authors are seasoned practitioners, experienced in representing international clients in the Dutch legal arena.

This series makes no pretence at being a survey of the entire Dutch business law – either in scope or in substance. It contains generalisations and simplifications and cannot be regarded as presenting complete and in depth advice in the areas covered.

Litigation in the Netherlands

Civil Procedure, Arbitration and
Administrative Litigation

By

Marieke van Hooijdonk and Peter Eijsvoogel

Partners at Allen & Overy Amsterdam

Wolters Kluwer
Law & Business

Published by:
Kluwer Law International
P.O. Box 85889
2508 CN The Hague
The Netherlands
E-mail: sales@kluwerlaw.com
Website: http://www.kluwerlaw.com

Sold and distributed in North, Central and South America by:
Aspen Publishers, Inc.
7201 McKinney Circle
Frederick, MD 21704
USA
E-mail: customer.service@aspenpublishers.com

Sold and distributed in all other countries by:
Extenza-Turpin Distribution Services
Stratton Business Park
Pegasus Drive
Biggleswade
Bedfordshire SG18 8TQ
United Kingdom
E-mail: kluwerlaw@turpin-distribution.com

Printed on acid-free paper.

ISBN 978-90-411-4143-9

Printed and Bound by CPI Group (UK) Ltd, Croydon, CR0 4YY

Foreword to the First Edition

'Quick', 'informal' and 'affordable' are key words for modern procedural law in the Netherlands, and they reflect not only the character of the Dutch people but also the needs of an urbanised society. To some lawyers, coming from common law jurisdictions and getting in touch with our litigation practice, the Dutch approach can seem hasty and too informal (though remarkably cheap). Such observations may be based on the difference between common law and Continental procedural systems such as ours. Dutch civil and administrative procedural law is part of the Continental tradition in which there is no jury and the position of the court has always been relatively dominant (especially in the fact-finding process). Therefore, proceedings are less 'adversarial' than in the common law tradition and are directed by an active judge. This may explain, for instance, the immense success in our country of the '*kort geding*', civil preliminary relief proceedings. The courts had the opportunity to develop preliminary relief proceedings, originally meant for interim injunctions in the true sense, in such a way that they have become a successful alternative to the lengthy and costly ordinary proceedings on the merits. The success of the *kort geding* partly explains the courts' current preference to apply *kort geding* techniques in ordinary procedures in order to avoid lengthy and irrelevant debates.

Although some aspects of Dutch litigation certainly need upgrading (in particular the fact-finding process), the machinery of justice is in general functioning very well. The attitude of the average lawyer or judge towards procedural matters is open-minded, flexible and pragmatic. The courts are clearly focused on settling disputes at an early stage of the proceedings rather than letting them drag on for years. By issuing detailed procedural regulations which are updated regularly, the judiciary has shown that it is prepared to adapt the rules quickly to changing needs.

An increasing proportion of procedural law is determined by European legislation and by the case-law of the European Court of Justice. The growing influence of the European Convention on Human Rights and the case-law of the European Court of Human Rights is also noticeable. These are developments which will eventually lead to the harmonisation of large parts of the procedural laws of the member states of the European Union. They will also inevitably lead to a better understanding of the legal cultures of other countries.

This book provides a detailed summary of the main features of litigation in the Netherlands, whether in civil or administrative courts, or in arbitration, and will certainly aid the understanding of procedural law in this country as well as its background, traditions and values.

Daan Asser
Judge with the Dutch Supreme Court
Hoge Raad der Nederlanden
September 2008

Table of Contents

Chapter 2
Arbitration 127

Preface

'Litigation in the Netherlands' provides a practical and comprehensive guide for all foreign lawyers, businesses and individuals involved in commercial litigation in the Netherlands. Its aim is also to be a resource for Dutch lawyers who wish to advise their English-speaking clients on Dutch litigation.

As in most other Western countries, litigation in the Netherlands has increased over the years. Statistics show that since 2000 the number of commercial cases dealt with by the District Courts increased by 74% to 664,000 in 2010, the vast majority of which relates to claims brought before the cantonal division. Preliminary relief proceedings in the Netherlands are very efficient and thus popular; annually about 15,000 claims are filed in summary proceedings. Whereas litigation was previously dealt with by various departments within a firm, the bigger law firms in the Netherlands now all have specialised litigation departments.

The Global Competitiveness Report 2012-2013 of the World Economic Forum shows that out of 144 countries, the Netherlands ranks eighth as regards the efficiency of its legal framework for settling disputes. Likewise, the Rule of Law Index 2011 of The World Justice Project shows that out of 12 countries investigated in Western Europe and North America, the Netherlands ranks in the top three for access to justice.

Most litigation is still brought in the public courts. Several surveys show that, compared with other Western European countries, the period of time required to settle a case through public court proceedings in the Netherlands is relatively short. The average length of contentious proceedings in a commercial dispute in the District Court (excluding the cantonal division) is about 14 months. More than half of the cases are dealt with within 10 months. Most practitioners and parties are satisfied with the accessibility, speed, quality and consistency of the administration of justice in the Netherlands. Judges are generally viewed as being professional and impartial. The World Economic Forum Report shows that out of 144 countries, the Netherlands ranks third for judicial independence.

Since 2002, the Council for the Judiciary (*Raad voor de Rechtspraak*) has continually been reviewing and promoting the quality of the Dutch judicial system. From 1 January 2013, the number of courts will be reduced significantly; larger-scale courts will be created to enhance the quality of legal decision-making.

Since 1 July 2011, the jurisdiction of the (more informal) cantonal division of the District Courts was increased and, on 1 July 2012, two new laws regarding the functioning of the Supreme Court entered into force. In conjunction with the Ministry of Justice and the courts, the Council is also investigating the use of ICT applications in court proceedings. To date, there are only limited opportunities to submit documents electronically; however the government's aim is that in 2015, it will be possible to communicate electronically with all the courts, i.e. in civil, administrative and criminal cases.

The Code of Civil Procedure itself is also subject to ongoing review. In 2002, important changes were made to the law to improve the efficiency of civil court proceedings, to minimise formal requirements and to modernise the relationship between judges and the parties. However, the Dutch parliament was of the opinion that these reforms were only a starting point and asked for a full review of the basic principles of civil procedure. The Government instituted a special committee (*Commissie Fundamentele herbezinning Nederlands burgerlijk procesrecht*) to carry out this review. One of the results of this study is that a bill is now pending which creates increased opportunities for discovery and disclosure.

In addition to litigation in the courts, arbitration has become increasingly important as a means of dispute resolution and is generally the quickest way of achieving this, especially if the arbitration is conducted under the efficient rules of the Netherlands Arbitration Institute. The advantages of arbitration are the ease of international enforceability under the New York Convention as well as confidentiality and the opportunity to use arbitrators with specific expertise, which avoids the costs and delays that would result from the court having to appoint experts to provide guidance on certain issues. The disadvantages of arbitration, however, are the absence of an appeals mechanism (even though this can be agreed upon) and the higher costs of arbitration in comparison with court proceedings. The Dutch rules on arbitration have not changed much during recent years. In March 2012, however, the Ministry of Justice presented a proposal to amend the Dutch Arbitration Act, mainly to bring it more in line with 'best practices' in (international) arbitration.

The chapter on arbitration in this book also deals briefly with mediation and with expert determination as an alternative means of dispute resolution. Since 1 April 2007, all courts, both in civil and administrative matters, can refer litigant parties to mediation. In practice, mediation is mostly used for specific kinds of dispute that relate to family and employment law. Dispute resolution by means of expert determination is common only within specific industries and is often used for more technical issues.

The rules of procedure relating to administrative disputes in the Netherlands are very different from those for civil disputes, more so than in most common law jurisdictions. Over the last 25 years, the Netherlands has seen an increase in various types of administrative litigation. In this period, many state-owned enterprises, such as the postal, telecommunications and energy businesses, have been privatised and subjected to competition in liberalised markets. State-owned enterprises that once saw hardly any litigation have now become competitive and highly regulated industries, and the decisions of the sector-specific regulatory authorities which govern many of these markets are generating significant volumes of administrative litigation. The same holds true for the Netherlands Competition Authority, which was created on 1 January 1998 to enforce competition law and merger control at national level. More recently, the banking, securities and insurance industries have been subjected to intense and detailed regulation, to a large extent as a result of European legislation. The Dutch supervisory authorities for the financial markets and industries (the Netherlands Authority for the Financial Markets and the Dutch Central Bank) have become increasingly active and more formal in their approach. This too has led to an increase in the volume of complex administrative litigation.

In practice, civil and administrative litigation are sometimes intertwined. For instance, a hostile takeover battle may well simultaneously involve civil litigation (in the Enterprise Court) as well as administrative litigation (against decisions of the Netherlands Authority for the Financial Markets in connection with its powers to approve a prospectus or to order a party to follow a particular course of action).

In view of the many differences between the procedural rules for each type of dispute resolution, this book is divided into three parts. Civil litigation is dealt with in Chapter 1, with a special section dedicated to corporate litigation in the Enterprise Court. The Enterprise Court has become a highly specialised court in enquiry proceedings, with far-reaching powers of investigation, and has made important contributions to the development of company law and corporate governance in the Netherlands. Arbitration is dealt with in Chapter 2 and administrative litigation in Chapter 3. As this book is intended to be a practical guide to litigation in the Netherlands, we have refrained from making references to textbooks and academic literature.

This work is a joint effort between two partners of the Amsterdam office of Allen & Overy LLP. Marieke van Hooijdonk, a partner specialising in Litigation and Arbitration, is responsible for Chapters 1 and 2, and Peter Eijsvoogel, a partner specialising in Regulated Industries and Economic Administrative Law, is responsible for Chapter 3.

The first edition of this book was published in February 2009. This second edition takes account of the changes in statutory, treaty and case law during the last four years. The authors would like to thank those colleagues who have assisted with the drafting of and commentary on this update. More specifically, they would like to thank Arnold Croiset van Uchelen, Richard de Haan and especially Joanna Jonker Roelants for their help on Chapter 1, Hilde van der Baan for her assistance on Chapter 2 and Jantine Vermont for her help on Chapter 3. The authors have stated the law as at 1 October 2012, although a limited number of provisions that were not in force at that date are covered.

Marieke van Hooijdonk
marieke.vanhooijdonk@allenovery.com

Peter Eijsvoogel
peter.eijsvoogel@allenovery.com

Chapter 1
Civil Procedure

1. INTRODUCTION

The civil court system in the Netherlands is a three-tiered system. In principle, cases at first instance are brought before one of the District Courts (*Rechtbanken*). Appeals against these judgments must be brought before one of the Courts of Appeal (*Gerechtshoven*). At the top of the hierarchy is the Supreme Court (*Hoge Raad*). The Netherlands has no jury trials.

On 1 January 2002, significant changes were made to the Code of Civil Procedure (the 'CCP') (*Wetboek van Burgerlijke Rechtsvordering*; 'Rv')[1] and to the structure of the court system as laid down in the Act on the Organisation of the Judiciary (*Wet op de Rechterlijke Organisatie*; 'RO').[2] The purpose of these changes was to simplify the rules of civil procedure, to minimise formal requirements, to modernise the relationship between judges and the parties, to improve efficiency, and to harmonise procedural rules as much as possible. A substantial change has been the abolition of separate Cantonal Courts (see § 3.1.1.2). Another important change is that a Council for the Judiciary (*Raad voor de Rechtspraak*) has been established, which aims, inter alia, to support the quality of legal decision-making.

Since 2002 there have been several other waves of reform. In 2006 an extensive study on the reform of Netherlands civil procedure was carried out by the Committee for the Review of Netherlands Civil Procedure (*Commissie Fundamentele herbezinning Nederlands burgerlijk procesrecht*). One of the results of this study is that a bill is now pending creating increased opportunities for discovery and disclosure. Also in 2006, another committee (*Commissie Deetman*) made suggestions for changes to the organisation of the court system, to divide the workload between the courts more evenly and to enhance their efficiency.[3] One of the suggestions became law on 1 July 2011: an extension of the powers of the cantonal division

1. *Wetboek Burgerlijke Rechtsvordering*, Stb. 1828, 14, most recently amended by Stb. 2012, 140.
2. *Wet op de Rechterlijke Organisatie*, Stb. 1827, 20, most recently amended by Stb. 2012, 140.
3. The suggestions led to the Act on the Evaluation of the Modernisation of the Judicial Structure (*Evaluatiewet Modernisering Rechterlijke Organisatie*) and Amendment Act, Stb. 2011, 255 and Stb. 2011, 256.

(*sector kanton*) of the District Court to hear claims up to EUR 25,000 and all claims relating to consumer purchase and consumer credit (see § 3.1.1.2).

On 1 July 2012, two new laws regarding the functioning of the Dutch Supreme Court entered into force. The Preliminary Questions Act (*Wet prejudiciële vragen Hoge Raad*) has made it possible for lower courts to ask the Supreme Court for a ruling on a question of law, on the condition that the issue is relevant to a significant number of claims or cases based on the same or similar facts (such as in collective actions). The Act on the Strengthening of Supreme Court Adjudication (*Wet versterking cassatierechtspraak*) attempts to diminish the workload of the Supreme Court, by entitling it to dismiss an appeal at an early stage of the proceedings, in cases where it is clear that the appeal will not be successful or the appellant has no sufficient interest (see § 6.4.2.1).

Last but not least, from 1 January 2013, a far-reaching change to the court system will take effect, as the current 19 District Courts will be reduced to 11 and the five Courts of Appeal to four (see §§ 3.1.1.1 and 3.1.2).[4]

The reforms mentioned are not the end of the road. The quality of legal decision-making is constantly being reviewed. At the end of 2011, the Ministry of Public Safety and Justice published a so-called 'innovation agenda', with the most important reforms for the coming years.[5] The government will focus on making proceedings in appeal quicker and more efficient, on further promoting mediation, on introducing simpler and quicker procedures for small claims, and on increasing the expertise of the courts in specific areas of the law.

Unsurprisingly, one of the spearheads of the agenda is a further digitisation of court proceedings. The recent Law on the Electronic Submission of Writs (*Wet elektronische indiening dagvaarding*) has made it possible for the government to designate by decree categories of cases in which a writ may be submitted electronically.[6] To date, this is only possible for claims before the cantonal divisions of the District Courts but the law is only one step in the road to digitisation. The government's aim is that in 2015, it will be possible to communicate electronically with all the courts, both in civil, administrative and criminal cases. Furthermore, in connection with its participation in an EU programme, the government promotes two projects, to increase the use of videoconferencing in cross-border litigation and to investigate the use of long distance interpreters.[7]

4. Act on the Revision of the Legal Landscape (*Wet Herziening gerechtelijke kaart*), Stb. 2012, 313, as amended (TK 33 451, No. 2).
5. *Innovatieagenda rechtsbestel*, published on <www.rijksoverheid.nl>.
6. Art. 125(3) Rv, in force since 1 July 2012 (Stb. 2012, 291).
7. <www.ec.europa.eu/justice/civil/commercial>.

2. DIFFERENCES BETWEEN NETHERLANDS AND COMMON LAW

There are many fundamental differences between the rules of civil procedure in the Netherlands and civil procedure in common law jurisdictions. A few important differences are discussed below.

2.1 No Jury and the Role of the Judge

The Netherlands has no jury trials, neither in civil nor in criminal cases. Reliance on the judge's independence and professionalism is part of the Dutch legal tradition. The Global Competitiveness Report 2012-2013 of the World Economic Forum shows that out of 144 countries the Netherlands ranks third for judicial independence.[8]

One of the basic principles of Dutch civil procedure is party autonomy: it is up to the parties to determine the scope of their dispute in court, and the facts and rights stated by one party, which are not or are insufficiently disputed by the opposing party, will be admitted by the court as true, without investigation. However, compared to common law jurisdictions (even after the Woolf reforms in England and Wales), the judge has a much more active role in proceedings. An example that illustrates this is the examination of witnesses (see § 2.2.4).

In general, Dutch civil lawsuits also tend to be less adversarial than proceedings in the United States and the United Kingdom. A Dutch judge is required to supplement the parties' legal arguments[9] and will also allow parties to supply missing evidence or take other procedural steps to ensure a fair procedure.

2.2 Evidence

2.2.1 Order

The order in which evidence is assembled and in which the case is argued is different from that in most common law jurisdictions. In Dutch civil procedure, even though the law does provide certain opportunities for gathering evidence ahead of trial (see §§ 5.2.2.5, 5.2.3.2 and 5.4), in most cases the parties first argue their case in court, whereupon the court decides which issues need to be sustained further by evidence. It is often only after this that witnesses are examined and other evidence is taken. In civil procedure in common law jurisdictions, the order is usually the reverse: first discovery or disclosure, then trial.

---

8. The Global Competitiveness Report 2012-2013, p. 273, <www.weforum.org>.
9. Art. 25 Rv. See § 6.1.4.2.

2.2.2 Admissibility

In American civil procedure, great emphasis is put on the admissibility of evidence. Before offering anything in evidence at the trial, a proper reason for its introduction must be given and the other party must be afforded an opportunity to object. By contrast, in the Netherlands, there is in principle no limitation on the kinds of evidence which can be submitted (see § 5.1.4). Evidence may be presented in any form, unless the CCP stipulates otherwise. Even evidence which has been unlawfully obtained can be admissible as evidence in civil proceedings. It is up to the court to evaluate the evidence presented at the time it renders its decision.

2.2.3 Burden of Proof

The rules of evidence operate differently as well. Under Dutch law, the burden of proof may for specific issues be on the claimant and for other specific issues on the defendant, and may even shift between them during the proceedings, as a result of evidence submitted (see § 5.1.3). In Anglo-Saxon systems, the burden of proof for a specific issue remains with one party throughout the trial.

2.2.4 Witness Hearings

Whereas in the United States and the United Kingdom it is largely up to the parties to examine and cross-examine the witnesses at trial, in the Netherlands it is primarily the court that puts questions to the witnesses, focusing on the issues it deems most important. In addition, instead of a verbatim transcript of witnesses' testimony, the court dictates a summary. In general, because of the widespread use of documentary evidence, the examination of witnesses seems to play a less important role than in common law jurisdictions. It certainly is much less time consuming.

2.2.5 No Document Discovery or Depositions

Another marked distinction is the limited availability of document discovery or disclosure under Dutch procedural law, although currently a bill is pending in which this availability is increased (see § 5.4). There is no obligation on a party to disclose documents which are damaging to its own case. Neither is there the option for a party to investigate its counterparty's documents: fishing expeditions are not allowed. Oral depositions, being the testimony of a witness before trial, in the presence of counsel without court order and without a court officer being present, are unknown in Dutch law. The ability to compel witnesses to provide testimony at or prior to trial, however, is widely available (see § 5.2.2).

2.3 Available Remedies

In terms of available remedies, Dutch civil law and Dutch civil procedure are more flexible than in most common law jurisdictions. In the overwhelming majority of cases of breach of contract, specific performance is available as a remedy under Dutch law without it being necessary to prove that damages would not constitute an adequate remedy. Independent from the law applicable to the merits of the case, injunctive (preliminary) relief is widely available, and can in urgent cases be obtained at very short notice. Extraterritorial measures can be granted in certain circumstances. Another major distinctive feature of Dutch procedural law, even in comparison to most other continental European jurisdictions, is that pre-judgment attachments on the assets of a defendant are rather widely allowed and difficult to release. The Netherlands is therefore an attachment-friendly country.

2.4 Duration of Proceedings

In terms of procedural efficiency, one advantage of the Dutch system is that the often time-consuming gathering of evidence (documents and witness statements) is limited to those issues that are deemed relevant by the court. On the other hand, Dutch proceedings can still be lengthy, if experts and witnesses need to be heard and if interim motions are filed. On the basis of the current docket rules, it is no longer possible for the litigating parties to ask for numerous postponements to submit their written statements or to deviate from set timetables. They run the risk of forfeiting their rights. This has quickened the pace of litigation. However, the court itself is allowed to postpone its decision again and again. It must be said that over the past few years, backlogs in the courts in civil matters have been greatly reduced. The average length of contentious proceedings in the District Court is now about 14 months[10] and much less for small claims dealt with by the cantonal division of the District Court. However, large or complex cases in the District Court may take significantly longer, not least because of the ability of courts to give interim judgments, e.g. ordering additional evidence after the parties have argued their case. Appeals proceedings before the Dutch courts may take longer than in other jurisdictions, as they consist of a full review on the merits (as regards both facts and law) of a case and the Court of Appeal may order new evidence through witness hearings or expert reports, rather than restrict itself to the evidence forwarded in the proceedings at first instance. The average length of appeals proceedings in the Netherlands is about 15 months,[11] but, again, often longer for large or complex cases.

---

10. <http://www.rechtspraak.nl/Actualiteiten/Persinformatie/Documents/Rechtspraak-%20doorlooptijden%202005-2010.pdf>.
11. See footnote 10.

2.5 Costs of Litigation

Although it is difficult to make an exact comparison, it can generally be said that the costs of civil litigation will be substantially lower in the Netherlands than in the United States or the United Kingdom. This is largely because the very expensive and time-consuming discovery or disclosure process does not exist in Dutch proceedings. The court registry fees are quite modest. A bill to increase these fees substantially was withdrawn in April 2012.

In the United Kingdom the general rule has remained that an unsuccessful party will be ordered to pay the costs of the successful party, and in the United States each side pays its own costs. In the Dutch system the prevailing party will generally recover its court registry fees but only a small part of its costs of attorney (see § 6.1.9). In the Netherlands, an attorney's fee cannot be fully dependent on the outcome of a lawsuit, and an attorney cannot receive a percentage of the claim. The prohibition on contingency fees is laid down in the rules of the Dutch Bar Association.[12] The discussion on the remuneration system is not closed however. According to the government, access to justice requires that alternative remuneration systems need to be investigated.[13]

3. COURT SYSTEM, PARTIES, SOURCES OF LAW AND FAIR TRIAL

3.1 The Court System

3.1.1 District Courts

3.1.1.1 General

In principle, all cases at first instance are brought before the District Court, unless stipulated otherwise (see § 4.3). Parties litigating before the District Court (other than the cantonal division) must be represented by an attorney (see § 3.2.2). In general, a case is heard by one judge, but, depending on the magnitude and/or complexity of the matter, it can be considered by three judges.[14]

---

12. Art. 2(1) Rules of the Bar on Legal Practice (Result Related Compensation) (*Verordening van de Orde op de praktijkuitoefening* (*Onderdeel Resultaatgerelateerde Beloning*)) and Rule 25(1)-(2) of the Code of Conduct (*Gedragsregels*) 1992 of the Dutch Bar Assocation.
13. MvT TK 32 382, No. 3, p. 3 (*Aanpassing van de Advocatenwet, de Wet op de rechtsbijstand en de Wet tarieven in burgerlijke zaken in verband met de positie van de advocatuur in de rechtsorde*).
14. Art. 15 Rv.

Since 1934 there have been 19 District Courts in the Netherlands. In recent years however, it was thought that the quality of decision-making would be better guaranteed by larger scale courts and a reorganisation of the court system. A law was thus passed which reduces the number of District Courts to 11 from 1 January 2013.[15]

3.1.1.2 Cantonal Division of the District Court

Claims involving EUR 25,000 or less, and disputes regarding employment, agency, rental and hire-purchase arrangements, consumer purchase and consumer credit, irrespective of their value, must be brought before the cantonal division of the District Court, previously known as the Cantonal Court.[16] Cases before the cantonal division are heard by one judge. Although the proceedings before the cantonal division and the District Court have been made largely consistent with each other since 1 January 2002, there are still some differences, the main one being that a party may litigate in person before the cantonal division without being represented by an attorney.[17] In general, proceedings before the cantonal division tend to be less formal than proceedings before the ordinary District Court.

3.1.2 Courts of Appeal

Following an adverse judgment in the District Court, a litigant may appeal to the Court of Appeal in the area of jurisdiction in which the District Court is located. Until 1 January 2013 there are five Courts of Appeal: Amsterdam, Arnhem, The Hague, 's-Hertogenbosch and Leeuwarden. As from that date, the Courts of Arnhem and Leeuwarden will be joined (Court of Arnhem-Leeuwarden), so that the number of Courts of Appeal is reduced to four.[18]

Each Court of Appeal sits with three judges. At appeal all issues can be fully reconsidered, irrespective of whether they relate to the facts or to legal arguments.

An important division of the Court of Appeal in Amsterdam is the so-called Enterprise Court (*Ondernemingskamer*). The Enterprise Court has jurisdiction, either at first instance or in appeal, to hear certain corporate litigation disputes (see § 7.).

Parties litigating before the Court of Appeal, including the Enterprise Court, must be represented by an attorney.

---

15. Art. 1 of the Act on Judicial Zoning (*Wet op de rechterlijke indeling*), Stb 1951, 347, as amended, lastly by Stb. 2012, 313: As from 1 January 2013 there will be the following District Courts: 1. Amsterdam; 2. The Hague; 3. Rotterdam; 4. Midden-Nederland; 5. Noord-Holland; 6. Noord-Nederland; 7. Oost-Brabant; 8. Overijssel; 9. Gelderland; 10. Limburg; and 11. Zeeland-West-Brabant.
16. Art. 93 Rv.
17. Art. 79 Rv.
18. Art. 2 of the Act on Judicial Zoning, see footnote 15.

3.1.3 Supreme Court

At the top of the hierarchy is the Supreme Court (*Hoge Raad*), located in The Hague. Parties litigating before the Supreme Court must be represented by an attorney who is qualified for Supreme Court proceedings (see § 3.2.2). The Supreme Court is only allowed to review decisions of a lower court on questions of law or insufficient or unclear reasoning.[19] Issues of fact are dealt with only by the lower courts. Usually, the Supreme Court reviews decisions of the Courts of Appeal. Parties may, however, agree to file for appeal immediately to the Supreme Court following a decision at first instance.[20] Parties do not have to request leave to appeal to the Supreme Court (as in the United States' system of *certiorari*). The Supreme Court is obliged to review all decisions presented to it. However, from 1 July 2012, it can dismiss an appeal at an early stage of the appeal proceedings if it is obvious that the appellant has no interest in the outcome of the appeal or that the appeal cannot be successful. In that case, a non reasoned decision is given by three judges, contrary to the general rule that the Supreme Court sits with five judges and must reason its judgments.[21]

From 1 July 2012, the Supreme Court also deals with preliminary questions from lower courts if the question relates to an issue which is of general interest; the answer to the question should have direct bearing on the resolution of a significant number of claims or cases based on the same or similar facts.[22] The very first question of this kind was posed on 3 August 2012 in preliminary relief proceedings, on whether a bank can use a mortgage deed to foreclose directly on other assets of its debtor once the house has been sold.[23]

3.2 Parties, Attorneys and Judges

3.2.1 Parties

In proceedings that are initiated with a writ of summons (see § 6.1.4.2), there are at least two litigating parties. The litigating party can be a natural person or a legal entity irrespective of whether it is a Dutch or a non-Dutch national. Non-naturals should, however, have legal personality (*rechtspersoonlijkheid*) in order to act as a litigating party. Most legal entities have such legal personality, such as companies (the Dutch B.V. and N.V.),[24] foundations and associations. Partnerships, however,

19. Art. 79 RO.
20. Art. 398(2) Rv.
21. Art. 80a RO.
22. Art. 81a RO and Arts 392-394 Rv.
23. District Court Utrecht 3 Aug. 2012, LJN: BX3391 (*Rabohypotheekbank/X*).
24. B.V.: *besloten vennootschap met beperkte aansprakelijkheid* (Art. 2:175 BW), a Dutch private limited liability company; N.V.: *naamloze vennootschap* (Art. 2:64 BW), a Dutch public limited liability company.

have no legal personality. Nevertheless, a general partnership (*vennootschap onder firma*) can sue and be sued in its own name. With respect to private partnerships (*maatschap*), the claims should in principle be instituted on behalf of (or against) all partners of the partnership instead of on behalf (or against) the partnership itself as such. However, if a private partnership acts in public under a joint name, the writ may include the name of the partnership only. In this kind of case, the partnership should provide on request a list of all the partners involved. If such a private partnership is the defendant, the writ can be served at the office of the partnership.[25] Under certain circumstances, a party may lose the power to act as a litigating party. This is the case, for example, when a legal entity is declared bankrupt. If the litigating party is a legal entity which is incorporated by another company during the proceedings, for example as the result of a merger, the legal successor automatically takes the place of the litigating party.

3.2.2 Attorneys

To become an attorney (*advocaat*), a candidate must have a law degree from a Dutch University. Thereafter, he must be registered with the Dutch Bar through one of the District Courts,[26] which is only possible if a practising, registered attorney with at least seven years experience acts as one's supervising principal. An in-house counsel is also allowed to register as an attorney, if certain requirements to safeguard his independence are met. Once registered, a Dutch in-house attorney has the same rights and duties as an attorney practicing within a law firm, such as the right to legal privilege.[27] After three years of practice (which must include at least some experience of litigation) and completion of the mandatory courses, the attorney's preliminary registration becomes permanent. The difference in registration is, however, only a formal one, as an attorney has the right to act in all kinds of cases from the first day of preliminary registration.

All attorneys are members of the Dutch Bar Association. As a result, they are also bound by the Code of Conduct (*Gedragsregels*) of the Dutch Bar Association of 1992. The Code of Conduct contains rules regarding, inter alia, how attorneys should act in relation to each other, in relation to their clients, and in cases of conflicts of interest.

In all proceedings, except those before the cantonal division of the District Court and as a defendant in preliminary relief proceedings, a party must be repre-

25. Art. 51(2) Rv.
26. As of 1 Sep. 2008, on the basis of the Act on the Abolition of the Attorney-of-record and the Introduction of Electronic Correspondence (*Wet afschaffing procuraat en invoering electronisch berichtenverkeer*), Stb. 2008, 100, the 19 local bars have been merged into one state bar (*landelijk tableau*).
27. This is different in the context of investigations by the European competition authority (CJEU 14 Sep. 2010, C-550/07, ECR 2010 I-08301, NJ 2010, 629, LJN: BN8974 (*Akzo Nobel Chemicals/European Commission*)).

sented by an attorney. From 1 September 2008, every attorney is allowed to act in each of the districts. Attorneys who litigate cases before the Supreme Court need additional qualifications.[28]

3.2.3 Judges

A law degree is necessary to become a judge in the Netherlands. Judges can be trained internally by the courts, but they are often also drawn from the practising bar or from the legal profession. All judges in the Netherlands are appointed, not elected, for life, although they are required to retire at the age of 70. Judges are civil servants, but in their judicial capacity they act with complete independence from the Government. Judges are less well-known by name than in the United States or the United Kingdom, probably because they do not deliver judgments in their own name but rather as a panel, and possible dissenting opinions are not expressed in the judgment.

3.3 Sources of Law

The Dutch legal system is a civil law system in which the primary source of law is codified legislation. Decisions of the courts are also important. A specific question is addressed by consulting the codified legislation together with court decisions, preferably those of the Supreme Court. In addition, legal writings can be used in arguing a party's case.

Dutch law is not based on a system of binding precedents. Lower courts are not bound by the decisions of higher courts, even those of the Supreme Court. However, in practice, judgments of the Supreme Court are almost invariably followed by the lower courts.

Of course, international sources of codification, such as Treaties and European Regulations and Directives, also need to be considered. EC Regulations and Treaties have supremacy over national law.[29] The courts must follow the decisions of the European Court of Justice, and national legislation must be interpreted in accordance with principles of European law.

3.4 Fair Trial, Due Process and Abuse of a Procedural Right

One of the Treaties which is of fundamental importance for the interpretation and review of Dutch civil procedure is the European Convention on Human Rights

28. Art. 9j Counsel Act (*Advocatenwet en Verordening vakbekwaamheidseisen civiele cassatieadvocatuur*), Stb.1952, 365 as amended, lastly by Stb. 2012, 116 and Stcrt. 2011, 20846.
29. Art. 94 Constitution of the Kingdom of the Netherlands (*Grondwet*), Stb. 1815, 45, as amended.

(the 'ECHR').[30] Article 6(1) ECHR safeguards the parties' right to a fair trial, by entitling them to a 'fair and public hearing within a reasonable time by an independent and impartial tribunal established by law' and, in principle, to a judgment pronounced publicly.[31]

Although it should be assumed that the Dutch rules on civil procedure as currently laid down in the CCP are in line with Article 6(1) ECHR, a party involved in civil litigation may invoke this provision if it is of the opinion that its right to a fair trial is being prejudiced by the court in its application of the law. In the past, Article 6(1) ECHR has generated significant case law, for example on the question of whether a party has the right to testify on its own behalf and whether it has the right to be heard in person.[32]

The right to a fair trial implies the right of each party to give its views on statements made and evidence submitted by the other party. A court's decision may not be based on documents or other evidence submitted by a party if the other party has not been given sufficient opportunity to comment thereon.[33] Likewise, a court may not base its decision on public information, such as information it found on the internet, if the parties have not first been able to comment thereon.[34] This principle of hearing both sides of the argument (*audi alteram partem*) has been codified in Article 19 CCP.

The fundamental principles covered by Article 6(1) ECHR can be considered to be a special category of the national rules or principles of due process (*goede procesorde*), which, in the past few decades, have become an important standard for review of the conduct of parties involved in civil litigation. 'Due process' is a concept largely developed in case law and is relied on mainly in situations where no written rule is available or where the law leaves room for interpretation.[35]

'Due process' is not only a standard for review for the parties but also for the conduct of the court. It can be used to correct the strict application of a rule in a specific case, if this would disregard the interests at stake.[36] In very exceptional cir-

30. European Convention for the Protection of Human Rights and Fundamental Freedoms (also called European Convention on Human Rights) concluded in Rome on 4 Nov. 1950, Trb. 1951, 154, most recently amended by Trb. 1994, 165.
31. The text is similar to that of Art. 14 International Covenant on Civil and Political Rights of 16 Dec. 1966, Trb., 1966, 99.
32. European Court of Human Rights 27 Oct. 1993, NJ 1994, 534, LJN: AD1977 (*Dombo*); Supreme Court 15 Mar. 1996, NJ 1997, 341, LJN: ZC2013 (*Boumans/'t Plenske II*).
33. Supreme Court 27 May 2011, JOR 2011, 275, LJN: BP8693 (*Van Dooren qq/Veco Lasconstructies*).
34. Supreme Court 15 Apr. 2011, NJ 2011, 180, LJN: BP5612 (*Donkersgoed/Kansen*) and Supreme Court 9 Sept. 2011, NJ 2011, 409, LJN: BR1654 (*Budgetbeheer Limburg*).
35. Since 1 Jan. 2002, the term 'due process' also appears in Art. 130 Rv, regarding the opportunity to amend one's claim, after having served the writ of summons. The defendant may object to such amendment if it is 'contrary to the requirements of due process'.
36. Supreme Court 18 Mar. 2011, NJ 2012, 315, LJN: BP0571 (*Antebi/NIHS*); Supreme Court 17 Jun. 2011, RvdW 2011, 776, LJN: BQ1774 (*Baarnsch Lyceum*).

cumstances, violation of due process may be qualified as an abuse of a (procedural) right or power (*misbruik van (proces)recht*).[37] Initiating proceedings will rarely be qualified as such. Every person who believes his rights are infringed has the right to start litigation. The mere fact that a claim objectively lacks all ground and is denied or declared inadmissible will not be sufficient to conclude that a party has abused its right to commence court proceedings. It will have to be assessed that the claimant knew or should have known that the facts underlying his claim were incorrect, or that he should have understood that there was no legal basis for his claim.[38] If a party is considered to have abused a procedural right, it may be held liable for the full amount of legal costs incurred by the other party.

4. JURISDICTION

4.1 Introduction

Whether or not matters with international aspects can be submitted to the Dutch courts depends on whether EC Regulations, international Treaties or national rules provide for international jurisdiction. As in any other area of law, as regards jurisdiction EC Regulations and Treaties have supremacy over national law.[39] The Dutch courts only have international jurisdiction where legal provisions allow or where the parties have selected a Dutch court as having jurisdiction.

This is different from the United States, for example, where the concept of personal jurisdiction is based on a fact-specific analysis of each case. Another difference, as compared to common law jurisdictions, is that in the Netherlands there is no separate doctrine of *forum non conveniens* (see § 4.2.3.4).

Once it has been determined that the Dutch courts have international jurisdiction, the rules regarding absolute jurisdiction decide which type of court (District Court, Court of Appeal or Supreme Court) should hear the case. The rules with regard to relative jurisdiction then determine the proper venue, if this has not already been decided by the rules governing international jurisdiction. The rules of absolute and relative jurisdiction also apply to national matters.

37. Art. 3:13 BW.
38. Supreme Court 29 Jun. 2007, NJ 2007, 353, LJN: BA3516 (*Waterschap Regge c.s./Milieutech Beheer*); Supreme Court 6 Apr. 2012, NJ 2012, 233, LJN: BV7828 (*Grand Café A./Achmea*).
39. Art. 1 Rv.

4.2 International Jurisdiction

4.2.1 Sources of International Jurisdiction

The most important source of international jurisdiction is the EC Council Regulation on jurisdiction and the recognition and enforcement of judgments in civil and commercial matters (the 'EC Regulation'), which entered into force on 1 March 2002.[40] This Regulation applies to all EU Member States.[41] With the exception of certain (former) Dutch and French overseas territories, the EC Regulation replaces the Brussels Convention on jurisdiction and the enforcement of judgments in civil and commercial matters (the 'Brussels Convention').[42] Another important source of international jurisdiction is the (new) Lugano Convention on jurisdiction and the enforcement of judgments in civil and commercial matters (the 'Lugano Convention'), applicable between the EU Member States and three of the four EFTA States,[43] namely Switzerland, Norway and Iceland. In this new Convention the rules for jurisdiction and recognition and enforcement are aligned with the rules of the EC Regulation.[44] Further, the EC Council Regulation on insolvency proceedings, which came into effect on 31 May 2002, deals with jurisdiction issues related to insolvency.[45]

---

40. EC Council Regulation of 22 December 2000 on jurisdiction and the recognition and enforcement of judgments in civil and commercial matters, No. 44/2001, O.J. EUR. COMM. (No. L 12) 1 (2001).
41. For a list of the EU Member States see <www.europa.eu>. Since 1 July 2007 the EC Regulation also applies to Denmark, on the basis of a separate agreement. The EC Regulation does not apply to the Dutch overseas territories Aruba, Curaçao and St. Maarten as these territories are subject to the special regime of Part IV TFEU, nor does it apply to the so-called BES islands Bonaire, Saba and St. Eustatius, which since the dissolution of the Netherlands Antilles on 10 October 2010 form special municipalities of the Netherlands. It cannot be excluded, however, that in the future the Regulation may also apply to some or all of the overseas territories, on the basis of Article 355(6) TFEU.
42. Brussels Convention of 27 September 1968 on jurisdiction and the enforcement of judgments in civil and commercial matters, amended in 1978, 1982, 1989 and 1996. The consolidated version of the Brussels Convention can be found in O.J. EUR. COMM. (No. C 27) 1 (1998), amended by O.J. EUR. COMM. (No. C 160) 1 (2000). From 1 July 2007 the Convention only continues to apply to the relations between the member states and certain overseas territories of the Netherlands and France, e.g. Aruba. The Convention does not apply to Curaçao nor St. Maarten nor the Dutch BES islands.
43. Another EFTA state is Liechtenstein. See <www.efta.int>.
44. The new Lugano Convention was signed on 30 October 2007 between the European Community, Denmark and the EFTA States Switzerland, Norway and Iceland (O.J. EUR. COMM. (No. L 339) 3 (2007)). For the Netherlands it replaces the old Lugano Convention of 16 Sept. 1988. The Lugano Convention, just as the old Convention, does not apply to the Dutch overseas territories Aruba, Curaçao and St. Maarten. Nor does it apply to the so-called BES islands Bonaire, Saba and St. Eustatius. It is possible, however, that in the future the Lugano Convention will also become applicable to these overseas territories, on the basis of Article 70(1)b of the Convention.
45. EC Council Regulation of 29 May 2000 on insolvency proceedings, No. 1346/2000, O.J. EUR. COMM. (No. L 160) 1 (2000). This Regulation does not apply in relation to Denmark.

4.2.2 The EC Regulation

The EC Regulation applies if a defendant is domiciled in one of the EU Member States. The main rule is that such a defendant, whatever his nationality, will be sued before the courts in his place of domicile.[46] There are, however, several exceptions to the main rule which create an alternative jurisdiction enjoyed by other courts. For example, if the dispute relates to a contract, the defendant can also be sued in the courts in the place of performance of the relevant contractual obligation.[47] If the dispute relates to tort, delict or quasi-delict, jurisdiction is enjoyed by the courts in the place where the harmful event occurred or may occur.[48] It is settled case-law that this rule must be interpreted as meaning that, where the place in which the event giving rise to liability in tort occurs, and the place where that event results in damage are not identical, the defendant may be sued, at the option of the claimant, in the courts of either of those places.[49] If the dispute relates to a pre-contractual obligation, jurisdiction must be based on Article 5(3) and not Article 5(1) of the EC Regulation.[50] The Dutch Supreme Court has ruled that the place where the harmful event occurred is the place where the negotiations were terminated and therefore usually the place where the notification of the termination was received, unless that place could be considered to be completely random.[51]

If the defendant is one of a number of defendants, he can generally be sued before the courts in the place of domicile of one of his co-defendants.[52] In addition,

---

46. As regards companies or other legal entities, the place of domicile is determined by Art. 60 EC Regulation.
47. Art. 5(1) EC Regulation.
48. Art. 5(3) EC Regulation. This Article also applies to an action for a negative declaration seeking to establish the absence of liability in tort (CJEU 25 Oct. 2012, C-133/11 (*Fofitec AG/Ritrama SpA*)).
49. See, inter alia, CJEU 30 Nov. 1976, C-21/76, ECR 1976, p. 1735, NJ 1977, 494 (*Bier/Mines de potasse d'Alsace*). No jurisdiction, however, is conferred to the place where the victim claims to have suffered financial damage following upon initial damage arising and suffered by him in another Contracting State (CJEU 19 Sep. 1995, C-364/93, ECR 1995 I-02719, NJ 1997, 52 (*Marinari/Lloyd's Bank*)), nor to the place where the claimant is domiciled or where 'his assets are concentrated' by reason only of the fact that he has suffered financial damage there resulting from the loss of part of his assets which arose and was incurred in another Member State (CJEU 10 Jun. 2004, C-168/02, ECR 2004 I-6009, NJ 2006, 335, LJN: AY0167 (*Kronhofer/Maier*)). As regards defamatory publications on the internet, the CJEU held on 25 October 2011, C-509/09 and C-161/10, NJ 2012, 224 (*E-date and Martinez/MGN*) that the claimant has the option of bringing an action for liability, in respect of all the damage caused, either before the courts of the Member State in which the publisher of that content is located or before the courts of the Member State in which the centre of his interests is based. The claimant may also, instead of an action for liability in respect of all the damage caused, bring his action before the courts of each Member State in the territory of which content placed online is or has been accessible. Those courts have jurisdiction only in respect of the damage caused in the territory of the Member State of the court seised.
50. CJEU 17 Sep. 2002, C-334/00, ECR 2002 I-07357, NJ 2003, 46, LJN: AF5792 (*Tacconi/HWS*).
51. Supreme Court 21 Sep. 2001, NJ 2002, 254, LJN: ZC3483 (*Bus/Chemconserve*).
52. Art. 6(1) EC Regulation.

a defendant can in principle be sued as a third party in any third-party proceedings (such as in an action relating to indemnity) in the court of the original proceedings.[53]

Finally, the EC Regulation contains specific jurisdiction rules concerning matters relating to insurance, consumer contracts and employment contracts. These rules can only be deviated from in limited circumstances.[54] The EC Regulation also contains several exclusive jurisdiction rules on, inter alia, immovable property, proceedings which have as their object the validity of the constitution, the nullity or the dissolution of companies or other legal persons or of associations of natural or legal persons, or the validity of the decisions of their corporate bodies, and on proceedings relating to the registration or validity of patents or trademarks. These rules cannot be deviated from.[55]

The EC Regulation applies not only if the defendant is domiciled in an EU Member State but also if one of the abovementioned exclusive jurisdiction rules is involved or if the parties, one of whom is domiciled in a Member State, have agreed that the court of a Member State has jurisdiction to settle disputes which have arisen or which may arise in connection with a particular legal relationship. Such a jurisdiction clause is only valid if it is concluded in a form stipulated by the EC Regulation.[56] The requirements are in short: (a) that the agreement must be in writing or evidenced in writing; or (b) in a form which accords with practices established between the parties, or (c) in international trade or commerce, in a form which accords with a widely known usage. The courts take a strict approach as to the validity of jurisdiction clauses. In particular, the validity of jurisdiction clauses in general conditions is often the subject of dispute. Recent case law has shown that even if an on-going business relationship is subject to general conditions, the jurisdiction clause is only valid if the conditions have been notified to the other party so that it knew or could have known that these included a jurisdiction clause. A mere reference on one's invoice to applicable general conditions is not sufficient to invoke the jurisdiction clause, irrespective of whether the invoices have been paid by the other party.[57] If there is a valid clause, it creates exclusive jurisdiction, unless agreed otherwise.

The EC Regulation does not prevent parties from making applications to the courts of Member States for provisional or interim measures that may be available under the national rules, even if under the EC Regulation the courts of another

53. Art. 6(2) EC Regulation.
54. Arts 8-21 EC Regulation.
55. Art. 22 EC Regulation. See CJEU 12 May 2011, C-144/10, NJ 2011, 363, LJN: BQ5459 (*Berliner Verkehrsbetriebe/JP Morgan Chase Bank*) on the strict interpretation of Article 22(2) EC Regulation in the context of proceedings in which a company raised an objection regarding the validity of the decisions of its organs.
56. Art. 23(1) EC Regulation.
57. Supreme Court 27 May 2011, NJ 2012, 391, LJN: BP8689 (*Demerara/Karl Heinz Haus*) and Supreme Court 30 Mar. 2012, NJ 2012, 392, LJN: BV2356 (*Giemulla-Bruns/Interpolis*).

Member State have jurisdiction as to the substance of the matter.[58] Examples of such interim measures under Dutch law are provisional remedies requested in preliminary relief proceedings or measures with respect to the attachment of goods (see § 9.). A request for a preliminary witness hearing, however, is considered by the CJEU to be a provisional measure only under certain conditions.[59]

On 14 December 2010 the European Commission published a proposal for a revision of the EC Regulation.[60] Since then, as a result of input from the European Council, the European Parliament and the Member States, quite some amendments have been made, and at the time of writing of this book it is not yet clear how the new Regulation will read. A likely change, however, is that the concept of provisional measures will be widened so as to include all preliminary witness hearings and *ex parte* attachment orders. Also the validity of jurisdiction clauses will be reinforced.

4.2.3 National Rules

4.2.3.1 General

If no EC Regulation or Treaty is applicable, national rules decide whether or not the Dutch courts have international jurisdiction. The Dutch rules on international jurisdiction were implemented in the CCP on 1 January 2002 and are largely based on the international jurisdiction rules in the EC Regulation (see § 4.2.2). The basic rule is that the Dutch courts have competence if the defendant is domiciled in the Netherlands.[61] The Dutch courts will also have competence if, in their agreement, the parties have chosen the Dutch courts as the forum.[62] There are no formal requirements for a jurisdiction clause to be valid (as opposed to a jurisdiction clause under the EC Regulation) but if it is disputed, a jurisdiction clause may only be proven by a document that has been accepted by the other party. The jurisdiction clause may be contained in the document itself or in general conditions to which the document refers.[63] Whether or not the jurisdiction clause is exclusive is a matter of interpretation for the court.

Newly introduced, and deviating from the EC Regulation, is the *forum necessitatis*.[64] This means that the Dutch courts also have jurisdiction if legal proceedings outside the Netherlands are impossible or unacceptable from the standpoint

58. Art. 31 EC Regulation.
59. CJEU 28 Apr. 2005, C-104/03, ECR 2005 I-03481, NJ 2006, 636, LJN: AV7679 (*St. Paul Dairy Industries/Unibel*) and Supreme Court 2 Dec. 2011, NJ 2012, 128, LJN: BU6545 (*Roucar/Guillouet*).
60. COM (2010) 748 final.
61. Art. 2 Rv.
62. Art. 8(1) Rv.
63. Art. 8(6) Rv.
64. Arts 9(b) and 9(c) Rv.

of the claimant. Only in limited circumstances will a claimant be able to show that the initiation of legal proceedings outside the Netherlands is unacceptable. The circumstances of the specific case are decisive. Generally speaking, one can think of situations involving war, natural disaster or discrimination in the foreign country.

4.2.3.2 *Attachment Creating Jurisdiction*

If the defendant is domiciled outside the Netherlands but has assets located in the Netherlands, attachment of these assets can also create jurisdiction.[65] This rule of *forum arresti* does not, however, apply if (a) the claimant can obtain a judgment in a non-Dutch court which is enforceable in the Netherlands on the basis of an applicable Regulation or Treaty or (b) if the parties have agreed on a jurisdiction clause on the basis of which a non-Dutch court has jurisdiction (irrespective of whether this judgment can be directly enforced in the Netherlands)[66] or (c) there is another basis in Dutch law on which a Dutch court can assume jurisdiction.

4.2.3.3 *Jurisdiction and Petition Proceedings*

In cases that are initiated with a petition (*verzoekschrift*) the Dutch courts have jurisdiction if (a) either the petitioner or the respondent is domiciled in the Netherlands, (b) the petition is related to proceedings initiated or to be initiated by a writ of summons for which the Dutch courts have jurisdiction or (c) the matter is otherwise sufficiently connected with the Netherlands (see § 6.5.2).[67]

4.2.3.4 *No Forum Non Conveniens*

There is no room for the doctrine of *forum non conveniens*, neither in cases initiated by writ of summons nor in cases initiated by petition. Thus, as long as the Dutch courts have jurisdiction according to the relevant rules, the defendant cannot argue that a court in another jurisdiction would be more convenient or appropriate.

4.2.4 *Lis Pendens*

Where proceedings brought in a Dutch court involve the same cause of action and the same parties as proceedings already pending in a foreign, non EU, court, the Dutch court may stay its proceedings until the foreign court has rendered a decision. If the decision of the foreign court can be recognised or enforced in the

65. Arts 10 and 767 Rv.
66. Supreme Court 16 Jun. 1995, NJ 1996, 256, LJN: ZC1761 (*SCI/AEC*).
67. Art. 3 Rv.

Netherlands (see § 10.3) the Dutch court must subsequently decline jurisdiction.[68] If proceedings are pending in a court of an EU Member State, the specific rules of the EC Regulation apply.[69] In that case the Dutch court may also order a stay if the two proceedings are closely connected.

4.3 Absolute Jurisdiction

The rules of absolute jurisdiction, setting forth which type of court has jurisdiction, are laid down in the Act on the Organisation of the Judiciary.[70]

The District Courts have absolute jurisdiction over all claims at first instance, unless stipulated otherwise.[71] Some of these first instance cases, such as those relating to employment contracts, are dealt with by the cantonal division of the District Court (see § 3.1.1.2). In certain cases, the Courts of Appeal also act at first instance. For example, the Enterprise Court of the Amsterdam Court of Appeal decides on certain corporate disputes, such as disputes involving the mismanagement of a company (see § 7.2) and disputes relating to the annual accounts of a company (see § 7.5). The most important task of the Courts of Appeal is, however, to deal with appeals from judgments of the District Courts, including appeals from their cantonal divisions.[72] The Supreme Court has absolute jurisdiction in reviewing judgments of the Courts of Appeal.[73]

Disputes concerning claims or rights that parties can freely dispose of, and over which the District Court would otherwise have absolute jurisdiction, may, at the parties' joint request, be submitted to the cantonal division of the District Court.[74] Unless the parties agree otherwise, appeal to the Court of Appeal is then excluded. Parties may also agree to bypass the District Court and submit any dispute directly to the Court of Appeal which falls within the appellate jurisdiction of that Court (prorogation).[75] Again, this only involves claims or rights which parties can freely dispose of, and the parties must jointly submit such a request. Both such judgments of the cantonal division of the District Court and of the Court of Appeal may be reviewed by the Supreme Court.

68. Art. 12 Rv.
69. Arts 27-30 EC Regulation.
70. See footnote 2.
71. Art. 42 RO.
72. Art. 60 RO.
73. Art. 78 RO.
74. Art. 96 Rv.
75. Art. 62 RO.

4.4 Venue (Relative Jurisdiction)

Once it is determined that the Dutch courts have international jurisdiction and absolute jurisdiction is established, the proper venue must be decided. In cases where the EC Regulation or the Lugano Convention applies, relative jurisdiction often follows from the same provision which establishes international jurisdiction. If not, the Dutch rules on venue as laid down in the CCP will be applied and these follow closely the above-mentioned rules on international jurisdiction.

Therefore, also under Dutch law, the basic rule for proceedings commenced by writ is that an action should be brought before the competent court in the place of the defendant's actual domicile.[76] If the parties have elected an alternative domicile, the court of that domicile is also competent. An alternative competent court in tort-related cases is the court where the harmful event occurred.[77] If there are several defendants, the action can be brought before the court that is competent for any of the defendants, provided the claims are so closely connected that it is expedient to hear them together.[78] In disputes regarding immovable property, an alternative court is the court where the property is located. The competence of the court is, however, exclusive if the dispute relates to the lease of a property.[79] If the parties have agreed upon a forum, that court will be competent. All other courts will not be competent, provided the defendant relies on the jurisdiction clause.[80] If the Dutch courts have international jurisdiction but no venue can be determined, the court in The Hague will be the competent court.[81] If a case is brought before the wrong court, the defendant will have to claim improper venue from the start if he wants the matter to be referred to the competent court. Only in cases which fall under the jurisdiction of the cantonal division of the District Courts (see § 3.1.1.2), such as employment disputes, the court will consider whether it is the right venue of its own initiative.[82]

Again, there is no room for the doctrine of *forum non conveniens*. Once a proper venue is determined, the defendant cannot argue that another venue would be more convenient or appropriate (see § 4.2.3.4).

---

76. Art. 99 Rv.
77. Art. 102 Rv.
78. Art. 107 Rv.
79. Art. 103 Rv.
80. Art. 108 Rv.
81. Art. 109 Rv.
82. Art. 110(1) and (2) Rv.

5. EVIDENCE

5.1 Rules of Evidence

5.1.1 General

The rules of evidence are laid down in the CCP. They deviate substantially from the way evidence is dealt with in common law systems such as those in the United States and the United Kingdom. Not only are there generally no restrictions on the admissibility of evidence but the concept of discovery or disclosure is also largely unknown. It used to be the case that parties could limit themselves to submitting only evidence that was favourable to them. The CCP restricts this by introducing the duty honestly to provide a full set of the facts. However, it is recognised that this duty is not as far-reaching as the concept of discovery and disclosure in the United States and the United Kingdom.

The court may base its decision only on facts that are not disputed by the parties or that are proven in the course of the proceedings. Furthermore it may use facts or circumstances that are generally known (such as the exchange rate of the pound for the euro on a specific day), even if these are not put forward by the parties.[83] Facts that are not disputed do not have to be proven and the court must accept them without question. Facts that are disputed need to be proven, either by documents or by witnesses. The court is not allowed to add facts on its own initiative.

In general, it is up to the court to assess the evidence presented to it, unless the CCP stipulates otherwise (see §§ 5.2.1.1 and 5.2.2.2).[84]

5.1.2 Range of Application

The rules of evidence are applicable to all proceedings initiated by a writ of summons, both at first instance and in appeals proceedings. They are also applicable to petition proceedings, unless the nature of the matter prevents this.[85] An example of the nature of the matter preventing the applicability of the rules of evidence is the second stage of enquiry proceedings (see § 7.2.7.2). Theoretically, the rules of evidence do not apply in preliminary relief proceedings, but in practice, the preliminary relief judge often applies these. The rules of evidence in principle also do not apply in arbitration proceedings. In the event that the rules of evidence do not apply, the court is free to make decisions on the admissibility of evidence and on the burden of proof as it deems fit, provided however that the principles of due process are taken into account (see § 3.4).

83. Art. 149 Rv.
84. Art. 152(2) Rv.
85. Art. 284(1) Rv.

5.1.3 Burden of Proof

The burden of proof is, in principle, on the party relying on the legal consequences of certain facts, unless specifically provided otherwise, or unless the requirement for such proof would be contrary to the principles of reasonableness and fairness.[86] The main rule entails that a claimant who claims damages from the other party on the basis of an alleged breach of contract will have to furnish the facts (*stelplicht*) and, if denied by the defendant, will have the burden of proof as regards both the breach and the causal connection between the breach and the damage suffered. If the defendant merely denies the breach or the causal connection, the burden of proof remains with the claimant. But if, for example, the defendant claims he is not liable for the damages due to force majeure, he will have the burden of proof for such force majeure.

Parties are, in most cases, free to deviate from the main evidence principle by contract, by excluding certain evidence or shifting the burden of proof.[87] Examples of specific legal provisions which deviate from the main principle can be found in the fields of employment law and consumer protection.

The risk of not providing sufficient evidence is on the party with the burden of proof. Once the claimant presents sufficient evidence, the defendant is allowed to provide counter-evidence.[88] The submission of counter-evidence should be distinguished from a situation in which the burden of proof is actually shifted to the other party, in deviation of the ground rule: in the first case, the defendant can limit himself to submitting sufficient evidence which contradicts the evidence put forward by the claimant while, in the latter case, to prevent the claimant's statements from being established as true, he will need to submit sufficient evidence himself for the facts he is relying on. Another device to lighten the burden of proof for the claimant is the so-called 'reversal rule', which applies in liability cases to the causal connection between the tort or breach of contract and the damages claimed. If damages are claimed as a result of actions which are in breach of a contractual or statutory provision that was drawn up to prevent the occurrence of a specific harm (e.g. traffic rules designed to prevent road accidents), if the violation of the norm largely increases such risk and the specific risk subsequently materialises, the causal link between the action and the damage suffered is presumed. In this case it is up to the defendant to submit counter-evidence that the damage would have occurred even without such action.[89]

---

86. Art. 150 Rv.
87. Art. 153 Rv.
88. Art. 151(2) Rv. Unlike the offer for evidence, the offer for counter-evidence need not be specified (Supreme Court 29 Apr. 2011, NJ 2011, 189, LJN: BP9860).
89. The 'reversal rule' started with Supreme Court 26 Jan. 1996, NJ 1996, 607, LJN: ZC1976 (*Dicky Trading II*) and is clarified in Supreme Court 29 Nov. 2002, NJ 2004, 304, LJN: AE7345 (*TFS/Nederlandse Spoorwegen*), Supreme Court 29 Nov. 2002, NJ 2004, 305, LJN: AE7351 (*Kastelijn/Gemeente*

In short, the above means that in one and the same case the burden of proof can for certain issues be on the claimant and for other issues on the defendant and can actually shift between them with respect to a single issue during the proceedings. This is different from most countries with an Anglo-Saxon legal system where the burden of proof for a specific issue remains with one party throughout the trial.

5.1.4 Admissibility of Evidence

Evidence may be presented in any form, unless stipulated otherwise by law.[90] The most common forms of evidence are documents and witness and expert testimonies (see § 5.2). There is in principle no limitation on the kinds of evidence which can be submitted. Even evidence which has been unlawfully obtained can often (though not always) be admissible as evidence in civil proceedings. Evidence which has been unlawfully obtained may for instance consist of recordings of private telephone conversations or video recordings of intimate situations, as these recordings will often be contrary to the right of respect for private and family life as stipulated in Article 8 ECHR. Recordings of telephone conversations made in the course of business or video recordings of employees suspected of fraudulent actions will not generally be seen as unlawful.[91] If the evidence submitted to the court is considered to have been unlawfully obtained, in reaching a decision on admissibility the courts will balance the interest of arriving at the truth, on the one hand, against the interest of protection of the other party, on the other hand. The relative importance of these competing interests is, however, still unclear under current case law.

On the other hand, evidence may sometimes be considered inadmissible, even if it has been lawfully obtained. This may be the case if submission of the evidence would violate the other party's right to a private life.[92]

Achtkarspelen) and Supreme Court 7 Apr. 2006, NJ 2006, 244, LJN: AU6934 (*Bildtpollen/Miedema*); Supreme Court 7 Dec. 2007, NJ 2007, 644, LJN: BB3670 (*Stichting Medisch Centrum Leeuwarden*). In literature there has been much criticism of this doctrine as many scholars believe it is an unnecessary and complicated rule that relates to issues which are better resolved by a factual appraisal of the evidence.

90. Art. 152(1) Rv. For example, an arbitration agreement can only be proven by a written document (Art. 1021 Rv). The same goes for a jurisdiction clause agreed by the parties (Art. 8(5) Rv).
91. Supreme Court 16 Oct. 1987, NJ 1988, 850, LJN: AC9997 (*Driessen/Van Gelder*) and Supreme Court 27 Apr. 2001, NJ 2001, 421, LJN: AB1347 (*L./Wennekes*).
92. See e.g. Supreme Court 22 Jan. 1999, NJ 1999, 715, LJN: ZC2831 (*F./S.*).

5.2 Types of Evidence

5.2.1 Documents

5.2.1.1 Value as Evidence

In principle, all documents may be presented as evidence and it is up to the court to decide the value of each document. An exception to this principle is that the contents of 'authentic deeds', i.e. documents drawn up by a public official acting within his official power (such as a civil law notary (*notaris*) drawing up the (mandatory) notarial deed on the transfer of shares) are presumed to be correct as regards the observations and declaration of the official, unless sufficient counter-evidence is presented.[93] Another exception is that the contents of authentic deeds constitute proof vis-à-vis the parties to the document (however, not vis-à-vis third parties). In fact, this latter rule also applies to the contents of written documents which are signed and drawn up for purposes of evidence, but which are not 'authentic deeds' since they are not drawn up by public officials (for example, a contract). However, if a document is not drawn up by a public official, a party may dispute the signatures on the document, in which case the party that relies on the document must prove that they are authentic.[94] The rule that the contents of a deed constitute proof between the parties does not apply to a deed of acknowledgement of indebtedness, unless the deed is written by hand or bears the approval of the debtor, including the amount being written fully in letters (not in numerals).[95]

5.2.1.2 Submission

The party relying on a document is required to submit a copy of it as an exhibit.[96] If a copy is not submitted on a party's own initiative, it runs the risk that the document will not be taken into account by the court. The court is not compelled to request the submission of documents, even if these documents would be relevant for its decision.[97] In contrast to common law jurisdictions, where the concepts of discovery or disclosure exist, parties are to a large extent free to submit or withhold documents. In 2002, however, the duty for both parties to provide a full and truthful account of the facts was introduced in the CCP.[98] The Explanatory Memorandum to

93. Art. 157(1) Rv.
94. Art. 159(2) Rv.
95. Art. 158(1) Rv.
96. Art. 85(1) Rv. In principle, a copy of the document will be sufficient. If the other party disputes the authenticity of the document, he can ask to inspect the original document.
97. Supreme Court 19 Mar. 1999, NJ 1999, 496, LJN: ZC2874 (*Tankink/Hartman*); Supreme Court 9 Mar. 2012, NJ 2012, 174, LJN: BU9204.
98. Art. 21 Rv.

the CCP states that this rule is designed to avoid the intentional misrepresentation of facts.[99] If the parties do not fulfil their duty to give a full account of the facts, the court is free to draw whatever conclusions from this it deems fit, also on its own initiative.[100] It could, for example, reverse the burden of proof on a specific issue. Only with respect to the submission of certain specific documents can this duty be enforced (see § 5.4).[101] Although it is not yet clear how far the obligation to disclose under the CCP extends, it should not be considered obligatory to submit all evidence which both supports and adversely affects a case. The parties can still provide a biased picture of the facts, as long as they do not intentionally misrepresent them.

The court on its own initiative can also order a party to submit certain documents.[102] However, if a party does not obey that order, the only thing the court can do is to draw its own conclusions. It cannot compel disclosure. Only in proceedings concerning annual accounts may a court order disclosure of books and documents the company is obliged to keep, on pain of a penalty (see § 7.5.2).[103]

There is no rule of law stating that all documents submitted as evidence must be in the Dutch language. In practice, since English is widely spoken in the Netherlands, English documentary evidence will usually be accepted in court proceedings. If counsel for one of the parties objects to the use of English documents or the court so requests, a Dutch translation will need to be submitted.

5.2.2 Witnesses

5.2.2.1 General

Witness evidence can be submitted in two forms: by means of a written declaration of a witness or by witness examination.

Parties may testify on their own behalf, although such testimony can never lead to conclusive evidence at their advantage, if it is not corroborated by other evidence.[104] When a company is one of the litigating parties, the statements of its managing directors (holding this position at the date of the witness hearing) are considered as statements on behalf of the company.[105] Certain persons, however, have the absolute right to decline to give evidence (*verschoningsrecht*) once they

99. MvT, TK 26 855, No. 3, Art. 1.3.3.
100. Supreme Court 25 Mar. 2011, RvdW 2011, 418, LJN: BO9675.
101. Art. 843a Rv.
102. Arts 22 and 162(1) Rv.
103. Art. 162(3) Rv.
104. Art. 164(1) and (2) Rv.
105. Supreme Court 22 Dec. 1995, NJ 1997, 22, LJN: ZC1928 (*Reprotechniek/Traugott*); Supreme Court 22 Dec. 1995, NJ 1997, 23, LJN: ZC1932 (*Masteco/Top-Pharm*); Supreme Court 23 May 2008, JBPr 2008, 41, LJN: BB3733 (*E&T/Milieutechniek*).

appear in court.[106] These include attorneys (see § 5.3), civil law notaries, doctors and clergymen. Accountants, bankers and tax advisers do not have the right to invoke such a privilege. Certain family members of the litigating parties and persons who could criminally implicate themselves or their close family members by their testimony also have the right to refuse to give evidence.

Unlike documentary evidence (including written witness statements) which can be submitted to a court on a party's own initiative, witness examinations can only be held on the basis of a court order. If a party offers to produce evidence by witnesses, the court must allow this, provided that the offer concerns challenged facts which may be decisive to the case and has been specified sufficiently.[107] Especially in appeal an offer for evidence must specify the arguments to which it relates, and, if possible, the name(s) of the witnesses. The court cannot refuse to hear witnesses on the basis of a prediction of what a witness will testify. A court order will usually take the form of an interim judgment. In this judgment, the court will determine which facts one or each of the parties should prove and on which day the witness examinations should take place.[108]

5.2.2.2 Value as Evidence

Witness testimonies do not have special value as evidence. Consequently, the general rule, that it is up to the court to decide the value of each statement (see § 5.2.1.1), applies.

An exception applies to statements of the parties made on their own behalf in witness hearings. Such statements can only be considered as corroborative evidence. The rule that a statement on a party's own behalf can only be considered as corroborative evidence only applies if the statement is used as evidence for a fact in relation to which that party has the burden of proof. It does not apply if the statement is used to contradict the evidence of another party bearing the burden of proof.[109] This exception does not apply to written declarations from a party although in practice, in deciding the value of the statement, the court will certainly take into account that it is a party statement.[110]

5.2.2.3 Written Witness Declarations

It is for the parties to decide whether they wish to submit a written witness declaration. There is no obligation to submit such statement, not even prior to a witness

106. Arts 165(2) and 165(3) Rv.
107. Art. 166(1) Rv.
108. Art. 166(2) Rv.
109. Supreme Court 17 Jan. 2003, NJ 2003, 176, LJN: AF0159 (*Durinck/Pavema*).
110. Supreme Court 24 Jan. 2003, NJ 2003, 166, LJN: AE9384 (*Adrichem/Reek*).

hearing. However, written witness declarations, usually drawn up with the help of counsel of the party who relies on the witness, are quite often submitted. Such statements must be considered as regular documentary evidence for which it is up to the court to decide their value.

Witness statements may be submitted to the Rotterdam District Court pursuant to the Office Statement Regulation (*Regeling inzake kantoorverklaringen*) of the Supervisory Board of the Rotterdam Bar Association. This regulation allows parties to hear witnesses in their counsel's offices rather than during a formal court hearing, if they both consent to such proceedings. As with regular documentary evidence, it is up to the court to decide the value of a statement drawn up in accordance with this procedure. However, the fact that counsel for both sides have the opportunity to question the witness may lend more weight to a statement drawn up in this way than to a written statement drawn up by one party only.[111]

5.2.2.4 Witness Hearings

The party which is ordered in an interim judgment to give evidence is responsible for calling the witnesses. This is usually done through a letter served by a bailiff. Each person who is called as a witness is obliged to appear in court on the date set by the court and to give testimony.[112] If a witness does not adhere to this request, he could ultimately be committed to prison for failure to comply with a judicial order.[113] Parties to the proceedings who refuse to testify on their own behalf can, however, not be committed for failure to do so.

A witness who does not appear may be ordered to reimburse the expenses of a party connected with the calling of the witness and may also be liable for damages.[114] A more effective way to induce a witness to appear is to request his appearance in preliminary relief proceedings on pain of a penalty.[115] Penalties cannot be imposed on a witness who refuses to testify on his own behalf.[116]

The witness hearing takes place before one judge. This is usually the judge who was involved in delivering the interim judgment, and as far as possible, this judge will also be involved in delivering the final judgment.[117] Except for witnesses testifying on their own behalf, a witness cannot attend other witness hearings prior

111. This regulation was introduced in 2004 mainly in an attempt to eliminate the Rotterdam Court's backlog, and is now mainly used in shipping cases. Counsel for both parties are present at the 'hearing' and can question the witnesses. Witnesses are requested by counsel to confirm that they are telling the truth, but they are not officially sworn in. At the end of the hearing a written statement is prepared and signed by the witness.
112. Art. 165(1) Rv.
113. Art. 173 Rv.
114. Art. 178 Rv.
115. Supreme Court 18 May 1979, NJ 1980, 213, LJN: AC6585 (*Hulskorte/Van der Lek*).
116. Supreme Court 6 Apr. 2012, NJ 2012/363, LJN BV3403 (*Claimants/Karadzic*).
117. Art. 155(1) Rv.

to being heard himself. After the witness has taken the oath (*eed*) or made a solemn affirmation (*belofte*), it is the judge who asks the witness questions. Counsel for each party can then ask additional questions.[118] The court may decide that questions do not have to be answered, for example when they are irrelevant for the issue in respect of which the order to produce evidence was given. Officially, the hearing is conducted in the Dutch language. If a witness speaks a foreign language, the party calling the witness should have an interpreter present. In practice, if the witness speaks English, the judge speaks English as well and if none of the parties objects to the use of the English language, the judge may decide to question the witness in English.

The Dutch courts do not use or allow court reporters to report literally what each witness says. The witness's answers are summarised by the judge and set out in a report (which will always be in Dutch). The report will be read to the witness and (through his counsel) he can then make changes to the report.[119] Finally, the report will be signed by the witness, the judge and the court clerk. A witness who intentionally gives a false declaration commits perjury and can be prosecuted.[120]

In general, the whole setting in which Dutch witness hearings are conducted is less adversary than is often seen in courts in the United States or the United Kingdom.

5.2.2.5 Preliminary Witness Hearing

Parties may request a court to order that witnesses are heard prior to or at any stage during the proceedings.[121] Preliminary witness hearings (*voorlopig getuigenverhoor*) should be distinguished from depositions under US law, as they are conducted before the court. These hearings are especially helpful in cases where the claimant is not yet sure whether he has enough evidence to initiate proceedings against a potential defendant. However, such hearings can also be used to hear witnesses soon after the disputed facts to avoid evidence from getting lost. The request should be filed by a petition to the court in the place where the majority of the witnesses are domiciled, or to the court which would be competent to hear the case if proceedings were initiated. The petition should list the nature of the claim, the facts to be proven and the names of the potential witnesses and defendant.[122] Although the (potential) defendant can object to such a request, the court usually

118. Art. 179 Rv.
119. Art. 180 Rv. If the changes deviate materially from what the witness testified before, the judge may be asked to make a note of this in the report.
120. Art. 207 Penal Code (*Wetboek van Strafrecht*).
121. Art. 186 Rv.
122. Art. 187 Rv.

grants a hearing[123] and there is no right of appeal against this.[124] The provisions regarding standard witness hearings also apply to preliminary witness hearings.[125]

Against the background of the purpose of preliminary witness hearings, the Supreme Court has decided that in principle no restrictions can be imposed by the court on the number of witnesses to be heard or the questions posed to the witnesses. The defendant has the right to submit counter-evidence, not only to support his position on the merits of the case, but also to discredit the witnesses already heard.[126]

5.2.3 Experts

5.2.3.1 General

If there are issues in dispute on which a court would like to get an expert opinion, it can order that an expert be appointed to produce a report on the specific issues it has identified or order that an expert should be heard. Such an order can also be issued at the request of one of the parties,[127] but unlike in the case of a request for a witness hearing, a court is under no obligation to grant a request for an expert's report or for a hearing of experts.

It is the court that decides who shall be appointed as expert(s). However, it must first discuss this with the parties. The expert who is finally appointed by the court is obliged to fulfil his obligations impartially. If necessary, the parties must cooperate with the expert, who is required to allow the parties to comment and make requests during the investigation. The parties are usually asked to provide written comments on the draft report. The final expert's report must be duly reasoned and indicate that the parties have had a reasonable opportunity to give their views.[128]

The court is not bound by the expert's report, which has no specific value as evidence. However, in practice, it will rely heavily on this report in rendering its judgment. If the court does not follow the expert's advice, the required extent of the reasoning of its decision will depend on the nature and extent of the parties' objections to the report.[129]

---

123. Compared to ten years ago, there is some more room for courts to deny a request; Supreme Court 11 Feb. 2005, NJ 2005, 442, LJN: AR6809 (*Frog People Mover/Stichting Floriade*); Supreme Court 21 Nov. 2008, NJ 2008, 608, LJN: BF3938 (*Udo/Renault Nissan*).
124. Art. 188(2) Rv.
125. Art. 189 Rv.
126. Supreme Court 16 Dec. 2011, NJ 2012, 316, LJN: BU3922 (*Boekhoorn/Cyrte Investments*).
127. Art. 194 Rv.
128. Arts 198(1) and 198(2) Rv.
129. Supreme Court 5 Dec. 2003, NJ 2004, 74, LJN: AN8478 (*Stichting Nieuw Vredenburgh/Nieuwe Hollandsche Lloyd Schadeverzekering*).

The option for parties to appoint their own expert witnesses was introduced by the CCP in 2002. Although the opportunity had existed for them to submit their own expert's reports prior to this, this new option allows them to ask a court to hear their experts during the proceedings, instead of waiting for a court order to that effect (see § 5.2.2.1). Such a hearing will be similar to a witness hearing but the court can also order the expert to provide further oral or written comments.[130]

5.2.3.2 Preliminary Expert's Report

As with a preliminary witness hearing, the parties can also request a preliminary expert's report by filing a petition prior to or at any stage during the proceedings.[131] If the request is granted, it is not subject to appeal.[132] Once the preliminary expert's report is agreed to, the rules regarding expert's reports in standard proceedings are applicable.[133] The procedure is similar to that of a preliminary witness hearing, which also means that such a request is almost always allowed (see § 5.2.2.5).

5.3 Attorney-Client Privilege

Attorneys – including in-house lawyers registered with the Dutch Bar[134] – are considered to have absolute privilege. Consequently, they have the right to decline to give evidence once they appear in court. This includes both the right to refuse to testify and the right to refuse to produce documents. It is accepted that the importance of attorneys' independent and confidential role in society outweighs the need for unfettered disclosure in court proceedings.

Attorney-client privilege applies equally in civil, administrative and criminal matters. It covers only information that has been entrusted to the attorney in his professional capacity and it is, in principle, up to him to decide whether such information has been entrusted to him in that capacity; there is only marginal review by the courts. The attorney will be allowed to rely on the privilege as long as the court has reasonable doubt as to whether testimony or production of documents would be possible 'without uncovering what should remain covered'.[135]

---

130. Art. 200 Rv.
131. Art. 202 Rv.
132. Art. 204(2) Rv.
133. Art. 205(1) Rv.
134. See § 3.2.2.
135. Supreme Court 1 Mar. 1985, NJ 1986, 173, LJN: AC9066 (*Notaris Maas*), Supreme Court 18 Dec. 1998, NJ 2000, 341, LJN: ZC2808 (*Van Olst/Ontvanger*) and Supreme Court 13 Jan. 2006, NJ 2006, 480, LJN: AU4533 (*Kuijper/De Wit*). This reserved attitude of the courts has been 'granted' to the legal profession in the absence of indications that the privilege is being used for purposes for which it is not intended. The criterion developed by the Supreme Court leaves enough room for courts to deny reliance on the privilege if abuse is suspected.

No distinction is made between confidential and non-confidential information. The privilege covers all information provided to and from an attorney in his professional capacity and includes notes, correspondence with the client, and correspondence to and from advisers (such as auditors) relating to the privileged information.[136]

In order to prevent attorney-client privilege from being eroded, it has been generally accepted under Dutch law that an attorney's duty of confidentiality and the legal privilege not only applies to himself, but also to those who work for him (e.g. his secretary) and to advisers instructed by him (e.g. auditors or experts). The derivative attorney-client privilege does not apply, however, if the adviser has been instructed directly by the client, instead of by the client's attorney.[137] Although not clear yet, it is likely that this derivative privilege also applies to the attorney's client. In the pending proposal to amend the disclosure duty under the CCP (see § 5.4), it is explicitly provided that documents that would normally be covered by privilege but are in the hands of someone else, who himself cannot invoke privilege, do not have to be disclosed. Hence, attorney-client product may not be requested from the client or a third party.

In contrast to US and UK law, the prevailing view under Dutch law is that privilege belongs to the attorney, not to the client. Consequently, an attorney cannot be forced by his client to speak. The fact that a client has waived privilege under US or UK law does not affect the right of a Dutch attorney to invoke privilege.

5.4 Pre-trial Discovery or Disclosure

The concept of document discovery or disclosure as it exists under US or UK law does not exist under Dutch law. The court may always order parties to submit documents relevant to the proceedings[138] but there is only one provision in the CCP covering the actual right by a party to request documents (including data such as movies, pictures and computer files).[139] Although the ability to request documents and data on the basis of this provision has been slightly enhanced by the revision of the CCP in 2002, it is still difficult, and often impossible, to obtain copies of

136. The Supreme Court has acknowledged an exception to the attorney-client privilege where an agreement was reached between the parties, which was laid down in writing under the supervision of a civil law notary. The civil law notary can then be obliged to testify about the form and contents of the agreement, including its interpretation. In specific circumstances, an exception to the attorney-client privilege may also apply if agreement has been reached but an attempt to put that agreement in writing under supervision of the civil law notary has failed (Supreme Court 25 Sep. 1992, NJ 1993, 467, LJN: ZC0690 (*Tomol/Notaris Van Eijck*)).

137. Supreme Court 29 Mar. 1994, NJ 1994, 552, LJN: ZC9693 (*AHV*).

138. Art. 22 Rv. If a party fails to comply with an order, the court may draw the conclusion it seems fit.

139. Art. 843a Rv.

documents or data which are in the possession of opponents who are unwilling to submit them.

Pursuant to Article 843a Rv, the requesting party must meet the following conditions. First, it should have a 'legitimate interest' in disclosure. The requesting party must make clear that the documents constitute relevant evidence for him, while his interests will have to be balanced against all the other interests at stake. Second, the requesting party must specify the relevant documents. This condition is designed to prevent fishing expeditions. As a rule of thumb it can be said that documents requested should be described in as much detail as possible. In any event the description of the documents must be concrete enough to be able to determine which documents are meant and whether or not the requesting party has a legitimate interest in obtaining them. Third, the documents must 'relate to' a legal relationship (based on either contract or (quasi) tort) to which it is a party or to which its legal predecessor was a party. It has been repeatedly held that the alleged breach of contract or (quasi) tort does not already have to be established by a court. In general, this condition is interpreted broadly, meaning that documents must be of significance to the legal relationship. For example, a due diligence report made by the financial adviser to the buyer of a company has been held to 'relate to' the legal relationship between the buyer and the seller laid down in the share purchase agreement and a copy of such a report could thus successfully be claimed by the seller from the buyer or from his adviser.[140] Nevertheless, this third condition may under current law prevent a request for documents to third parties (not involved in pending or future proceedings between claimant and defendant). In 2001, in a case involving a letter of request from an English court, the Supreme Court upheld a decision which denied a request to a third-party bank to produce account statements of one of its customers.[141] Following the opinion of most scholars, however, lower courts have quite often allowed requests to third parties. In the future, this debate will be ended, as a bill is pending before Parliament, which explicitly provides that documents may also be requested from third parties (see below and footnote 148).

The duty to disclose documents does not apply if it conflicts with other laws, such as the Law on Data Protection (*Wet bescherming persoonsgegevens*) or the Police Files Act (*Wet politiegegevens*). It also does not apply to those who have a right to refuse to give evidence because of their professional occupation (see § 5.2.2.1), or if there are compelling reasons to refuse disclosure.[142] Protection of trade secrets, confidentiality of internal consultations and a duty of secrecy towards a contracting party are in themselves not compelling reasons. The test is whether

140. Court of Appeal 's-Hertogenbosch 28 Sep. 2004, JOR 2005, 23, LJN: AS6740 (*BVR/Ho-Cla*); District Court Amsterdam 13 Apr. 2005, JOR 2005, 142, LJN: AT8064 (*Verder Holding/Hagemeyer*); District Court Utrecht 12 Sep. 2007, JOR 2007, 265, LJN: BB3722.
141. Supreme Court 18 Feb. 2000, NJ 2001, 259, LJN: AA4877 (*News International/ABN AMRO*).
142. Arts 843a(3) and 843a(4) Rv.

in the circumstances of the case and after due consideration, the interests protected by secrecy and confidentiality outweigh the interests of society in revealing the truth.[143] As every situation is different, it is not possible to know beforehand whether a court will honour a defendant's argument that the information should remain confidential. One should also bear in mind that in response to such a defence, the court has the means to impose a duty of confidentiality on the requesting party, to decide that confidential parts of the documents should be blackened, to decide that the documents should only be given to a third party, or – if both parties agree – that the court alone will be allowed to see the documents.[144]

Finally, under current law disclosure may also be refused if the evidence can be obtained by other means, for example through witness hearings.[145] This ground for refusal will disappear once the new disclosure provisions enter into force.

If the conditions for application of Article 843a Rv are fulfilled and none of the grounds for refusal apply, the party to whom the request is directed will have to submit all the requested documents and data it has at his disposal. This means that documents and data that are in the possession of a group company or a predecessor should also be produced, if it is legally possible for the requested party to obtain these documents and data. Whether the fact that the documents are located in another country impacts on this decision, is as yet unclear.

A request for submission of documents can be made by a motion during the proceedings on the merits or in separate (e.g. preliminary relief) proceedings, if necessary on pain of forfeiture of a penalty. A claimant may also file a request for documents which he would like to use for proceedings pending outside the Netherlands, provided there is jurisdiction for the request.[146]

If a request for submission of documents is made during the proceedings on the merits, the decision on this request must generally be considered as an interim judgment.[147] This means that an appeal can only be lodged simultaneously with the final judgment, unless the court has explicitly allowed for interim appeal (see §§ 6.1.8.3 and 6.4.1.1).

At the time of writing of this book, a bill is pending before the Lower House to amend Article 843a Rv.[148] In the proposed Article 126a Rv, it is first of all made clear that documents may also be requested from third parties (such as banks, not

143. Supreme Court 11 Jul. 2008, NJ 2009, 451, LJN: BC8421 (*De Telegraaf/Staat der Nederlanden*).
144. Supreme Court 20 Dec. 2002, NJ 2004, 4, LJN: AE3350 (*Lightning Casino/Nederlandse Antillen*); Supreme Court 11 Jul. 2008, NJ 2009, 451 LJN: BC8421 (*Telegraaf/Staat der Nederlanden*).
145. Supreme Court 31 May 2002, NJ 2003, 589, LJN: AD9609 (*K./AEGON*), Court of Appeal Leeuwarden 28 Jun. 2012, LJN: BW9764.
146. Supreme Court 8 Jun. 2012, RvdW 2012, 824, LJN: BV8510 (*Abu Dhabi Islamic Bank/ABN AMRO*).
147. Supreme Court 13 Jul. 2012, RvdW 2012, 1005, LJN: BW3263 (*ABN AMRO/A*) and Supreme Court 13 Jul. 2012, RvdW 2012, 1006, LJN: BW 3264 (*Koedjikov c.s. /Optiver Holding*).
148. *Aanpassing van het Wetboek van Burgerlijke Rechtsvordering in verband met de wijziging van het recht op inzage, afschrift of uittreksel van bescheiden,* TK 33 079, No. 2.

involved in the proceedings). Whether such a third party request is granted will depend on a careful consideration of all the interests involved and will have to be duly reasoned. There are a few other changes in the bill: the requesting party will have a duty of confidentiality and may not communicate the information obtained to third parties; and the court may decide to make the order to disclose conditional upon the paying by the requesting party of a deposit for the costs involved with the production of documents (ultimately, just as under current law, it will be the losing party who pays for these costs). Finally, some procedural amendments are made: in the future it will be easier to ask for production of documents during the proceedings, as a simple request to the court will be sufficient.

Some parties have expressed the concern that if passed, the new law will make fishing expeditions easier. The legislator has firmly denied this. The court has the power to deny a request for document production on grounds of legal privilege and data protection, and because of compelling reasons or proper administration of justice. Moreover it has the power to decide the specific way the information should be made available. All this should be a sufficient guarantee against fishing expeditions.

If a party is not sure whether it has enough evidence to initiate proceedings, it should not ask for production of documents but rely principally on preliminary witness hearings or on a preliminary expert's opinion. The US concept of formal depositions, where the testimony of witnesses is taken without supervision by the court by means of pre-trial discovery, does not exist under Dutch law.

5.5 International Aspects

5.5.1 Formal and Substantive Rules of Evidence

Although the difference is not always clear, a distinction must be made between the formal and substantive rules of evidence. Most rules are considered to be formal and relate to the way the taking of evidence is conducted. The formal rules are governed by Dutch law, being the law of the forum (*lex fori*).[149] The ability to decline to give evidence (e.g. on the basis of attorney-client privilege) and the way in which witness hearings take place and in which experts are appointed are all issues which are subject to the law of the forum. Some rules however are considered to be substantive, for instance the rules which raise presumptions of law or which determine the burden of proof. These rules are governed by the *lex causae*, i.e. the law governing the substantive legal relationship at stake.[150] If the relationship is contractual, the applicability of the *lex causae* to presumptions of law and burden

149. Art. 10:3 BW.
150. Art. 10:13 BW.

of proof also derives from the EC Regulation on the law applicable to contractual obligations ('Rome I').[151] As regards the admissibility of evidence, Rome I stipulates that a contract or an act intended to have legal effect may be proven by any mode of proof recognised by the law of the forum or by any of the laws under which that contract or act is formally valid, provided that such mode of proof can be administered by the forum.[152] Similar rules regarding the burden of proof and admissibility of evidence apply in the case of non-contractual obligations under the EC Regulation on the law applicable to non-contractual obligations ('Rome II'), which applies in all EU Member States except Denmark from 11 January 2009.[153]

5.5.2 Taking of Evidence Abroad

Several Treaties exist which allow the Dutch courts to request non-domestic authorities, by means of a letter of request (*rogatoire commissie*), to obtain evidence or to perform some other judicial act.[154] The most important Treaty in this respect is the Hague Convention on the Taking of Evidence Abroad (the 'Hague Evidence Convention'), to which many countries are party, including the United States. The letter of request should include the names and addresses of the parties, the nature of the proceedings, the evidence to be obtained, the questions to be posed to the witnesses or the documents which should be inspected and, if necessary, any specific requirement with respect to the evidence. The letter of request is usually issued by a court on the request of one of the parties. On the basis of the Hague Evidence Convention, the Dutch authorities may also themselves be requested to take evidence for the purpose of non-domestic proceedings. Witness hearings pursuant to a letter of request are held in accordance with Dutch procedural law and the only documents and data a claimant can request to produce are specific documents and data which fall under the disclosure duty of the CCP (see § 5.4).[155]

---

151. Art. 18(1) EC Council Regulation of 17 Jun. 2008 on the law applicable to contractual obligations (Rome I), No. 593/2008, O.J. EUR. COMM. (No. L 177) 6 (2008). Rome I replaces the Convention on the Law applicable to Contractual Obligations of 19 June 1980, (the 'Rome Convention'), O.J. EUR. COMM. (No. L 266) 1 (1980), by turning it into a Community instrument and modernising some of its rules. Its substantive provisions apply directly from 17 Dec. 2009 in all EU Member States, except Denmark, to all contracts concluded after this date. To contracts concluded before that date, the EC Convention still applies.
152. Art. 18(2) Rome I.
153. Art. 22(1) EC Council Regulation of 11 July 2007 on the law applicable to non-contractual obligations (Rome II), No. 864/2007, O.J. EUR. COMM. (No. L 199) 40 (2007); CJEU 17 Nov. 2011, C-412/10, NJ 2012, 109, LJN: BU5964 (*Homawoo/GMF*).
154. Hague Convention on Civil Procedure of 1 Mar. 1954, Trb. 1954, 40 and Hague Convention on the Taking of Evidence Abroad in Civil or Commercial Matters of 18 Mar. 1970, Trb. 1975, 38. All Hague Conventions can be found on the website of the Hague Convention, <www.hcch.net>.
155. Supreme Court 11 Mar. 1994, NJ 1995, 3, LJN: ZC1296 (*Kilbarr/Holland*).

The Netherlands, like many other countries, will not execute letters of request issued for the purpose of obtaining pre-trial discovery of documents as would be the case in some common law countries such as the United States.[156]

Within the EU, the taking of evidence in international situations is governed by the EC Council Regulation on cooperation between the courts of the Member States in the taking of evidence in civil or commercial matters (the 'EC Evidence Regulation').[157] The EC Evidence Regulation applies to all EU Member States, with the exception of Denmark. The content of the EC Evidence Regulation is very similar to that of the Hague Evidence Convention, however the EC Evidence Regulation contains some clarifications and amendments to simplify and expedite the procedure for the taking of evidence. For example, the letter of request is transmitted directly from the court in the state of origin to the court in the state of execution and does not need to pass through the Central Authority of the state of execution. The Supreme Court was recently faced with the question whether a witness residing in another EU Member State could refuse to appear as a witness before the Dutch court and insist that he be summoned as a witness under the EC Evidence Regulation, i.e. that he be heard before his own court. In response to a preliminary question, the CJEU held that a court is not compelled to use the EC Evidence Regulation, and that it has the right to summon the witness before it and hear him in accordance with its own law. If the witness refuses to appear, the court can then draw its own conclusions. A foreign witness can thus not demand to be heard before his own court.[158]

If neither the Hague Evidence Convention nor the EC Evidence Regulation applies, the rules of the CCP will be applicable.[159] In all situations, with respect to witnesses who reside abroad, there are basically three options to have them testify. If the non-domestic witness is willing to travel to the Netherlands, the normal rules of witness hearings of the CCP apply. If the witness is prepared to testify but refuses to travel, the court can either ask the competent authority of the state where the

---

156. Art. 23 Hague Evidence Convention: "A Contracting State may at the time of signature, ratification or accession, declare that it will not execute Letters of Request issued for the purpose of obtaining pre-trial discovery of documents as known in Common Law countries." In their subsequent declaration, the Netherlands have stated: "For the purposes of Article 23 of the Convention, 'Letters of Request issued for the purpose of obtaining pre-trial discovery of documents as known in common law countries', which the Netherlands will not execute, are defined by the Government of the Kingdom of the Netherlands as being any Letters of Request which require a person: (a) to state which of the documents which are of relevance to the proceedings to which the Letter of Request relates have been in his possession, custody or power; or (b) to produce any document other than particular documents specified in the Letter of Request as being documents which the court which is conducting the proceedings believes to be in his possession, custody or power."
157. EC Council Regulation of 28 May 2001 on cooperation between the courts of the Member States in the taking of evidence in civil or commercial matters, No. 1206/2001, O.J. EUR. COMM. (No. L 174) 1 (2001). The Regulation entered into force on 1 Jan. 2004.
158. CJEU 6 Sep. 2012, C-170/11 (*Lippens c.s./Kortekaas*).
159. Art. 176 Rv.

witness resides to allow the hearing to take place before a designated official (e.g. a consular agent, a diplomatic officer or a court officer) or issue a letter of request to the relevant foreign authority, which will then need to be executed. If the witness not only refuses to travel but also declines to testify, the evidence may only be obtained by transmitting a letter of request. The value of a witness report from another country is equal to that of a Dutch report, which means that it is up to the court to determine the value of such a statement (see § 5.2.2.2). However, if the foreign authority has not enabled all parties to attend the witness hearing abroad, the relevant Dutch court may not base its decision on the resulting witness report.[160]

5.5.3 Foreign Law

If a dispute is international, the court will apply Dutch conflict of law rules on its own initiative. All procedural issues are governed by Dutch law as *lex fori*.[161] For issues regarding the merits of the case, this will be different. If the conflict of law rules lead to the applicability of extraterritorial law, the parties must 'prove' the contents and implications of that law and may use all evidentiary means to do this, including the submission of written legal opinions (by foreign scholars). In principle, the court also has a duty to investigate the contents of such foreign law on its own initiative and it is not bound to the parties' explanation.[162] Pursuant to the European Convention on Information of Foreign Law of 1968,[163] which applies to almost all Member States of the Council of Europe (*Raad van Europa*) and to a few other countries,[164] a court can request information on applicable foreign law directly from the competent authority in the country concerned.[165]

The parties have an additional interest in informing the District Court and the Court of Appeal on the contents of the applicable foreign law to the best of their abilities, as, contrary to cases governed by Dutch law, it will not be possible at a later stage to appeal to the Supreme Court on the grounds that the foreign law was not applied correctly.[166]

160. Supreme Court 25 Oct. 1991, NJ 1992, 6, LJN: ZC0383 (*Peters/Hagemans*).
161. Art. 10:3 BW.
162. Art. 10:2 BW.
163. European Convention on Information of Foreign Law of 7 June 1968, Trb. 1968, 142.
164. As of 1 Oct. 2012, Belarus, Costa Rica and Mexico, <www.conventions.coe.int>.
165. Art. 67 Rv.
166. Art. 79(1)(b) RO. It is, however, possible to file an appeal with the Supreme Court if the way in which the extraterritorial law was applied, was incorrectly or insufficiently reasoned: Supreme Court 2 Mar. 1989, NJ 1990, 688, LJN: AL7834 (*USSR/ICC Handelmaatschappij*).

6. THE PROCEEDINGS

6.1 Course of the Proceedings at First Instance

6.1.1 General

Most legal proceedings are initiated with a writ of summons (*dagvaarding*). After the claimant has arranged for service of the writ on the defendant, he must register the writ with the competent court and pay a court registry fee. The defendant has the opportunity to file his defence. Depending on the nature of the proceedings, this will be followed by an appearance before the court and/or further written statements and the process will sometimes be rounded off with closing arguments. The proceedings will conclude with a judgment being delivered.

Not all proceedings are, however, initiated by a writ of summons. For example, in some cases involving family law, in disputes regarding foreclosure on collateral, and for certain issues relating to company law (see §§ 7.2 and 7.5), claims will be initiated with the filing of a petition with the court. These petition proceedings will be dealt with separately in § 6.5.

The proceedings are conducted in the Dutch language. This means that all written submissions drawn up by counsel of the parties must be in Dutch.[167] However, the documentary evidence on which the submissions rely may generally also be in English (see § 5.2.1.2).

6.1.2 Service of Process

6.1.2.1 Commencement of the Proceedings

A lawsuit commences with the serving of a writ of summons on a defendant by a claimant.[168] Service of process is the formal delivery of the writ to the defendant, by which the latter is formally notified that a lawsuit has been started against him. Thereafter, the claimant must register the writ with the court on the date stated in the writ (see § 6.1.4.2). This is different from the practice in most Anglo-Saxon jurisdictions, where the proceedings commence with the filing of a complaint with the court, after which the complaint is served on the defendant by that court.

167. See e.g. District Court Utrecht cantonal division 14 Dec. 2005, Prg 2006, 121, LJN: AY5238; District Court Haarlem cantonal division 3 Jul. 2008, Prg 2008, 138; LJN: BD6218 (*Ohra Schadeverzekeringen/defendant*).
168. Art. 125(1) Rv.

6.1.2.2 Service of Process on Dutch Defendants

Contrary to common law jurisdictions, service of a writ can only be performed by a court bailiff.[169] Court bailiffs are appointed by government to act, among other things, as official process servers. The bailiff usually visits the domicile of the defendant and delivers the summons to him. If the defendant is not present, the bailiff may leave the summons behind with someone else living at the house or with any other person present whom the bailiff can reasonably expect to give the writ to the defendant; if that is not possible, he may leave the summons behind in the mailbox. If that is also not possible, he must instantly mail the writ to him.[170] If the defendant is a corporation, the writ can be served at the offices of the company, or served personally on any of its directors or at a director's domicile.[171] The address of the offices of a company, as well as the addresses of its directors, are registered in the trade register of the Chamber of Commerce, which is available for public inspection.

6.1.2.3 Service of Process on Foreign Defendants

If the defendant has no known domicile or residence in the Netherlands, but does have a known address abroad, a distinction must be made between a defendant who resides in (i) a State to which the EC Council Regulation on the Service in the Member States of Judicial and Extrajudicial documents in Civil or Commercial Matters (the 'EC Service Regulation')[172] applies or (ii) a State which is a party to the Hague Convention on the Service Abroad of Judicial and Extrajudicial Documents in Civil or Commercial Matters of 1965 (the 'Hague Service Convention') or the

169. Art. 45 Rv.
170. Arts 46(1) and 47(1) Rv.
171. Art. 50 Rv.
172. EC Council Regulation of 13 Nov. 2007 on the service in the Member States of judicial and extra-judicial documents in civil or commercial matters, No. 1393/2007 (O.J. EUR. COMM. (No. L 324) 79 (2007)). The EC Service Regulation applies to all EU Member States from 13 November 2008, including Denmark (Denmark does not take part in the application of measures pursuant to Part III Title V TFEU such as the Service Regulation, but has concluded an agreement with the EU, to the effect that it will apply the provisions of the Service Regulation). The new EC Service Regulation repeals EC Service Regulation No. 1348/2000. It incorporates certain case law of the CJEU on the EC Service Regulation and makes some improvements to service, amongst others with regard to speed and language of the documents served. It provides a procedure for the service of documents primarily via designated 'transmitting agencies' and 'receiving agencies'.

Hague Convention on Civil Procedure of 1954 (the '1954 Hague Convention')[173] or (iii) another State.[174]

While the EC Service Regulation contains mandatory and exclusive rules for service to be completed in EU Member States, the Hague Service Convention and the 1954 Hague Convention contain rules that are additional to the service requirements for foreign defendants in the CCP.[175] Under the CCP, service on defendants residing abroad is completed if a bailiff serves the writ at the office of the public prosecutor of the court that is competent to hear the case and at the same time mails a copy of the writ to the defendant's address outside the Netherlands. The public prosecutor's office then sends a copy of the writ to the Ministry of Foreign Affairs, which notifies the defendant through diplomatic or consular channels.[176]

A defendant in a state that is party to the Hague Service Convention or the 1954 Hague Convention, who has only been served under the CCP rules has been served in a valid manner but if he does not appear he cannot be declared in default until the court is convinced that the requirements of the Hague Service Convention or the 1954 Hague Convention have also been met (see § 6.1.3).

In cases of urgency, a court may order provisional or protective measures against a defendant who has not appeared, even if the requirements of the Hague Service Convention or the EC Service Regulation have not been met, as long as it has sufficient grounds to conclude that the defendant has been notified of the writ in a timely manner, providing sufficient time to prepare his defence.[177]

The requirements of the Hague Service Convention do not apply if a foreign defendant has explicitly elected domicile in the Netherlands, frequently at his attorney's offices, in which case it is sufficient to follow the ordinary rules for service on Dutch residents.[178] It is likely, although never explicitly decided, that the same applies in the case of the 1954 Hague Convention. As for the EC Service Regulation,

173. Hague Convention on the Service Abroad of Judicial and Extrajudicial Documents in Civil or Commercial Matters of 15 Nov. 1965, Trb. 1966, 91 and Hague Convention on Civil Procedure of 1 Mar. 1954, Trb. 1954, 40. The Hague Convention on Civil Procedure of 17 July 1905, Stb. 1909, 120 has lost its significance now that Iceland has become a party to the 1954 Convention on 10 July 2008. Between the Kingdom of the Netherlands and the United Kingdom there exists a Convention on legal proceedings in civil and commercial matters, which was concluded on 31 May 1932; this Convention still applies in the relations between the Netherlands and some former colonies and protectorates of the United Kingdom, such as Kenya, Lesotho, Fiji, Tonga, Swaziland, and the Commonwealths of Dominica and the Bahamas (Stb 1933, 36; Trb 1966, 295; Trb. 1967, 196; Trb. 1980, 194; Trb. 1998, 19).

174. Arts 54 and 55 Rv.

175. The Hague Service Convention was incorporated into Dutch law by the *Uitvoeringswet Haags Betekeningsverdrag*, Stb. 1975, 5 and the 1954 Hague Convention was incorporated into in Dutch law by the *Uitvoeringswet Haags Rechtsvorderingsverdrag 1954*, Stb. 1958, 677.

176. Art. 55(1) Rv.

177. Art. 15(3) Hague Service Convention and Supreme Court 14 Dec. 2007, NJ 2008, 13, LJN: BB7192 (*Yukos/Rebgun*). Art. 19(3) EC Service Regulation contains a provision similar to that of Art. 15(3) Hague Service Convention.

178. Supreme Court 2 Feb. 1996, NJ 1997, 26, LJN: ZC1982 (*Nieuwersteeg/Colonia c.s.*).

the recitals make clear that it does not apply to service on a party's authorised representative in the Member State where the proceedings are taking place.

Although neither the EC Service Regulation nor the Hague Service Convention prescribes a translation of the writ of summons, it is nevertheless advisable to provide one as, under the EC Service Regulation, a defendant may otherwise refuse to accept the writ[179] and under the Hague Service Convention, the Central Authority has the power to require such a translation if it deems this necessary.[180] For service under the 1954 Hague Convention, a translation is compulsory.[181]

The third situation is where the foreign defendant has no known address in the Netherlands or abroad, and neither the above-mentioned Conventions nor the Regulation apply. In that case, the writ must be served at the office of the public prosecutor. In addition, an abstract of the writ must be published in a Dutch national or local newspaper.[182]

6.1.2.4 Minimum Period between Service and Appearance in Court

The period between service of a writ on a defendant in the Netherlands and the first day of appearance before a court is a minimum of one week.[183] In proceedings at first instance, if the defendant resides in a European State to which the EC Service Regulation or the Hague Service Convention applies, the period between service and the first day in court is a minimum of four weeks. For defendants residing in other states (such as the United States), a minimum period of three months between service and appearance in court must elapse.[184] If a non-domiciled defendant has chosen domicile in the Netherlands, which often happens in international contracts, or if the same defendant is served personally during a (temporary) stay in the Netherlands, the minimum term of one week applies.[185] It is also possible for the

179. Under Art. 8 of the EC Service Regulation 1393/2007 an addressee may refuse to accept the document to be served if it is not translated into a language the addressee understands or if it is not in the official language of the Member State addressed. The CJEU has held that if a document has been refused for lack of translation, the transmitting agency can remedy this by sending the translation as soon as possible. A period of one month from receipt by the transmitting agency of the information relating to the refusal may be regarded as appropriate but this period can be determined by the national court according to the circumstances (CJEU 8 Nov. 2005, C-443/03, ECR 2005 I-9611, RvdW 2006, 98, LJN: AU5958 (*Götz Leffler/Berlin Chemie AG*)).

180. Art. 5 Hague Service Convention provides that the Central Authority may require a translation in the official language of the Member State addressed.

181. Art. 4(3) *Uitvoeringswet Haags Rechtsvorderingsverdrag 1954*, in combination with Art. 3 of the 1954 Hague Convention, requires a sworn translation into the language of the Member State addressed or a language agreed to between the two Member States.

182. Art. 54 Rv. In the near future publication in a newspaper will be substituted by publication on the internet (Innovation agenda of the Ministry of Public Safety and Justice § 4.3, see footnote 5).

183. Art. 114 Rv.

184. Arts 115(2) and 115(3) Rv.

185. Art. 115(3) Rv.

claimant's attorney to ask the defendant's attorney if his client accepts to choose domicile and allow service at his offices, in which case the term will also be just one week (see also § 6.1.2.3).

The court can be requested to shorten the minimum period.[186] In urgent matters to be decided in preliminary relief proceedings, the period between service and appearance can be reduced to an absolute minimum.

6.1.3 Default

If the defendant's attorney does not notify the court on the day of appearance that the defendant will be represented, the claimant may obtain a default judgment. Before entering a default judgment, the court must verify whether all formalities of service of process have been fulfilled and whether all requirements regarding the writ of summons have been met.

If this is the case, the defendant is declared to be in default and the claims of the claimant will be granted. If the EC Service Regulation or the Hague Service Convention applies, the court must verify the formalities in accordance with specific provisions.[187] Within a certain period thereafter, usually at least two weeks, the court will enter a default judgment.

A defendant whose whereabouts are unknown and has thus been served with proceedings by public notice, may also be declared in default. If the defendant is likely to live within the EU, the court must then, however, first satisfy itself that all investigations required by the principles of diligence and good faith have been undertaken to trace the defendant.[188]

If the defendant is represented by an attorney but does not pay the court registry fee in time, he may also be declared in default.[189]

No default judgment will be entered if the court considers the claim on its face to be unlawful or unfounded.[190] A default judgment may be opposed by the defendant before the same court within four weeks (or eight weeks if he is domiciled abroad) after the judgment has been served upon him. If the defendant performs an act that proves he knew about the contents of the judgment or the execution, the term for opposition (*verzet*) is four/eight weeks from that day.[191] If there is more than one defendant and some of them fail to appear, the absent defendants are declared to be in default while proceedings continue between the claimant and the defendants

186. Art. 117 Rv.
187. Art. 19 EC Service Regulation and Art. 15 Hague Service Convention.
188. CJEU 15 Mar. 2012, C-292/10, NJ 2012, 286, LJN: BW0381 (*G/De Visser*).
189. Arts 139 and 128(6) Rv.
190. Art. 139 Rv.
191. Art. 143(2) Rv. See also Supreme Court 9 Oct. 2009, NJ 2009, 491, LJN: BJ0652 (*Shamshum/Mahuko*).

who have appeared in court.[192] The judgment in such a case will not be considered a default judgment in relation to the absent defendants.[193] This means that the absent defendants cannot oppose, but only appeal the judgment. They thus miss one instance to defend their case. Until a (default) judgment is entered, defendants who were absent on the first day of appearance are allowed to correct their omission; they may still appear in court and defend their case. If this happens they will, however, in principle, be ordered to pay the costs related to their late appearance.[194]

6.1.4 Written Statements

6.1.4.1 General

The written statements (comparable to those known in certain common law jurisdictions as 'pleadings' or 'statements of case') are the papers by which the litigants set out their case to the court. The claimant and the defendant can each submit at least one written statement. It should be noted that many of the judgments entered in civil law cases are based solely on the written statements submitted.

Although from 1 September 2008 some of the communication with the court proceeds digitally through standardised forms, it is not yet possible to submit the actual written statements digitally. The recent Law on the Electronic Submission of Writs has made it possible to designate by decree categories of cases, in which a writ of summons may be submitted electronically. As yet, this is only made possible for monetary claims before the cantonal division of the District Courts, therefore not above EUR 25,000.[195]

6.1.4.2 Writ of Summons

Most legal proceedings are initiated with a writ of summons (comparable to a claim form in the United Kingdom). The writ must contain the names and addresses of the parties, the competent court and the day of formal appearance in court, the nature of the dispute (including all the necessary facts), the relief sought (e.g. specific performance or damages, see § 6.3), and the cause of action.[196] Although the CCP stipulates that the court is required to supplement the parties' legal arguments,[197] it can only do so if the new ground is supported entirely by the facts and the positions

192. Art. 140(1) Rv.
193. Art. 140(2) Rv.
194. Art. 142 Rv.
195. Art. 125(3) Rv and *Besluit elektronische indiening dagvaarding*, Stb. 2012, 292. Both the law and the decree entered into force on 1 July. 2012 (Stb. 2012, 291). See also footnote 6.
196. Art. 111(2) BW.
197. Art. 25 Rv and, for example, Supreme Court 15 Feb. 2002, NJ 2002, 228, LJN: AD6625 (*De Rond cs/Flottille*).

taken by the parties in the proceedings. The court is not allowed to alter or supplement the factual basis or the positions taken by the parties.[198]

In 2002, the CCP introduced the requirement to include in the writ the arguments of the defendant against the claim, unless his arguments are not known. In addition, the claimant must sum up the evidence on which he intends to rely, including the names of the witnesses who will support his claim.[199] The reason this requirement was introduced is that the legislature wants parties to provide all information on the dispute at the beginning of the process, preventing them from 'keeping their powder dry' until the last moment.

The writ is an important document in the litigation. The description it contains of the dispute is a decisive factor in establishing the competent court (see § 4.). Service of a writ also interrupts the limitation period. Finally, a writ that clearly states the facts and that specifies the relief sought can enable the court to enter a default judgment if the defendant does not appear.

The writ does not have legal effect unless it is registered with the court before the date of appearance mentioned therein.[200] On the date of appearance, the court becomes involved and the defendant has the opportunity to engage an attorney to represent him.

As mentioned above, it is as yet only possible to file a writ through electronic means for monetary claims up to and including EUR 25,000.

6.1.4.3 Statement of Defence

The defendant is allowed to respond to the claim in his statement of defence, after he has paid the court registry fee.[201] He will have six weeks from the date of his formal appearance in court, which term may be extended for six weeks, and extended further on certain conditions.[202] The statement of defence must address the claim and must in principle contain all the arguments that the defendant intends to rely on. Like the claimant, the defendant must assert the evidence on which he intends to rely, including the names of the witnesses who will support his defence.[203] If he wants to make certain interlocutory applications (motions) or bring forward certain procedural defences, the defendant will need to make sure that he does so prior to

198. Art. 24 Rv and Supreme Court 3 Oct. 2003, NJ 2004, 50, LJN: AF9712 (*De Nieuwe Woning/Staat der Nederlanden*); Supreme Court 10 Feb. 2006, NJ 2006, 154, LJN: AU5702 (*Univé Schade/Axa Schade*) and Supreme Court 9 Dec. 2012, JBPr 2012, 35, LJN: BR2045 (*Doornenbal/Van der Spek*). The Court can, however, invite a party to supplement its own position if the other party does not object thereto, see Supreme Court 14 Mar. 2008, NJ 2008, 466, LJN: BC1231 (*X/Aerts qq*).

199. Art. 111(3) Rv.

200. Art. 125(2) Rv.

201. Art. 128(2) Rv.

202. Arts 2.7 and 2.8 Docket rules for the District Court (*Landelijk Procesreglement voor civiele dagvaardingszaken bij de Rechtbanken*), version 1 January 2012, <www.rechtspraak.nl>.

203. Art. 128(5) Rv.

or simultaneously with the submission of his statement of defence on the merits of the case. A motion to decline jurisdiction can be raised as a separate defence and submitted independently of the statement of defence. The statement of defence will then need to be submitted only after the court has declared itself competent. The raising of such a motion can thus substantially delay the proceedings. Motion practice is discussed in more detail in § 6.2.

If the defendant wishes to file a counterclaim, he is also required to do this in his statement of defence.[204] The counterclaim should refer to the arguments on which the claim is based, the defence of the defendant in the counterclaim (the original claimant) and the evidence and witnesses on which the defendant relies. In the event of a counterclaim, the original claimant (defendant in the counterclaim) will have the opportunity to submit a statement of defence to the counterclaim. The claim and the counterclaim will be adjudicated upon by the court in one judgment.[205]

6.1.4.4 *Statement of Reply and Statement of Rejoinder*

The claimant and the defendant will only be allowed to submit further written statements (statement of reply and statement of rejoinder, respectively) if the court permits them to do so (see § 6.1.5). Although the court has wide discretion in making that decision, the parties can suggest in their first written statement that they wish to submit a statement of reply and rejoinder and the court should take their wishes into account in making its decision.

6.1.4.5 *Amendment of Claim*

The claimant may use the statement of reply to increase or change his claims or the grounds for his claims. As long as it is in writing he may also do so at an earlier or at a later stage, until the final judgment. The defendant may object to such an amendment of the claim if it is contrary to 'the requirements of due process', because it would unduly delay the proceedings or because it would unduly hinder him in his defence.[206] The court's decision may not be appealed. If the claimant reduces his claim, the defendant may not object.[207]

---

204. Art. 137 Rv.
205. Art. 138(1) Rv.
206. Art. 130(1) Rv.
207. Art. 129 Rv.

6.1.5 Order to Appear in Court

After the submission of the statement of defence, the general principle is that the court orders the parties to appear in court (*comparitie na antwoord*).[208] This is an important difference compared to proceedings under the old CCP, where such personal appearances were the exception and multiple written submissions the rule. The purpose of this change is to shorten the length of average proceedings. During the parties' appearance, the judge can investigate whether the dispute can be settled, further information can be requested, issues can be narrowed down and, generally, discussions can take place on how the proceedings should be continued.[209] Prior to their appearance, the parties can submit additional documents. Directors or other persons attending court on behalf of a company are required to submit proof that they are authorised to act on its behalf (in the event of a settlement). Only if the court considers it necessary are the parties granted an opportunity to follow up the appearance in court with a statement of reply and a statement of rejoinder.

If the court does not require a personal appearance at all, it will allow the claimant and the defendant to submit a statement of reply and a statement of rejoinder respectively.[210] Although a court has wide discretion in determining which cases should be heard before it, an order for personal appearance is unlikely in disputes involving complex legal issues or where the facts are extensive and disputed by the parties. The parties can also give their reasons for choosing or declining a personal appearance in their first written statement.

6.1.6 Closing Arguments

6.1.6.1 Request for Closing Arguments

Before the court enters its judgment, the parties may ask it to set a date for closing arguments (*pleidooi*). The right to argue one's case orally before the court is considered a fundamental right. The general rule is therefore that a request for closing arguments must be granted except in two cases. First, the request may be denied if there has previously been a personal appearance in accordance with the CCP during which the parties have had sufficient opportunity to present their case (see § 6.1.5).[211] This exception does not apply, however, if further evidence was provided by one of the parties after the personal appearance.[212] Secondly, in exceptional cases, a court may deny a party closing arguments on grounds of due

208. Art. 131 Rv.
209. Arts 87 and 88 Rv.
210. Arts 131 and 132 Rv.
211. Art. 134(1) Rv.
212. TK 26 855, No. 5, p. 61.

process, for example if permitting it to present such arguments would unnecessarily delay the proceedings (see § 3.4). The court may do so on its own initiative or on request of the other party. The court should, however, clearly justify its denial in its judgment.[213]

6.1.6.2 Nature of Closing Arguments

Closing arguments should not be used merely to repeat the arguments made in the written statements. They should rather be used to stress certain aspects of the case in order to paint the bigger picture. Prior to the oral hearing, documents can be submitted while, during the closing arguments, the parties can put forward new facts and, in exceptional instances, even submit new documents. The court will, however, not take into account any facts or documents if their late submission is considered a violation of fair trial or due process (see § 3.4).[214] The closing arguments are usually based on the pleading notes, of which a copy will have been given to the court. Although the parties may personally plead their closing arguments,[215] this is usually done by their attorneys in their presence.

Despite the fact that the parties are often entitled to closing arguments, it should be noted that, in the majority of cases, the parties do not make them and judgments will be based solely on written statements.

6.1.7 Termination of Proceedings

In certain situations, either the claimant or both parties may wish that the proceedings be terminated prior to a judgment being rendered. One instance of this would be when a claimant realises that he has summoned the wrong defendant, or when the parties settle the dispute that is the subject of the litigation. Under the CCP, there are three ways of terminating the proceedings: (i) removing the case from the docket list (see § 6.1.7.1); (ii) withdrawing the proceedings (see § 6.1.7.2); or (iii) prejudicing the right of continuing an action (see § 6.1.7.3).

6.1.7.1 Removal from Docket List

If the parties jointly decide that the proceedings should be terminated, for example as part of a settlement, they can jointly apply to the court to remove the case from

213. Supreme Court 5 Oct. 2001, NJ 2002, 514, LJN: ZC3669 (*Verbeek/SCH*) and Supreme Court 2 Dec. 2011, NJ 2011, 575, LJN: BT7596 (*Waarborgfonds Motorverkeer/X*).
214. See also Art. 19 Rv. In principle, documents should be submitted no later than two weeks before the hearing (Art. 2.9 Docket Rules for the District Court).
215. Art. 134(3) Rv.

the docket list (*doorhaling op de rol* or *royement*).[216] The court can also remove a case from the docket list on its own initiative, provided that it informs the parties beforehand and neither of them wants to continue the proceedings.[217]

Removal from the docket list is an administrative measure only, which means that the cause of action does not lapse, and any party can revive the proceedings at any time thereafter unless such is prevented by an agreement.[218] Obviously, in the case of a settlement, the parties usually agree that the claimant will waive his rights and they will also decide on how the litigation costs should be settled between them.

6.1.7.2 Withdrawal

If a claimant wishes to terminate proceedings, for example because he has instituted litigation proceedings against the wrong defendant, he can do so by withdrawing the proceedings (*afstand van instantie*). This option is, however, only available prior to the defendant submitting his statement of defence.[219] The claimant will then be obliged to pay the legal costs of the defendant, which at that stage usually only consist of the court registry fee.[220] After the statement of defence has been submitted, proceedings can only be terminated by the claimant with the consent of the defendant by removing the case from the docket list (see § 6.1.7.1).

The consequence of this kind of termination is that the parties will automatically be in the same position they were in before the proceedings were initiated.[221] It also means that the claimant will not forfeit his rights of action and that he could, in principle, initiate new proceedings provided that he has paid the legal costs of the original defendant and, of course, his claim has not become time barred.

6.1.7.3 Prejudice of the Right To Take Action

Where no action has been taken in proceedings for 12 months by the party that should act (e.g. file a written statement), the other party can file a motion in order to prejudice the right to continue the action (*verval van instantie*).[222] The party that should act should, however, be given at least two weeks notice before the court can render a judgment prejudicing the right to take action.[223] If the party that should act does not wish the proceedings to be terminated, he should take the relevant action

216. Art. 246(1) Rv.
217. Art. 247 Rv.
218. Art. 246(2) Rv.
219. Art. 249(1) Rv.
220. Art. 249(2) Rv.
221. Art. 250(3) Rv.
222. Art. 251(1) Rv.
223. Art. 251(3) Rv.

(e.g. file his written statement) or explain to the court that there is a good reason for the delay in the proceedings, failing which the court will allow the claim for termination of the proceedings.[224] If the proceedings are terminated, each party in principle bears its own legal costs unless the court decides otherwise.[225]

Again, in first instance this termination does not involve the claimant losing his right of action. He can file his claim in new proceedings, provided that the claim has not become time barred in the meantime.[226] In such new proceedings, the claimant may use judicial admissions (*gerechtelijke erkentenissen*) and evidence provided in the former proceedings.[227]

6.1.8 Judgments

6.1.8.1 General

After written statements have been submitted and, where applicable, the parties have appeared before the court following an order to do so or to plead closing arguments, the court will set a date on which it will enter judgment.[228] The judgment will be either interim or final, which distinction is relevant to the question of appeal. The docket rules prescribe that the judgment should be given within four weeks if the judgment is interim and six weeks if the judgment is final.[229] However, this date is often postponed, frequently more than once.

6.1.8.2 Requirements of a Judgment

The judgment will be reached as a result of a majority vote where the court is made up of more than one judge. The judgment must contain the reasons for the decision, with the exception of default judgments and certain Supreme Court judgments.[230] Dissenting opinions are not published. A judgment should be in writing and signed by the judge or, where there are several judges, by the presiding judge and the court clerk.[231] Generally, a judgment must contain the following information:[232] (i) names and domiciles of the parties and their attorneys; (ii) the course of the proceedings;

224. Art. 251(4) Rv.
225. Art. 252(1) Rv.
226. Art. 253 Rv. In appeals proceedings, this is different. Termination of the appeals proceedings means that the decision in first instance becomes final and conclusive and will have binding force in new proceedings.
227. Art. 253(2) Rv.
228. Art. 229 Rv.
229. Art. 6.4(2) Docket rules for the District Court (*Landelijk Procesreglement voor civiele dagvaardings-zaken bij de Rechtbanken*), version 1 January 2012, <www.rechtspraak.nl>.
230. Art. 30 Rv. See also §§ 3.1.3 and 6.4.2.4.
231. Art. 230(3) Rv.
232. Art. 230 Rv.

(iii) the claim and the arguments of the parties; (iv) the reasons for the decision, including the facts on which the decision is based; (v) the decision; (vi) the name(s) of the judges; and (vii) the date of the judgment. In the case of default judgments, only (ii), (vi) and (vii) must be included, while for the remaining requirements (including the reasons for the decision) reference may be made to the information in the writ of summons.[233]

6.1.8.3 Interim Judgments

If certain actions need to be taken before the delivery of a final judgment or if motions have been made that need to be ruled upon, the court will enter an interim judgment.[234] A common interim judgment is one where one of the parties is ordered to submit certain evidence. The Supreme Court recently decided that a decision on a request for disclosure of documents made during and for the purpose of the main proceedings is not a final but an interim judgment, since it does not put an end to any part of the claim.[235] The same goes for a decision ordering an expert investigation and a down payment for the expert's costs.[236]

The difference between final and interim judgments is important for determining when an appeal can be lodged. The general rule is that an appeal against an interim judgment can only be lodged simultaneously with the final judgment, unless the court has specifically allowed for interim appeal, on its own initiative or upon request of a party (see § 6.4.1.1).

It may be that an interim judgment contains explicit and unconditional decisions by the court on certain aspects of the dispute, without these decisions leading to a grant or denial of the claim. These 'binding final decisions' (*bindende eindbeslissingen*) do not alter the character of the interim judgment, and the appeal rules for interim judgments still apply. In its further judgment(s) the court is bound to these decisions, unless they were based on incorrect facts or incorrect legal grounds.[237] A party that is adversely affected by an interim judgment and fears it may prejudice the final judgment may request a court to reconsider the binding decisions leading to the interim judgment.

Interim judgments must be distinguished from docket decisions (*rolbeschikkingen*), which are decisions of the docket judge (*rolrechter*) that deal merely with the order of the proceedings, such as a decision to grant a party an extension for filing a certain statement or an order to hold the oral hearing at a certain date.

233. Arts 230(2) and 30 Rv.
234. Art. 232 Rv.
235. Supreme Court 13 Jul. 2012, RvdW 2012, 1005, LJN: BW3263 (*ABN AMRO/X*) and Supreme Court 13 Jul. 2012, RvdW 2012, 1006, LJN: BW3264 (*Y/Optiver Holding*).
236. Supreme Court 22 Jan. 2010, NJ 2011, 269, LJN: BK1639 (X/Y).
237. Supreme Court 25 Apr. 2008, NJ 2008, 553, LJN: BC2800 (*De Vries/Gemeente Voorst*); Supreme Court 26 Nov. 2010, NJ 2010, 634, LJN: BN8521 (*Kojen/ABB*).

Docket decisions are not appealable. Decisions that deny a party to hear witnesses for evidence or counter-evidence cannot be considered to be merely docket decisions as they affect the rights and interests of the litigating parties. They should be qualified as interim judgments and are therefore appealable.[238]

6.1.8.4 *Final Judgments*

Judgments qualify as final (*eindvonnis*) once they end the dispute brought before the court. A distinction can be made between judgments ordering a party to do something, such as an award for damages (*condemnatoir vonnis*), judgments which create or cancel a legal relationship (*constitutief vonnis*), and declaratory judgments, which merely confirm the existence of a legal relationship (*declaratoir vonnis*). Judgments can also contain a combination of these elements.

6.1.8.5 *Binding Force*

If a judgment from the District Court or the Court of Appeal is no longer subject to appeal, it becomes final and conclusive (*kracht van gewijsde*). Decisions made in a judgment which is final and conclusive have binding force (*gezag van gewijsde*) on the parties to the proceedings and on their legal successors in other proceedings.[239] Findings as to fact or law in preliminary relief proceedings do not, however, bind the courts in proceedings on the merits.[240]

6.1.8.6 *Provisionally Enforceable Notwithstanding an Appeal*

A judgment is immediately enforceable notwithstanding that it is still open to appeal. However, the moment that a legal remedy, such as an appeal, is lodged, the enforceability is suspended.[241] To prevent this suspension, parties can request the court to declare its judgment provisionally enforceable notwithstanding an appeal (*uitvoerbaar bij voorraad*) and this request is almost always granted.[242] Such request is usually made in the initial claim, but it is also possible to make such request by making a motion on appeal.[243] The court can make the enforceability conditional upon the provision of security by the party who wishes to enforce the judgment. The enforcement of a judgment which is subject to a legal remedy, even if it is declared provisionally enforceable by the court, is, however, made at the

238. Supreme Court 18 Mar. 2011, NJ 2012, 315, LJN: BP0517 (*Antebi/NIH*); Supreme Court 16 Dec. 2011, NJ 2012, 316, LJN: BU3922 (*Boekhoorn/Cyrte Investments*).
239. Arts 236(1) and 236(2) Rv.
240. Art. 257 Rv.
241. Art. 350 Rv.
242. Art. 233 Rv.
243. Art. 234 Rv.

risk of the enforcing party, who is strictly liable for all damages resulting from the enforcement, if the judgment is later overturned in appeal.[244]

6.1.8.7 Rectification, Correction and Supplementation of Judgment

If a judgment contains a manifest computing or clerical error, rectification or correction of the judgment can be requested by either of the parties or be made on the initiative of the court.[245] If the court has failed to decide on one or more matters which have been submitted to it, either party may request the court to supplement its judgment.[246] No time limit applies for a judgment to be corrected or supplemented. Before deciding on such requests, or before correcting the judgment on its own initiative, the court should give the parties the opportunity to be heard. No appeal is possible against a decision to allow or refuse the correction or a decision to refuse to supplement the judgment.[247] If a corrected or supplementary decision is rendered, it will be regarded as a regular judgment and the prior judgment can no longer be enforced.[248]

6.1.9 Litigation Costs and Attorneys' Fees

The party which loses the proceedings will be ordered to pay the costs of the prevailing party.[249] These costs include the court registry fee, together with the costs of service of the writ, costs of attachments, costs relating to compensation of witnesses and experts, and experts' and attorneys' fees. If relevant, the claimant is also entitled to extrajudicial collection costs (*buitengerechtelijke incassokosten*), calculated as from 1 July 2012 as a percentage of the claim on the merits.[250]

Unlike the other costs, the attorneys' fees are as a rule not the actual fees but calculated on the basis of a court approved scale of costs (*liquidatietarief*) that is set out in non-binding but generally applied court guidelines. This scale awards a fixed amount per written statement or court appearance, depending on the magnitude of the claim involved.[251] In practice, this scale leads to a remuneration that only covers a small amount of the attorneys' costs actually incurred by the winning party. For example, in proceedings on a claim of EUR 1 million, where two statements

244. Supreme Court 13 Jun. 1913, NJ 1913, 782 (*Maatschappij van Weldadigheid/Nicola*).
245. Art. 31 Rv.
246. Art. 32 Rv.
247. Arts 31(4) and 32(3) Rv.
248. Arts 31(3) and 32(2) Rv.
249. Art. 237 Rv.
250. Art. 6:96 BW and the Decree on the Refund of Extrajudicial Collection Costs (*Besluit vergoeding voor buitengerechtelijke incassokosten*), Stb. 2012, 141. There is a minimum of EUR 40 and a maximum of EUR 6.775.
251. The *liquidatietarief* is published on <www.rechtspraak.nl>.

are submitted by the parties, followed by closing arguments, the amount awarded would be some EUR 11,000. Unless there is a provision in the contract to that effect, there is no legal right to recover the remainder of the costs from the losing party, even if it was clear from the beginning that this party would lose. In intellectual property cases, due to the implementation in Dutch law of the EC Directive on the Enforcement of Intellectual Property rights, the recovery of litigation costs is regulated differently.[252]

The court can order the losing party to pay the costs on its own initiative. Usually, however, the claimant will request the court to order the defendant to pay the costs. The defendant usually makes the same request in his statement of defence. It is not necessary for the defendant to file a counterclaim to this effect.

6.2 Motion Practice

6.2.1 Introduction

In the course of the proceedings, instead of or in addition to arguing their case on the merits, the parties may file various interlocutory applications (*incidentele vorderingen*) with the court. For ease of reference, such claims or requests are referred to below as 'motions'. Examples are motions to dismiss the case for lack of jurisdiction, motions to commence indemnification proceedings against a third party, and motions to join the proceedings with other proceedings already pending. Third parties may also file motions, such as motions to be allowed to join the litigation.

The CCP does not contain a closed system of interlocutory applications. Apart from the motions explicitly provided for in Articles 210-224 Rv, it allows motions based on statutory rights found elsewhere in the CCP, such as motions for the production of documents under Article 843a Rv (see § 5.4). It is even possible to file motions not provided for in law, as long as they deal with procedural issues. Most motions must be made at an early stage of the proceedings, but some can be made at a relatively late stage.

Motion practice in Dutch civil litigation differs in a number of respects from United States style motion practice. One important difference is that it is not possible in Dutch proceedings to arrive at an early termination of the litigation by filing a motion to dismiss (if the alleged facts do not support the claimant's claims) or a motion for summary judgment. The only undisputed ground which can result in a dismissal by a separate motion is lack of jurisdiction.

252. EC Directive of 29 Apr. 2004 on the enforcement of intellectual property rights, No. 48/2004, O.J. EUR. COMM. (No. L 157) 45 (2004). Art. 14 of this Directive relates to legal costs and was implemented in Art. 1019(h) Rv and the Regulation on Indicative fees in Intellectual Property Cases (*Regeling Indicatietarieven in IE-zaken*), see <www.rechtspraak.nl>. Specifically in patent litigation, costs are fully recovered.

6.2.2 Procedural Aspects of Motion Practice

The CCP contains some general rules on motion practice in proceedings commenced with a writ of summons. These rules apply by analogy to petition proceedings.

Motions must be made by writ of summons (*dagvaarding*) or by a further written statement (*conclusie*). Usually motions will be decided upon before the decision in the main proceedings and if the court deems it necessary the main proceedings will be stayed.[253] As a result, motion practice is sometimes used by parties as a delaying tactic. However, if a party files a motion instead of a statement on the merits, and the CCP does not expressly provide that the motion is of a type which needs to be decided on before the decision on the merits, the filing party runs the risk that the court will decide that it has forfeited its right to file a statement on the merits.[254]

Motions must, to the extent possible, all be made at the same time.[255] However, there is no penalty for breaching this rule other than an award of costs against a party who files his motions consecutively without reasonable grounds. Both the claimant and the defendant can file motions during the proceedings, but not at every stage. Some of the defendant's motions must be part of the statement of defence. This is the case, for example, if a motion contains a procedural defence, such as the invalidity of the writ or the non-admissibility of the appeal by reason of exceeding the period for appeal.[256]

The party opposing the motion is usually granted a short extension of two weeks for filing a statement of defence to the motion. This period may be extended for another two weeks, and extended further on certain conditions. Only in special circumstances may the parties submit further statements. They are, however, entitled to require the court to allow closing arguments on the motion.[257] After the statement of defence against the motion has been submitted or closing arguments have been made, the court will decide the motion in an interim judgment, in which it will also set a date for the main proceedings to be continued. Under the national docket rules, an interim judgment must be given within four weeks.[258] In practice, however, interim judgments often take longer to prepare in view of the backlogs at some courts.

---

253. Art. 209 Rv.
254. Supreme Court 2 Mar. 2012, NJ 2012, 158, LJN: BU8176 (*Bakker/Royal Bank of Scotland*).
255. Art. 208(3) Rv.
256. Art. 128(3) Rv. It must be observed that the scope of this Article is debated. Also, there is an exception as regards a motion to dismiss for lack of jurisdiction; this may be filed prior to the statement of defence (see footnote 259).
257. Art. 208(1) Rv in conjunction with Art. 134 Rv.
258. Art. 6.4(2) Docket rules for the District Court (*Landelijk Procesreglement voor civiele dagvaardingszaken bij de Rechtbanken*), version 1 January 2012, <www.rechtspraak.nl>.

In general, an appeal against an interim judgment may only be lodged simultaneously with an appeal against the final judgment (see § 6.4.1.1).

6.2.3 Motion to Dismiss for Lack of Jurisdiction

If a court does not have international, absolute or relative jurisdiction over a dispute, a defendant may file a motion to dismiss for lack of jurisdiction, either prior to or in his statement of defence.[259] As discussed above, it is not possible to file a motion to dismiss on the grounds of *forum non conveniens* (see § 4.2.3.4).

If the court declines international jurisdiction, it will dismiss the case. The claimant then has the option to start proceedings in another (foreign) court that will have jurisdiction or to appeal the judgment. If the court decides it does have jurisdiction, the entire dispute will generally have to be litigated on its merits before the decision on jurisdiction can be appealed (see § 6.4.1.1).

The CCP contains rules to cover a situation where there is a lack of absolute jurisdiction or venue, i.e. where a claimant has sued in a court without proper jurisdiction when another Dutch court would have been competent. The aim of these rules is to provide a practical solution by passing the matter on to the competent court or allowing the claimant to bring the action in that competent court.

The general rule is that a court that dismisses a case for lack of absolute jurisdiction or venue, refers it to another court with proper jurisdiction.[260] Only if that court is a lower court (e.g. if a Court of Appeal refers the matter to a District Court) is that referral appealable. In such a case, the referral is nevertheless appealable only to the Supreme Court on issues of law, not on issues of fact.[261] A referral to a higher court is not appealable.[262] An appeal is also not possible against a referral by a court to a court of equal ranking in another venue, such as a referral by the Amsterdam District Court to the District Court of The Hague.[263]

Comparable to cases of lack of jurisdiction are cases where an action is commenced by writ of summons instead of by petition (see § 6.1.1) or vice versa, or where a civil suit is commenced against public authorities in cases where the claimant should have commenced administrative proceedings. In the first situation, the claimant will be entitled to exchange his writ of summons for a petition (or vice versa) and, to the extent necessary, amend his arguments.[264] The court can re-route the claim at the request of one of the parties (by way of a motion or a simple request in a statement) or on its own initiative. In the second situation, where administra-

259. Arts 11, 110 and 1022 Rv.
260. Art. 73 Rv for absolute jurisdiction and Art. 110 Rv for venue.
261. Art. 75(1) Rv.
262. Art. 75(2) Rv.
263. Art. 110(3) Rv (and Art. 270(3) Rv for petition proceedings).
264. Art. 69 Rv.

tive proceedings would have been appropriate, the court will mention this in the judgment dismissing the claim, and the term for filing a notice of objection or for commencing administrative court proceedings will be extended to allow the claimant to file such proceedings.[265]

6.2.4 Motion to Consolidate with Another Pending Case

If, prior to the commencement of litigation, proceedings were already pending in the same court between the same parties with respect to the same subject matter, or if the subject matter of the new action is strongly connected (*verknocht*) with the subject matter of other proceedings in that court (even if between different parties), either party to the later proceedings can ask that these proceedings be consolidated with the already pending proceedings.[266] If the earlier proceedings are pending in a different Dutch court with equal ranking, both parties can even ask the court to refer the matter to that other court, so that the cases may be consolidated there.[267]

A claimant can only file such a motion in his writ of summons or in a motion prior to the defendant's statement of defence. The defendant must file the motion prior to or in his statement of defence.[268]

Matters are only considered to be 'strongly connected' if the factual or legal issues in one case are identical to those in the other or are sufficiently closely connected that for efficiency purposes it is desirable to hear the cases together, for example to prevent contradictory judgments or to simplify the submission of evidence.[269]

After the cases have been consolidated, not only the same court but the same judge or panel of judges will deal with both matters. However, the cases remain independent and the findings of fact in both instances may still be different, depending on the way the parties have argued their points and how the evidence is weighed in both cases. Judgments in both matters are given separately, even though they may be contained in one document. Of course, the fact that one (panel of) judge(s) deals with the same matter concurrently in practice implies a high degree of consistency between the two judgments.

265. Art. 70 Rv.
266. Art. 222 Rv.
267. Art. 220 Rv. For the purpose of joining, the cantonal division of the District Court ranks equally with the regular District Court, Art. 220(1) Rv.
268. Arts 220(2), 220(3) and 222(2) Rv.
269. Supreme Court 27 Oct. 1978, NJ 1980, 102, LJN: AC6384 (*Vierhout/Crosland Filters*); District Court Zwolle, 23 May 2007, NJF 2007, 386, LJN: BA8971 (*X/Rabo Vastgoed*).

6.2.5 Motion to Join or Intervene as a Party

A party with a sufficient interest may join the litigation in order to put forward facts and arguments supporting the position of one of the litigating parties (*voeging*). A party with a sufficient interest may even intervene in the litigation with a claim of its own against either the claimant or the defendant (*tussenkomst*).[270] By way of example, an insurance company, or a third party that has given collateral for the defendant's obligations vis-à-vis the claimant, may have an interest in joining the litigation by supporting the defendant. In a situation where the dispute between the claimant and defendant concerns title to certain goods, a third party that also claims title to those goods may wish to intervene with a claim of its own.

The party wishing to join or intervene in the litigation must make a motion to that effect no later than the date set by the court for the submission of the last written statement by the main parties, setting out the grounds for such joining or intervention.[271] In contrast to the joining of proceedings (see § 6.2.4), in this instance there is only one case and one judgment between the original parties and the joining or intervening party.

There has been some controversy as to what constitutes sufficient interest to join or intervene in litigation. Older Supreme Court case law indicated that the joining or intervening party had to demonstrate that its legal rights or legal position were directly being threatened as a result of the proceedings.[272] However, this position has been much criticised in legal literature, and in practice the lower courts often allow joining or intervention when there are reasonable grounds for doing so, e.g. when it is efficient from a procedural perspective as an alternative to the joining or intervening party commencing separate litigation. The Supreme Court has held that a party has sufficient interest to join the proceedings in support of one of the parties if an unfavourable outcome of the litigation for the party he wishes to join would possibly harm his legal position.[273] Earlier, the Supreme Court had confirmed that not only a legal interest but also an interest in fact may constitute sufficient grounds for intervention.[274]

A party that has joined or intervened in litigation has a right of appeal, even if the main litigating parties have not themselves appealed.

---

270. Art. 217 Rv.
271. Arts 218 and 219 Rv.
272. Supreme Court 2 Mar. 1956, NJ 1956, 199 (*Lloyd Levensverzekering/Ter Laag-De Leeuw*) (intervention) and Supreme Court 3 May 1957, NJ 1959, 62 (*Cicero/Bach*) (joining in support of one of the parties).
273. Supreme Court 14 Mar. 2008, NJ 2008, 168, LJN: BC6692 (*Heijmans Holding/Heijmans Management*).
274. Supreme Court 14 Mar. 2003, NJ 2003, 313, LJN: AF2833 (*Cremers/Gasster*); see also judgments of Supreme Court 16 Feb. 1994, NJ 1994, 485, LJN: AD2037 (*Molenschot/VWB*) and Supreme Court, 15 Nov. 1996, NJ 1997, 482, LJN: ZC2200 (*Multivision/De Nederlandse Antillen*).

6.2.6 Motion for Indemnification Proceedings

A defendant may often wish to take recourse against a third party in the event that he loses the litigation case against the claimant. For instance, the defendant may have recourse claims against his insurers or his employer. Or he may have a claim for contribution against a third party that is, in his view, liable to the claimant and should contribute all or part of the damages that may be awarded against him as a defendant. Sometimes, the defence put forward by the defendant may urge the claimant to commence proceedings against a third party. For instance, in a tort case, a defendant may argue that the tort was not committed by himself but by a third party that the claimant was not previously aware of.

In these cases, the defendant (or the claimant, as the case may be) may have an interest in having his recourse or other rights against the third party determined in proceedings that are ancillary to the main proceedings and decided by the same panel of judges, so as to avoid contradictions between (the facts assessed in) both cases. For that purpose, the CCP has created the opportunity for both the defendant and the claimant to file a motion for what the CCP calls indemnification proceedings (*vrijwaringsprocedure*).[275]

If a defendant files a motion before the first day of appearance, it is automatically granted. Thereafter, he can do so at the latest at the date set for his statement of defence, but the motion may then be contested by the claimant. The claimant may only file the motion at the latest at the day set for his statement of reply.[276] It is not possible to file the motion for the first time in appeal.[277]

It is not necessary for there to be a direct connection between the claim in the main proceedings and the indemnification claim. The only requirement is that the defendant shows that, if the claimant's claim is awarded, he has an arguable claim against a third party for that reason. A comparable rule exists for a motion by the claimant.

If the motion is granted, the defendant or claimant is allowed to summon the third party in indemnification proceedings before the same court, at a date set by the court. The third party will not become a party in the main proceedings between the original claimant and defendant, unless he joins those proceedings.[278] Only in a situation where a claimant has commenced proceedings against a defendant on the grounds that the defendant owns goods encumbered with rights of the claimant, and where a third party is held liable by the defendant for this situation, may the

275. The term 'indemnification' is, strictly speaking, a misnomer for such ancillary proceedings if they are based on other grounds than a right to indemnification, as is the case with contribution claims and with ancillary proceedings commenced by a claimant.
276. Arts 210(1) and 210(2) Rv.
277. Supreme Court 14 Dec. 2007, NJ 2008, 9, LJN: BB7189 (*Gubbels/Aichi*).
278. Art. 214 Rv.

third party have the right to take over the defence in the main proceedings from the defendant.[279] In this situation, the defendant remains a party to the proceedings and is bound by the judgment.[280]

An important effect of the granting of a motion is that a court is automatically competent to hear the claim against the third party, even if it would not have otherwise been competent in a separate dispute between the party seeking indemnification proceedings and the third party.[281] This may be different, however, in an international context, where the third party can contest the court's international jurisdiction on the basis of a Treaty, Regulation or provision in the CCP (see § 4.2).[282] Also, if a jurisdiction clause has been agreed with the third party and the chosen forum is different from the one where the main proceedings are pending, the court of the main proceedings will not have jurisdiction.

Even though the two sets of proceedings remain technically independent, they are decided by the same judge(s), often in one judgment. If the main proceedings are ready for judgment but the indemnification proceedings have not yet been concluded the court may decide the main proceedings before the indemnification proceedings, and is even compelled to do so if one of the parties so requests.[283] Although this rarely happens, even the reverse is possible: a judgment in the indemnification proceedings may be rendered before the main proceedings.[284] The party that decided to file the motion for indemnification remains liable for the costs involved with the indemnification proceedings if it loses them; it will not be allowed to pass these costs on to the losing party in the main proceedings.[285]

6.2.7 Motion for Security for Litigation Costs

Under the CCP, a defendant can file a motion to claim security for his litigation costs against a claimant that is not domiciled in the Netherlands. The motion must be filed before the defendant asserts any material defences. By filing the motion, the defendant does not recognise the competence of the court and he may as yet file a motion to dismiss for lack of jurisdiction.[286]

---

279. Art. 212 Rv.
280. Art. 213 Rv.
281. Art. 216 Rv.
282. Art. 6(2) EC Regulation provides that a third party can be sued in the court seised of the original proceedings, unless these were instituted solely with the object of removing it from the jurisdiction of the court which would be competent in its case. Art. 7(2) Rv provides that in international cases the court seised of the original claim is also competent to decide on the claim for indemnification, unless the two claims are not sufficiently connected.
283. Art. 215 Rv.
284. Supreme Court 6 Feb. 1998, NJ 1998, 350, LJN: ZC2569 (*Paulissen/Gemeente Tilburg*).
285. Supreme Court 28 Oct. 2011, NJ 2012, 213, LJN: BQ6079 (*Zegveld c.s./ZLTO*).
286. Art. 224 Rv.

Security has to be provided for the (estimated) amount that may be awarded by the court only, which is usually substantially lower than the actual litigation costs (see § 6.1.9). The motion cannot be granted if there is a Treaty prohibiting the ability to request such security between the residents of the countries involved, for example, the 1954 Hague Convention or the Treaty of Friendship, Commerce and Navigation between the United States and the Netherlands of 1956.[287] The EC Regulation also prohibits the requesting of security. In practice, there are therefore only limited opportunities for filing this motion.

6.2.8 Motion for Provisional Relief

After proceedings have been instituted, either party can, at any stage, file a motion for provisional relief if it has an urgent interest for such relief that cannot await the (final) judgment in the main proceedings.[288] The test for deciding whether to grant such a motion is the same one that is applied by the preliminary relief judge in preliminary relief proceedings (see § 9.1): there must be sufficient urgency and the legal grounds to support the relief claim must be sufficiently likely. The consequences of granting or not granting the relief for both parties will also be a relevant factor to be taken into account.

The difference between this motion and separate preliminary relief proceedings is that it must be connected to the claim in the main proceedings and has the advantage of being dealt with by the same judge(s) who will deal with the main proceedings.[289] However, such relief will only be granted for a limited time period up to the final judgment in the main proceedings. Unlike judgments on other motions, a judgment on this motion can be appealed separately.[290]

6.2.9 Other Motions

Apart from the above-mentioned motions provided for in Articles 210-224, the CCP provides for motions in several other Articles. Examples are motions in appeal to provide security for or to stay the enforcement of a judgment that is declared enforceable notwithstanding appeal.[291] Furthermore, the CCP does not contain a closed system of motions and the parties may therefore file other motions based on rights they have under various statutory provisions or case law, as long as these motions concern procedural issues or defences and do not relate to the merits of a claim.

287. 'Dutch American Friendship Treaty' of 27 March 1956, Trb. 1956, 40.
288. Art. 223(1) Rv.
289. Art. 223(2) Rv.
290. Art. 337(1) Rv.
291. Arts 235 and 351 Rv.

Since the opportunities for document discovery or disclosure were increased in 2002 (see § 5.4), motions to provide copies of relevant documents are quite often being filed. Other examples are motions to disallow claims due to the invalidity of the writ of summons and motions to dismiss appeals because the appeal period has been exceeded or because the judgment is not appealable.[292]

6.3 Main Available Remedies

6.3.1 Specific Performance

Under Dutch law a party to a contract or a creditor of another (non-contractual) obligation has the right to claim specific performance (*nakoming*) as long as performance is possible.[293] The creditor is, in principle, not obliged to be satisfied with a substitute remedy such as damages. This is different from most common law jurisdictions, where the primary remedy for breach of contract is damages and the right to request specific performance exists only in a limited number of cases.

Specific performance will only be refused if statutory law allows for this, if the nature of the obligation prevents specific performance, or if specific performance has been disallowed by the contract. These limited grounds for refusal appear, however, to have been enlarged by the Supreme Court case *Multi Vastgoed v. Nethou*.[294] In this case, the Supreme Court ruled that a creditor is not completely free in his choice of specific performance or damages but, in making his choice, is bound by the principles of reasonableness and fairness, so that the justified interests of the other party also have to be taken into account.

Upon the request of the creditor, a party which has obligations towards the creditor is ordered by the court to meet these.[295] In the case of a failure by this other party to meet its obligation to do something, the judge may authorise the creditor himself to bring about what would otherwise be the result of the performance by the other party.[296] Likewise, if the obligation on the other party consists of refraining from doing something, the creditor can be authorised to reverse the consequences of an act made in breach of this obligation.[297] In the case of an obligation to perform a legal act, such as the transfer of property, the judge may determine that his judgment will have the same force as a legal deed or he may appoint a representative to perform the act on behalf of the debtor.[298]

---

292. Since these motions concern procedural defences, it is debatable whether motions should be part of the statement of defence or whether they can also be filed separately, before the defence (see § 6.2.2).
293. Art. 3:296(1) BW.
294. Supreme Court 5 Jan. 2001, NJ 2001, 79, LJN: AA9311 (*Multi Vastgoed/Nethou*).
295. Art. 3:296 BW.
296. Art. 3:299(1) BW.
297. Art. 3:299(2) BW.
298. Art. 3:300 BW.

6.3.2 Damages

Instead of specific performance, a creditor may claim alternative damages. If the creditor elects to pursue the remedies of specific performance or rescission, additional damages may be claimed if these remedies do not eliminate all the damage suffered by the creditor.

All damage consisting of material loss and, to the extent that the law so provides, other harm (such as emotional damage) must be compensated.[299] Pecuniary damage comprises both losses and foregone profits.[300] Damages shall, in principle, be paid in monetary form, although the court has discretion to award them in a form other than money.[301] The court can assess the damages independently without being bound by the rules of evidence. The basic principle, however, is that the aggrieved party is placed, as far as possible, in the situation which it would have been in if the event that caused the damage had not taken place. In specific instances, the law prescribes what is known as 'abstract damages'. For instance, in the case of late payment of a money debt, the damage is fixed at a certain interest rate, even if as a result of the late payment the creditor has actually suffered larger or smaller 'concrete damage'.[302] At the request of the aggrieved party, the damage may also be determined as the amount of the profit (or a part thereof) which the other party derived from its unlawful act or breach of contract.[303] If the amount of damage cannot be exactly determined, it will be estimated.[304] If neither determination nor estimation is possible, the court will refer the case to special follow-up proceedings for the determination of the damages (*schadestaatprocedure*).[305]

---

299. Art. 6:95 BW.
300. Art. 6:96(1) BW.
301. Art. 6:103 BW.
302. Pursuant to Arts 6:119 and 120(1) BW, the debtor is obliged to pay statutory interest over the amount due, which interest is established by governmental decree. As of 1 October 2012, the interest rate is 3%. As of 8 Aug. 2002, the EC Directive of 29 Jun. 2000 on combating late payment in commercial transactions, No. 35/2000, O.J. EUR. COMM. (No. L 200) 35 (2000) prescribes the interest rate to be paid in the case of late payment in commercial transactions. Pursuant to this Directive, a new Article 6:119(a) was implemented in the Civil Code and Article 6:120 was amended accordingly (Stb. 2002, 545). The interest rate in the case of late payment in commercial transactions is the sum of 7% and the reference rate per 1 January or 1 July of the year in question. The reference rate is the interest rate applied by the European Central Bank to its most recent main refinancing operation (in case of fixed rate tenders) or the marginal interest rate resulting from the tender procedure for its most recent main financing operation (in case of variable rate tenders). This interest rate for commercial transactions is thus substantially higher than the ordinary statutory interest rate. A new Directive on combating late payment in commercial transactions, No. 7/2011, O.J. EUR. COMM. (No L) 48 (2011) was adopted on 16 February 2011. This directive should be implemented in national legislation before 16 March 2013. One of the changes is that the commercial interest rate will be the sum of the reference rate plus 8%.
303. Art. 6:104 BW.
304. Art. 6:97 BW.
305. Art. 612 Rv.

A claimant can also request the court to refer the case to these special follow-up proceedings if he is not yet able to estimate the damage, or if he wishes that the questions of liability and damages be dealt with separately (see § 6.3.5). However, as with the determination of damages, the court has wide discretion in this respect. A claimant who does not sufficiently substantiate his damage claim in the main proceedings runs the risk that the court will not refer his case to the follow-up proceedings and award a limited amount of damages in the main proceedings.

6.3.3 Rescission

If a party does not fulfil its contractual obligations, the other party may partly or wholly rescind (*ontbinden*) the contract unless the breach is of a subordinate nature and does not justify the rescission.[306] Case law has determined, however, that this does not mean that rescission is only possible in the event of a sufficiently material breach.[307] Along with rescission, damages caused by the rescission can be claimed.

The consequence of rescission is that both parties are released from their obligations arising from the contract. To the extent that these obligations have already been performed, the legal ground for this performance remains intact, but an obligation arises on the parties to undo the performance which has already been carried out.[308] Where the performance, by its nature, cannot be undone, for example in the case of services rendered, it can be substituted by compensation up to its total value at the time of performance.[309]

A contract can be rescinded by a written statement of the creditor out of court. It may also be rescinded by a court upon demand.[310] In practice, a contract is usually rescinded by written statement, after which the court is requested to enter a declaratory judgment to the effect that the contract has been validly rescinded through that written statement (see also §§ 6.1.8.4 and 6.3.5).

6.3.4 Annulment

Comparable to rescission is the remedy of annulment (*vernietiging*). Contracts and other legal acts can be annulled by a court on the application of one of the parties and, in the case of certain legal acts, even by other interested parties. In most cases the party seeking annulment can either ask the court to annul the contract or other legal act, or do so itself out of court by way of a written statement. Thereafter, if

306. Art. 6:265(1) BW.
307. Supreme Court 27 Nov. 1998, NJ 1999, 197, LJN: ZC2789 (*De Bruin/Meiling*); Supreme Court 22 Oct. 1999, NJ 2000, 208, LJN: ZC2993 (*Twickler/R.*); Supreme Court 22 Jun. 2007, NJ 2007, 343, LJN: BA4122 (*Fisser/Tycho*).
308. Art. 6:271 BW.
309. Art. 6:272 BW.
310. Art. 6:267 BW.

necessary, the court can be asked to confirm the effectiveness of the out-of-court annulment in what is then a declaratory judgment (see §§ 6.1.8.4 and 6.3.5).

Contracts can, for instance, be annulled if they have been concluded on the basis of duress (*bedreiging*), fraud (*bedrog*), undue influence (*misbruik van omstandigheden*) or misrepresentation or error (*dwaling*).[311] Examples of other legal acts that may be annulled are corporate resolutions that violate certain statutory provisions or provisions in a company's articles of association or that violate the principles of reasonableness and fairness.[312]

An important difference between rescission and annulment is that an annulment in principle has retroactive effect. If a sales contract is rescinded, the purchaser who has obtained title to the goods must transfer title of the goods back to the seller; by contrast, in the case of an annulment the transfer of title by the seller to the purchaser is deemed to have been ineffective *ab initio* for lack of a valid contract.

6.3.5 Declaration of Law

Another remedy that can be sought from a court is a declaration of law (*verklaring voor recht*). This can be given in what is called a declaratory judgment. Such a judgment merely confirms the existence or absence of a certain legal relationship. For example, a claimant can request the court to declare that he is the legal owner of certain property or that an agreement is null and void. Declaratory judgments are also often requested in cases where a claimant wishes the issue of liability to be decided before damages are litigated. A reason for such a distinction could, for example, be that the amount of damages cannot yet be established. In such a case, a claimant can first ask for a declaratory judgment that the alleged behaviour of the defendant constitutes a tort. If this is granted, the claimant can then commence follow-up proceedings for the determination of damages (*schadestaatprocedure*).[313]

6.3.6 Injunction

In cases related to a breach of contract or tort, a court can also issue a (mandatory or prohibitory) injunction, ordering a defendant to perform or to abstain from certain acts, such as to vacate the claimant's property or to refrain from infringing a patent or other intellectual property right of the claimant.

In exceptional cases a court may also grant an anti-suit injunction. Such will be granted if the party starting the litigation abuses his rights. This is not necessarily the case when a party files a claim twice, or when he files a claim that is most likely

311. Arts 3:44 and 6:228 BW.
312. Art. 2:15 BW.
313. Art. 612 Rv.

unsuccessful.[314] Anti-suit injunctions cannot be granted in relation to proceedings in the courts of other EU Member States.[315]

6.4 Appeal

6.4.1 Appeal to the Courts of Appeal

6.4.1.1 Appealable Judgments

Unless expressly stated otherwise in the law or unless the parties have agreed to skip the appeal,[316] all final judgments delivered by a District Court, whether entered by the cantonal division or not, can be appealed to the Court of Appeal in whose area the District Court is located (see § 3.1.2). Exceptions, for example, are judgments regarding claims of less than EUR 1,750,[317] orders involving the dissolution of employment contracts, orders permitting a preliminary witness hearing (see § 5.2.2.5) and orders granting leave for attachment (see § 9.2).[318]

Interim judgments can also be appealed but in principle appeal must be lodged simultaneously with an appeal against a final judgment. However, an exception applies if the court specifically stipulates otherwise (possibly on the request of one of the parties)[319] or if the court grants or denies a provisional measure.[320] In these circumstances, the interim judgment can be appealed within three months of its delivery. If the court allows an appeal from an interim judgment before the final award, the party concerned may choose to lodge the appeal either within three months of the interim judgment or simultaneously with an appeal against the final judgment. An interim judgment in which the court denies jurisdiction because the case should have been brought before a lower court may only be appealed to the Supreme Court, within eight weeks of the decision; an interim judgment in which the court denies jurisdiction because the case should have been brought before a higher court is not appealable (see § 6.2.3).[321] A judgment in which the court dis-

314. Supreme Court 29 Jun. 2007, NJ 2007, 353, LJN: BA3516 (*Waterschappen/Milieutech Beheer*). See also § 3.4.
315. CJEU 27 Apr. 2004, C-159/02, ECR 2004 I-3565, NJ 2007, 152, LJN: AP4711 (*Turner/Harada*); CJEU 10 Feb. 2009, C-185/07, ECR 2009 I-663, RvdW 2009, 546, LJN: BH3000 (*Allianz SpA/West Tankers*).
316. Art. 333 Rv.
317. Art. 332 Rv .
318. Art. 7:685(11) BW, Art. 188(2) Rv and Art. 700 (2) Rv. In exceptional circumstances, a legal provision that probihits appeal may be broken through (Supreme Court 29 Mar. 1985, NJ 1986, 242, LJN: AG4989 (*Enka/Dupont*)); Supreme Court 27 May 2011, JOR 2011, 275, LJN: BP8693 (*Van Dooren qq/Veco Lasconstructies*).
319. Supreme Court 23 Jan. 2004, NJ 2005, 510, LJN: AL7051 (*Ponteecen/Stratex*).
320. Arts 337(1) and 337(2) Rv.
321. Art. 71(1)-(2) Rv.

misses the case for lack of international jurisdiction or because the parties agreed on arbitration is not an interim but a final judgment (since this will end litigation in the Netherlands altogether) and must be appealed accordingly.[322]

6.4.1.2 Period for Lodging an Appeal

In general, an appeal must be lodged within three months of the date of the judgment at first instance.[323] The appeal is considered lodged not on the day that the writ is filed with the court but on the day that the writ is served on the respondent, in accordance with the applicable service rules. If the judgment is delivered in preliminary relief proceedings, the appeal must be lodged within four weeks of the date of the judgment.[324] The respondent in appeal proceedings may lodge a cross-appeal together with his statement of defence on appeal and is therefore not limited by the three month appeal period.[325]

6.4.1.3 Standard and Scope of Review

The Court of Appeal will conduct a full review of the merits of the case. This means that both issues of fact and of law will be fully reviewed for the second time. The Court of Appeal, however, can only make a decision on issues which are the subject of the appellant's complaint(s). With respect to those issues, the party filing the appeal has the opportunity to improve and supplement its arguments, or to submit new or additional facts omitted at first instance, and the respondent has the opportunity to elaborate his defence. This may be disallowed in rare cases, however, if at first instance the parties explicitly waived certain arguments (e.g. by admitting that they were false) or if it followed from their adopted course of action at first instance that they unmistakably gave up certain arguments.[326] In deciding on the appellant's complaint, the Court of Appeal must take into account all arguments raised by the respondent at first instance and appeal, also those arguments which were disregarded or rejected by the court of first instance, even if the respondent fails to cross-appeal. In specific cases the facts may dictate an exception to this rule.[327]

---

322. See District Court The Hague, 18 Apr. 2002, NJ 2002, 347, LJN: AE5279 (*Intros/Group GM*).
323. Art. 339(1) Rv. Only in exceptional circumstances, if there has been a serious mistake of the court and the right to a fair trial as meant in Article 6 ECHR would be prejudiced, may an appeal be admitted after the appeal period has expired (Supreme Court 27 May 2011, JOR 2011, 275, LJN: BP8693 (*Van Dooren qq/Veco Lasconstructies*)).
324. Art. 339(2) Rv.
325. Art. 339(3) Rv.
326. Art. 348 Rv and Supreme Court 19 Jan. 1996, NJ 1996, 709, LJN: ZC1964 (*Royal Nederland/Campina*); Supreme Court 22 Jan. 1999, NJ 1999, 715, LJN: ZC2831 (*F./S.*).
327. Supreme Court 20 Mar. 2012, RvdW 2012, 94, LJN: BT8413 (*Ydo ambachtelijke en Machinale Timmerfabriek/Baljeu & Staal Assurantiën*); Supreme Court 30 Mar. 2012, RvdW 2012, 497, LJN:

6.4.1.4 The Proceedings

The proceedings at appeal resemble those at first instance (see § 6.1), but with the following differences: although the writ must include the remedy sought by the appellant (usually to reverse the judgment at first instance), it does not have to include the complaints, which may be provided in a later statement.[328] Service of the writ may take place at the office of the respondent's attorney at first instance, also if the respondent is domiciled in a state where the EC Service Regulation or the Hague Service Convention apply.[329] In appeal it is not necessary to effect service under these international instruments; service at the attorney's office is thought to be the best way to ensure that the writ reaches the respondent in time. Service at the attorney's offices will speed up the proceedings as the long time between service and formal appearance which would otherwise apply (ranging from four weeks for respondents in Europe to three months for respondents outside Europe), can be shortened to one week.[330] Another advantage is that no translation of the writ is needed.

If not already contained in the appeal writ, the complaints must be filed in a statement of claim which is then submitted to the Court of Appeal. Thereafter, the respondent can submit a statement of defence. In the case of a cross-appeal, the original claimant can submit a statement of defence on the cross-appeal. Two important differences compared to proceedings at first instance are the absence of a hearing of the parties following the exchange of written documents (although the Amsterdam Court of Appeal is conducting a pilot in which a hearing will be standard practice as from 1 January 2013) and the absence of further written statements such as a reply or a rejoinder.[331]

BU8514 (*Fafianie/Consumenten Advies Nederland*).

328. Of course, if the appellant wishes to expedite the appeal proceedings, it is better to include the complaints in the writ.
329. For situations under the EC Service Regulation 1393/2007, this follows from recital 8 of the Regulation and Article 63 Rv, as it reads since 10 June 2009 (Supreme Court 18 Dec. 2009, NJ 2010, 111 LJN: BK3078 (*Demerara/Haus*)). For situations under the Hague Service Convention, the Supreme Court decided this on 4 February 2011, NJ 2011, 368, LJN: BP0006 (*Goudberg/Van Breukelen*), overturning its long standing decision of 27 June 1986, NJ 1987, 764, LJN: AC9459 (*Segers/Mabanaft*).
330. A *caveat* still applies for situations under the EC Service Regulation: In the Explanatory Memorandum of the law revising the *Uitvoeringswet* EC Service Regulation (MvT 31 522, No. 3, p. 11) it can be read that also in appeal the time period between service and appearance in court should be based on Art. 115(1) Rv, meaning four weeks. However, on 15 April 2011 the Supreme Court issued a decision (NJ 2011, 369, LJN: BP4952 (*Kleinhout/Bernardin*)) under the Hague Service Convention (the respondent resided in Canada), which held that if service is effected at the offices of the respondent's attorney at first instance, Art. 115(3) Rv is applicable, so that a period of one week is sufficient. It is unlikely that with this decision in mind, the Supreme Court would request four weeks for service under the EC Service Regulation. However, until there is an explicit decision, it may be best to ask the respondent's attorney explicitly if he will allow service to be effected at this office (see § 6.1.2.4).
331. Art. 347 Rv. Further written statements are only permitted if agreed by both parties with the Court of Appeal. It is, however, allowed to submit a short statement (*akte*) if the opposing party has submitted

This latter rule entails that both the appellant and respondent are required to concentrate all their arguments in the statement of claim and defence and that a change of (the grounds of) the claim by the claimant at first instance will need to be laid down in that one statement. Further arguments, defences and changes of claim will not be admitted, unless exceptional circumstances so dictate.[332]

It is not possible to submit a counterclaim for the first time in appeal proceedings, as the defendant to the counterclaim would be deprived of one instance.[333] It is also not possible to file a motion for indemnification proceedings for the first time in appeal.[334]

Both the appellant and the respondent should sum up the specific (counter) evidence they wish to rely on, failing which the Court of Appeal may refuse to give the parties a further chance to present evidence, e.g. by means of witnesses. This will be the case particularly where a party at appeal relies on witnesses who have already been heard at the lower stages or who have submitted written witness statements.[335]

If they feel this would contribute to their case, the parties can request closing arguments after the statement of defence (in appeal or cross-appeal). A request for closing arguments may only be refused in exceptional circumstances.[336]

After submission of the written statements, and possibly the closing arguments, the Court of Appeal has the option to enter either an interim judgment or a final judgment (see §§ 6.1.8.3 and 6.1.8.4). If the final judgment reverses the judgment of the District Court, the Court of Appeal must in principle settle the dispute itself, unless the reversed judgment was a judgment in which the lower court concluded that it had no jurisdiction.[337] In such a case, the matter may be referred back to the lower court.

---

new facts or exhibits in his last written statement.

332. Supreme Court 14 Mar. 2008, NJ 2008, 466, LJN: BC1231 (*X/Aerts qq*), Supreme Court 20 Jun. 2008, NJ 2009, 21, LJN: BC4959 (*Willemsen/NOM*), Supreme Court 19 Jun. 2009, NJ 2010, 154, LJN: BI8771 (*Wertenbroek qq/Van den Heuvel c.s*), Supreme Court 23 Sep. 2011, NJ 2012, 376, LJN: BQ8092 (*X/Ru-Pro Holding* BV) and Supreme Court 9 Dec. 2011, RvdW 2011, 1543, LJN: BR2045 (*Doornenbal/Van der Spek*).

333. Article 353(1) Rv.

334. Supreme Court 14 Dec. 2007, NJ 2008, 9, LJN: BB7189 (*Gubbels/Aichi*).

335. Supreme Court 9 Jul. 2004, NJ 2005, 270, LJN: AO7817 (*OZ Export/Roozen*); Supreme Court 25 May 2011, NJ 2011, 138, LJN: BO5804 (*Westening/Weslo*). For a situation where a party was allowed to call for witness hearings after it had submitted written statements from these witnesses at first instance, see Supreme Court 27 May 2011, NJ 2011, 512, LJN: BP9991 (*X/Cofely Installatietechniek*).

336. Supreme Court 27 Jan. 2012, NJ 2012, 76, LJN: BU8513 (*Weef/Maico Investments*) and Supreme Court 27 Jan. 2012, NJ 2012, 77, LJN: BU7254 (*X/Verster*).

337. Art. 356 Rv and Supreme Court 16 Apr. 1993, NJ 1993, 654, LJN: ZC0926 (*Van der Belt/De Open Ankh*); Supreme Court 7 May 1993, NJ 1993, 655, LJN: ZC0949 (*Meulen/Keijsers*).

6.4.2 Appeal to the Supreme Court

6.4.2.1 Appealable Judgments

Judgments of a Court of Appeal and judgments of a court of first instance which cannot be appealed to the Court of Appeal (see § 6.4.1.1) can be appealed to the Supreme Court.[338] Unlike the system in the United States and the United Kingdom, all appeals can be lodged without first having to obtain leave to appeal. However, on 1 July 2012, the *Wet versterking cassatierechtspraak* entered into force (see § 1.). This law entitles the Supreme Court to dismiss an appeal at an early stage of the appeal proceedings in cases where it is clear that the appellant has insufficient interest in the appeal or that the appeal will not be successful.[339]

6.4.2.2 Period for Lodging an Appeal

Like an appeal to the Court of Appeal, the period for lodging an appeal to the Supreme Court is in principle three months, but is eight weeks in the case of a judgment delivered in preliminary relief proceedings.[340] The respondent in the appeal proceedings before the Supreme Court may lodge a cross-appeal together with his statement of defence.[341]

6.4.2.3 Standard and Scope of Review

The grounds for appeal to the Supreme Court are limited to insufficient or unclear reasoning of the lower court and violation of the law (excluding extraterritorial law).[342] The assessment of issues of fact by the lower courts is not tested by the Supreme Court unless a lower court has failed in its duty to properly justify its conclusions.

6.4.2.4 The Proceedings

Other than in appeal proceedings before the Court of Appeal, the writ of summons must include the complaint(s) and the reasons for the complaint(s). Once the writ is registered with the Supreme Court, the respondent may submit his answer. In general, this is merely a formal document in which the respondent states that the judgment should not be reversed. Thereafter, unless the Supreme Court decides

---

338. Art. 398 Rv.
339. Art. 80a RO.
340. Arts 402(1) and 402(2) Rv.
341. Art. 410(1) Rv.
342. Art. 79 RO.

to dismiss the appeal (see § 6.4.2.1), the parties are requested to submit written statements simultaneously, in which they set out their arguments in more detail.[343] Each party may respond to this in writing, and such reply and rejoinder are also submitted simultaneously.[344] Before the Supreme Court arrives at its decision, the Procurator-general or the Attorney-general will deliver a non-binding opinion to the Supreme Court. This will be very well argued, often with numerous references to case law and doctrine. These opinions are important as they are often, but not always, followed by the Supreme Court. If the parties so wish, they may respond to this opinion. Thereafter, the Supreme Court will deliver its reasoned judgment. No dissenting opinions are published. The Supreme Court will deny the appeal if the issues at stake do not fall within the scope for review (see § 6.4.2.3). In that case it will be sufficient to mention this as reason in the judgment.[345]

If the appeal is granted, depending on the situation, the Supreme Court will either give a new decision itself, or refer the case back to the Court of Appeal. This can be either the court which has given the reversed decision or a different court.[346] The court to which the case has been referred must in its decision take account of the Supreme Court judgment.[347] It should decide the case based on the situation that existed before the reversed decision. Therefore, as a general rule, there is no room for new facts or legal arguments or the submission of new evidence that could also have been submitted earlier. However, a party is allowed to clarify its arguments and in that respect, depending on the facts of the case, he may sometimes also submit new exhibits.[348]

Parties litigating before the Supreme Court must be represented by a qualified Supreme Court attorney (see § 3.1.3).

6.4.3 Revocation

Even after the appeal period has lapsed and a decision from a District Court or a Court of Appeal has become final and conclusive, such a decision may be revoked (*herroepen*) upon request of a party. The grounds for revocation are limited: either the decision was based on fraud committed by a party during the proceedings,[349] or it was based on documents which appeared to be false afterwards, or a party received documents after the judgment that had been withheld by the other party and

343. Art. 412(2) Rv.
344. Art. 408a(5) Rv.
345. Arts 30 Rv and 81 RO.
346. Arts 420-423 Rv.
347. Art. 424 Rv.
348. Supreme Court 25 Mar. 2011, RvdW 2011, 419, LJN: BP8991 (*Ploum/Smeets*).
349. The fraud should not already have been discovered during the proceedings (Supreme Court 15 Feb. 2008, NJ 2008, 112, LJN: BC0393 (*Veenbrink/Spijkerman*).

were decisive for the outcome of the proceedings.[350] The time period for a request for revocation is three months after the ground for revocation became apparent and known to the claimant.[351] The request is in principle brought before the court that gave the decision. The request does not automatically lead to a stay of the execution of the decision but a stay may be asked for in summary proceedings.[352] If the court decides to reopen the case, this will lead to a stay of the execution.[353] Neither the decision to dismiss the request for revocation nor the decision to reopen the case are appealable.[354]

6.5 Petition Proceedings

The proceedings described so far in this chapter are of an adversarial nature, where one party, the claimant, is seeking relief vis-à-vis another party in court. Those proceedings are commenced by a writ of summons. In addition, however, there is a second category of proceedings known as petition proceedings (*verzoekschriftprocedures*) which are in part of a different nature and which have, in some respects, different procedural rules even though they are also typically brought at first instance in the District Courts and are appealable to the Courts of Appeal and the Supreme Court.

6.5.1 Nature of Petition Proceedings

Petition proceedings are generally prescribed, where the issue to be resolved (*res judicata*) has a direct impact on the legal position of third parties. Such proceedings are relatively informal in nature and allow other parties to join the litigation relatively easily. There is usually one party against whom the relief is aimed in particular, and this party is referred to as the respondent (*verweerder*). In some cases, however, the formal respondent actually supports the petition, whereas other interested parties (*belanghebbenden*) may oppose it.

An example of petition proceedings are the proceedings where a pledgee petitions a court to allow him to sell collateral by way of a private sale rather than by way of an auction.[355] Clearly, not just the rights of the pledgor are at stake here, but also the rights of other persons who may have rights to the collateral and the interests of the pledgor's creditors generally. Another example are enquiry proceedings (discussed in § 7.2) where the decisions of the Enterprise Court may affect the

350. Art. 382 Rv.
351. Art. 383 Rv.
352. Art. 386 Rv.
353. Art. 388(1) Rv
354. Art. 388(2) Rv and Supreme Court 21 Sep. 2012, LJN: BW4896 (*X/Stichting Joodse Omroep*).
355. Art. 3:251 BW.

rights of not just the shareholder who has filed the petition and of the company, but also that of other shareholders, the employees and/or management. Many proceedings pursuant to the Dutch Bankruptcy Code are also petition proceedings since, typically, the interests of many creditors are involved.

Apart from the fact that third parties can join the litigation more easily and the proceedings are less formal, the main difference between petition proceedings and proceedings commenced by writ of summons is that the courts have wider discretion with respect to the course of the proceedings and the relief that may be granted.

6.5.2 Jurisdiction

In the CPP, petition proceedings have different jurisdiction rules to proceedings commenced by writ. In international situations, if no Treaty or EC Regulation applies, the general rule is that the Dutch court has jurisdiction if either the petitioner or the respondent is domiciled in the Netherlands or if the petition relates to proceedings which are commenced by writ and are instituted or will be instituted before a competent Dutch court or, finally, if the case is in any other way sufficiently connected with the Dutch jurisdiction.[356] This last condition relates to a situation of *forum conveniens*, which will be considered by the court on a case-by-case basis. The general ability to dismiss a case on grounds of *forum non conveniens* used to be available in petition proceedings but was abolished in 2002. Elaborate rules on venue are also laid down in the CCP.[357] The most important one is that not only the court of the place of domicile of the respondent, but also the court of the place of domicile of the petitioner has jurisdiction, whereas this is usually not the case in proceedings commenced by writ.[358]

6.5.3 The Proceedings

Petition proceedings are commenced by the petitioner filing his petition with the court. The petitioner must usually be represented by an attorney, but unlike a writ, a petition need not be served by a court bailiff. The petition sets out the relief that is being claimed, the grounds for the claim and, in most cases, the name of the principal respondent.[359] The petition may also list other interested parties.

After receipt of the petition, the court sends by registered letter a copy to the respondent(s) and to other parties that in the court's opinion qualify as interested parties and invites them to file a statement of response. Once a party has submitted a statement of response or has appeared at the oral hearing, further communications

---

356. Art. 3 Rv. See also § 4.2.3.3.
357. Arts 262-270 Rv.
358. Art. 262(a) Rv.
359. Art. 278 Rv.

will in general be by ordinary letter, unless the court decides otherwise. If a party does not submit a statement of response or appear in the proceedings, communications will be by registered letter.[360] Special rules apply if the respondent or the interested party is domiciled in a country where the EC Service Regulation or the Hague Service Convention apply.[361]

In order to join the proceedings, an interested party does not need to file a motion that can first be contested by the other parties before it is admitted. It simply files its statement with the court and the court will determine whether the party was entitled to bring forward its views as an interested party.[362]

The court informs all parties of the date of the oral hearing, which is key to the petition proceedings. The respondent and every interested party can file a written statement of response until the very date of the oral hearing, or – with the permission of the court – even during that oral hearing. Statements of response are, again, simply sent to the court by mail. In contrast to proceedings commenced by writ, there are no fixed dates for submitting statements, as the case is not placed on the court's docket list.

In their statements of response, the respondent and the interested parties may themselves petition the court for relief related to the subject matter of the original petition. In this case, the court may allow the petitioner and the other parties to file a statement in response to that request.[363]

Many of the rules related to proceedings commenced by writ are also applicable to petition proceedings. One difference is that all interested parties are entitled to receive copies of all the petitions and statements filed in the course of the proceedings. The ordinary rules of evidence are also applicable in petition proceedings, unless the nature of the case requires otherwise. Other than in proceedings commenced by writ, the court can, on its own initiative, determine to have certain witnesses examined.[364]

6.5.4 Orders

A court's decision in petition proceedings is not referred to as a judgment (*vonnis*) but as an order (*beschikking*). It can be declared enforceable notwithstanding an appeal and can contain an award for costs against one or more of the parties on the same footing as in proceedings commenced by writ.[365]

360. Arts 271 and 272 Rv.
361. Art. 277 Rv as regards the EC Service Regulation and Supreme Court 18 May 2001, NJ 2002, 478, LJN: ZC3542 (*Erven L.*) as regards the Hague Service Convention.
362. Art. 282(1) Rv.
363. Art. 282 Rv.
364. Art. 284 Rv.
365. Arts 288 and 289 Rv.

The court's decisions are binding upon all the parties that have appeared in the proceedings and, in the case of some decisions, such as those dealing with the method of foreclosure on the collateral, also on third parties.

The right of appeal is granted not only to all parties that have appeared in the proceedings at first instance, but also to other interested parties.[366] Another difference from proceedings commenced by writ is that the grounds on which a party wishes to appeal must already be contained in the appeal petition, which leaves the appealing party less time to prepare, especially if the appeal period is brief.[367] Unless provided otherwise, the period for filing an appeal is three months, but for some specific proceedings in insolvency law matters, the appeal period may be as brief as a few weeks. The procedure in appeal is more or less the same as that at first instance.

7. CORPORATE LITIGATION IN THE ENTERPRISE COURT

7.1 Role of the Enterprise Court

For the purpose of this section, corporate litigation can be defined as all litigation with respect to the capital and governance of companies and other legal entities and to the position of the various stakeholders in those legal entities. Corporate litigation can take place by means of standard proceedings in the District Court. This is the case, for example, for claims to annul corporate resolutions on the grounds of violation of the law or of the articles of association, or violation of the principles of reasonableness and fairness, and also for directors' and shareholders' liability claims and other damages claims.

Nevertheless, corporate litigation in the Netherlands is to a large extent concentrated in one forum, the specialised Enterprise Court (*Ondernemingskamer*).

The Enterprise Court was established as a special branch of the Amsterdam Court of Appeal and is comprised of three professional judges and two laymen who are experts in entrepreneurial and financial matters. Decisions of the Enterprise Court can only be appealed to the Supreme Court and, therefore, are subject to review only on issues of law, proper procedure and proper reasoning (see §§ 3.1.3 and 6.4.2.3). The appeal does not include a full review of the merits, as is the case with District Court judgments which are subject to appeal at one of the Courts of Appeal.

The Enterprise Court can only adjudicate certain specific proceedings, the most important of which are so-called enquiry proceedings (*enquêteprocedures*), pursu-

366. Art. 358 Rv.
367. Art. 359 Rv.

ant to which it can investigate alleged mismanagement of a company (a concept it defines broadly) and take a wide range of measures to address that mismanagement (see § 7.2). The Enterprise Court is also the forum for squeeze-out proceedings in which a shareholder with at least 95% of the shares can buy out the remaining shareholders at a price set by the Enterprise Court. The Enterprise Court also hears applications by shareholders and other interested parties to revise or annul annual accounts of companies.

Finally, the Enterprise Court acts as the Court of Appeal for certain corporate litigation claims brought in the District Court. One such form of corporate litigation in the District Court which merits specific attention are the so-called forced exit proceedings (*geschillenregeling*), in which a shareholder who has a dispute with another shareholder can demand a buy out by the other shareholder or can, conversely, force that other shareholder to sell his shares to him (see § 7.3).

7.2 Enquiry Proceedings

7.2.1 Introduction

Under Dutch company law certain stakeholders in a company have the right to request the Enterprise Court to order an enquiry into the management and affairs of the company, if it can be established that there are 'sufficient grounds to doubt as to whether the company is pursuing a proper policy or a proper course of affairs'. Such an enquiry procedure may not only be commenced in respect of the management and affairs of a company established in the Netherlands (N.V. or B.V.), but also in respect of certain other Dutch legal entities, such as commercial foundations, co-operatives and certain other associations.[368] For the purpose of this book, only companies will be considered.

The statutory provisions on enquiry proceedings (Articles 2:344 – 2:359 BW) have been amended recently.[369] These amendments take effect on 1 January 2013. The text of this chapter is based on the amended situation as per 1 January 2013.

The Enterprise Court has been given exclusive jurisdiction to deal with requests for enquiries and consequently has become a highly specialised court in this particular area of the law. It has made important contributions to the development of company law and corporate governance in the Netherlands. Case law in enquiry proceedings from the Enterprise Court and, in appeal (*cassatie*), the Supreme Court,

---

368. Art. 2:344 BW. In addition to the legal entities listed in Art. 2:344 BW, the rules concerning the enquiry proceedings also apply to European Economic Interest Groupings (EEIGs), see Art. 3(3) of the Act of 28 June 1989, Stb. 1989, 245, implementing the EC Council Regulation of 25 July 1985 on the European Economic Interest Grouping, No. 2137/85, O.J. EUR. COMM. (No. L 199) 1 (1985).
369. Stb. 2012, 274.

provides important legal standards concerning the proper performance of duties by management and supervisory boards.

In order to avoid disruption of the business of companies as much as possible, the Dutch legislature has made the enquiry procedure a relatively informal and quick procedure with limited scope for appeal (see § 7.2.10). The proceedings consist of three stages (see §§ 7.2.6-7.2.8).

7.2.2 Aim of the Enquiry Proceedings

The original aim of enquiry proceedings was to disclose the state of affairs of a company in cases of mismanagement in the strictest sense of the word: cases of fraud and of mismanagement through the taking of unacceptable risks. However, in view of the growing expertise of the Enterprise Court and especially the introduction in 1994 of the possibility of obtaining provisional measures at short notice, the Enterprise Court has become an important forum for corporate disputes in a much broader sense, such as takeover battles, issues between shareholders, disputes concerning the disclosure of information to shareholders, and clashes of power between the shareholders' meeting and the management board.

Enquiry proceedings serve in the main three aims: the restoration of sound relationships within a company through re-organisational measures, disclosure of the state of affairs of the company, and the identification of those responsible for mismanagement. In addition, the possibility of an enquiry may have a preventative effect.[370] The enquiry proceedings are not aimed at establishing liability of the board for mismanagement or for mistakes made and the Enterprise Court cannot award damages. Nonetheless, enquiry proceedings are often an overture to civil proceedings in which liability for mismanagement can be established (see § 7.2.11). Resolution of disputes solely concerning the question of which party is entitled to a certain property or goods is not an aim of enquiry proceedings.[371] A request to the Enterprise Court to resolve such a dispute will be declared inadmissible.

7.2.3 Parties Entitled to Ask for an Enquiry

7.2.3.1 Shareholders, Holders of Depositary Receipts for Shares, Pledgees and Holders of a Right of Usufruct

Shareholders holding alone or together at least one-tenth of the issued shares or shares with a nominal value of at least EUR 225,000 in a company (N.V. or B.V.)

370. Supreme Court 10 Jan. 1990, NJ 1990, 466, LJN: AC1234 (*Ogem*), confirmed in Supreme Court 26 Jun. 2009, JOR 2009, 192, LJN: BD5516 (*KPNQwest*).
371. Supreme Court 18 Nov. 2005, NJ 2006, 173, LJN: AU2465 (*Unilever*).

with an issued capital of no more than EUR 22,5 million can ask the Enterprise Court to order an enquiry into the affairs of that company.[372]

In case of a company (N.V. or B.V.) with an issued capital of more than EUR 22,5 million, an enquiry can be requested by one or more shareholders who solely or jointly represent at least one-hundredth of the issued capital or, if the shares have been admitted to trading on a regulated market or a multilateral trading facility as defined in in Article 1:1 of the Dutch Financial Supervision Act (*Wet op het Financieel Toezicht*)[373] or a system similar to a regulated market or a multilateral trading facility of a state that is not a Member State, his shares represent a value of at least EUR 20 million according to the closing price on the final day of trading prior to the application for an enquiry.[374]

Not only shareholders but also holders of depositary receipts for shares and even beneficial owners of depositary receipts for shares that meet these criteria have the right to ask for an enquiry.[375] Shareholders and holders of depositary receipts for shares can also authorise a third party to exercise their right to ask for an enquiry on their behalf.[376]

If the shares have been pledged or a right of usufruct has been created (meaning the dividends are not distributed to the shareholders), not only the shareholder but also the holder of the right of usufruct and the pledgee of the shares can ask for an enquiry, provided that they have voting rights. If the holder of the right of usufruct or the pledgee do not have voting rights, an enquiry can only be requested if certain conditions are met, which conditions differ for the B.V. and the N.V.[377]

A company can lower the threshold for shareholders and the holders of depositary receipts for shares to ask for an enquiry in its articles of association.[378] It is not possible for a company to raise this threshold. A higher threshold would be in violation of mandatory law and consequently would be invalid.

7.2.3.2 The Company

As from 1 January 2013, the company itself is also entitled to ask for an enquiry.[379] Such a request will have to be made by a duly authorised representative of the company. Normally speaking this will be the board of directors, or if the company's

372. Art. 2:346((1)(b) BW.
373. *Wet op het Financieel Toezicht*, Stb. 2006, 475, as amended.
374. Art. 2:346(1)(c) BW.
375. Art. 2:346(1)(b) BW, Art. 2:346(1) (c) BW and Supreme Court 6 Jun. 2003, NJ 2003, 486, LJN: AF9440 (*Scheipar*).
376. Enterprise Court 6 Jan. 1994, NJ 1995, 119, LJN: AB9299 (*Kustlicht*) and Enterprise Court 22 Dec. 1983, NJ 1985, 383, LJN: AC8232 (*Ogem*).
377. Arts 2:88(4) and 2:89(4) BW (N.V.) and Arts 2:197(4) and 2:198(4) BW (B.V.).
378. Art. 2:346(1)(b) BW Art. 2:346(1)(c) BW.
379. 2:346(1)(d) BW.

articles of association provide for this, one or more individual directors. The application for an enquiry may also be filed on behalf of the company by the supervisory board or, if a one tier board has been put in place, by the non-executive directors.[380]

In the event of insolvency of the company the application for an enquiry may also be filed by the receiver (*curator*).[381]

7.2.3.3 Trade Unions and Works Councils

A request for an enquiry can also be made by a trade union whose members are employees of the company (or its group companies), provided that the trade union has had full legal capacity for at least two years and, according to its articles of association, has as its purpose the promotion of the interests of its members as employees, and is active as such in the industry or company.[382]

The question of whether the works council of a company should have the right to ask for an enquiry has been debated in legal literature but, as yet, works councils do not have this right.[383] However, they do have certain rights in the case of enquiry proceedings. First of all, a request for an enquiry made by a trade union will be declared inadmissible if the trade union does not, before submitting the request, provide the works council with the opportunity to give its written view on the matter at hand.[384] Secondly, it is possible for a works council to conclude an agreement with the company in which the company grants the works council the right to ask for an enquiry.[385] Finally, a works council can intervene in enquiry proceedings as an interested party and submit a statement of defence against the request for an enquiry.[386]

7.2.3.4 Other Parties

The right to ask for an enquiry can also be granted to other persons or entities in the articles of association of the company, or in an agreement concluded with the company.[387]

---

380. 2: 346(2) BW.
381. Art. 2:346(3) BW.
382. Art. 2:347 BW.
383. Supreme Court 1 Feb. 2002, NJ 2002, 225, LJN: AD8831 (*De Vries Robbé*).
384. Art. 2:349(2) BW.
385. Art. 2:346(1)(e) BW.
386. Art. 279 Rv.
387. Art. 2:346(1)(e) BW.

7.2.3.5 *Attorney-general*

The Attorney-general can request an enquiry into the affairs of the company if matters of public interest are involved.[388] Such matters may be involved if the company investigated is of significant interest to the national or regional economy, if the preservation of a large number of jobs is at stake, or if the finding of mismanagement in a particular company could have spill-over effects to other companies or even discredit an entire industry or sector.[389]

Although the phrase 'matters of public interest' limits the situations in which the Attorney-general can ask for an enquiry, it follows from parliamentary history that it must be interpreted broadly. Subsequently, requests for enquiries by the Attorney-general have also been allowed in cases in which the public interest was more remote.[390]

The Attorney-general has the right but not the obligation to ask for an enquiry if a matter of public interest is involved and can also ask for an enquiry independently and regardless of other persons who also have such a right.

7.2.4 Prior Written Notice

In order that the request does not come to the management board as surprise, before submitting a request to the Enterprise Court the petitioner must first notify the board (and the supervisory board if there is one) in writing of his objections against the policies of the company.[391] If a company has been declared bankrupt, the prior written notice can be sent to the bankruptcy trustee.[392] The management board (and the supervisory board if there is one) must be given a reasonable opportunity to examine the objections and to take measures to remedy them.

In practice, the requirement to send prior written notice is easily met.[393] The Enterprise Court has accepted a writ of summons in preliminary relief proceedings served upon a company as prior written notice.[394] Complaints communicated to the board orally during a shareholders' meeting and subsequently recorded in the

---

388. Art. 2:345(2) BW.
389. Examples of cases where matters of public interest were involved can be found in Supreme Court 10 Jan. 1990, NJ 1990, 466, LJN: AC1234 (*Ogem*) and Enterprise Court 3 Aug. 1995, De NV 1995, p. 203 (*Vie d'Or*).
390. Examples can be found in Enterprise Court 28 Dec. 1981, NJ 1983, 25, LJN: AC7470 (*Diesel Holland*); Enterprise Court 26 Jun. 1986, NJ 1988, 99, LJN: AC9448 followed by Enterprise Court 8 Oct. 1987, NJ 1989, 270, LJN: AC0548 (*Van der Klis*); Enterprise Court 16 Jul. 1987, NJ 1988, 579, LJN: AB7750 (*Briljant*).
391. Art. 2:349 BW.
392. Supreme Court 19 May 1999, NJ 1999, 670, LJN: AD3052 (*De Haan*).
393. Enterprise Court 17 Jun. 2008, JOR 2008, 265, LJN: BG0453 (*KPN Narrowcasting*).
394. Enterprise Court 25 Aug. 1998, NJ 1989, 308, LJN: AD0416 (*Corocor*).

minutes of the meeting also qualify, according to the Enterprise Court, as prior written notice.[395]

The requirement that the board must be given an opportunity to respond to the complaints of the petitioner implies that the board must be given a reasonable period of time to take measures. What constitutes a reasonable period of time depends on the circumstances of the case. The Enterprise Court will take into account how long the company has been aware of the complaints, regardless of the date on which these complaints were communicated to the company in writing.[396]

The abovementioned requirements do not apply if the application for an enquiry was made by the company itself. In that event the supervisory board or the management board and the works council must be informed as soon as possible of the intention to file the application or of the filing of the application.[397]

7.2.5 Subject of the Enquiry

A request for an enquiry from one or more shareholders will typically relate to the affairs and policies of the company in which the applicant directly holds shares. But an enquiry may in some circumstances also look into the affairs and policies of 100% subsidiaries of that company. This will be the case, for instance, if, at the level of the subsidiary, there is no management policy independent of the policy of the parent company, and consequently the affairs and policies of the subsidiary will affect the interests of the parent company in the same way that they affect the interests of the subsidiary.[398]

The Enterprise Court has ordered several group enquiries, even in a case where the holding company has not held 100% but only 75% of the shares in the subsidiary.[399] At the request of a works council that has contractually been given a right to ask for an enquiry, it has also ordered an enquiry not only into the affairs and policies of the company in which the works council was active, but also into the affairs and policies of its holding company.[400]

Similarly, an enquiry requested by a trade union does not necessarily have to be limited to the affairs and policies of the company which employs members of the

395. For example, Enterprise Court 3 Jan. 1977, NJ 1977, 342, LJN: AB6893 (*Oostrums Algemene Beleggingsmaatschappij*); Enterprise Court 2 Feb. 1989, NJ 1990, 146, LJN: AB7886 (*Friesendorp*); Enterprise Court 29 Apr. 2002, ARO 2002, 53, LJN: BD4710 (*I.H.D. Schipholservice*) and Enterprise Court 11 Apr. 2003, ARO 2003, 64, LJN: AL7170 (*T&L Verzekeringen*).
396. Enterprise Court 31 Mar. 1994, TVVS 1994, p. 190 (*Kluft/Distrifood*).
397. Art. 2:349(1) BW.
398. Supreme Court 4 Feb. 2005, NJ 2005, 127, LJN: AR8899 (*Landis*).
399. Enterprise Court 22 Mar. 2006, JOR 2006, 180, LJN: AY6788 (*Van Doorn*).
400. Enterprise Court 5 Oct. 2005, JOR 2005, 296, LJN: AU5264 (*Smit Transformatoren*).

trade union. It may in certain circumstances also look into the affairs and policies of other companies within the same group including the holding company.[401]

7.2.6 First Stage: Request for Enquiry

7.2.6.1 Interested Parties

The first stage of the enquiry proceedings begins with a written petition (*verzoekschrift*) in which the petitioner requests the Enterprise Court to order an enquiry into the affairs and policies of the company.[402] The Enterprise Court will immediately identify interested parties (shareholders, managing directors, supervisory directors, etc.) and inform them of the fact that a request for an enquiry has been submitted. Interested parties may also proactively inform the Enterprise Court that they want to be included in the proceedings.

Since enquiry proceedings are a form of petition proceedings, all legitimate interested parties have the right to submit a written statement, in order to present their views (see § 6.5.3).[403] Such statement may be submitted up to a date stipulated by the Enterprise Court prior to the beginning of the hearing.[404] Under certain circumstances, interested parties also have the right, by way of counterclaim, to ask for an enquiry into different or additional matters or for a different period of time, and provisional measures.

In determining whether or not a party is an interested party and should be able to participate in the proceedings, the court will take into account the extent to which the interests of that party can be affected by the outcome of the proceedings, as well as the extent to which the party is or has been closely involved with the subject of the proceedings.[405]

7.2.6.2 Sufficient Grounds to Doubt as to Whether the Company Is Pursuing a Proper Policy or a Proper Course of Affairs

The request for an enquiry may relate to all or part of the affairs and policies of the company. It may include plans, proposals, implemented decisions, single actions or a series of actions, and may relate to a specific or unspecified period of time. However, a request for an enquiry can only relate to facts and circumstances that

401. Enterprise Court 17 Mar. 1994, NJ 1995, 408, LJN: AD2058 (*Janssen Pers*), Enterprise Court 10 Sep. 1999, JOR 1999, 228, LJN: AG3517 (IJsselwerf) and Enterprise Court 10 Jan. 2008, JOR 2008, 39, LJN: BC1657 (*PCM*).
402. Art. 2:345 BW.
403. Art. 279 Rv.
404. Art. 2:349a(1) BW.
405. Supreme Court 6 Jun. 2003, NJ 2003, 486, LJN: AF9440 (*Scheipar*).

have taken place before the date of submission of the request.[406] The enquiry does not have to be limited to the policies and affairs of the management board of the company. It may concern any corporate body and any person who holds office in such corporate body. The enquiry may relate to the governance of the company as well as to the business it operates.

The Enterprise Court can only allow a request for an enquiry if there are 'sufficient grounds to doubt as to whether the company is pursuing a proper policy or a proper course of affairs'.[407] This means that the circumstances must be such that there is a reasonable chance that the enquiry, if ordered, will lead to the conclusion that the company has failed to pursue a proper policy or proper course of affairs in one or more respects.[408] It is at the sole discretion of the Enterprise Court to determine whether this criterion is met, although it is up to the petitioners to demonstrate plausibly that the facts and circumstances support such conclusion.[409] In its assessment, the Enterprise Court will take into account all the circumstances of the case.

Typical situations that may lead the Enterprise Court to conclude that there are sufficient grounds to doubt whether a proper policy or a proper course of affairs is being followed are: a deadlock in the decision-making process, either at the level of the shareholders' meeting,[410] at the level of the management board[411] or at the level of both corporate bodies,[412] conflicts between the management board and its sole shareholder,[413] insufficient or unequal disclosure of information to shareholders,[414] conflicts of interest,[415] the company's failure to sufficiently take the interests of the minority shareholders into account[416] and failing corporate governance.[417] In

406. Supreme Court 16 Apr. 2010, JOR 2010, 223, LJN: BL6182 (*ASMI*).
407. Art. 2:350 BW.
408. Art. 2:350 BW.
409. Enterprise Court, 17 Apr. 2008, JOR 2008, 157, LJN: BD4198 (*ABN AMRO*).
410. Enterprise Court 20 Jun. 2007, JOR 2007, 203, LJN: BB3207 (*Cordial*); Enterprise Court 21 Nov. 1991, NJ 1992, 254, LJN: AD1535 (*ITP Holland*); Enterprise Court 11 Feb. 1993, NJ 1993, 414, LJN: AC1859 (*RLA*).
411. Enterprise Court 4 Feb. 2008, JOR 2008, 95, LJN: BC9457 (*Focwa*).
412. Enterprise Court 18 Nov 2008, JOR 2009, 37, LJN: BG4598 (*Living City*).
413. Enterprise Court 28 Dec. 1981, NJ 1983, 25, LJN: AC7470 (A.BV).
414. Enterprise Court 8 Dec. 2006, JOR 2007, 41, LJN: AZ4007 (*Versatel*); Enterprise Court 10 Dec. 1981, NJ 1983, 24, LJN: AC1722 (*Ford* Nederland).
415. Enterprise Court 28 Dec. 2006, JOR 2007, 68, LJN: AZ5403 (*Begemann*); Enterprise Court 14 Dec. 2005, JOR 2006, 7, LJN: AU8151 (*Versatel*); Enterprise Court 26 Sep. 1991, NJ 1992, 310, LJN: AD1498 (*VHS*); Enterprise Court 6 Jan. 1994, NJ 1995, 119, LJN: AB9299 (*Text Lite*); Enterprise Court 6 Jun. 2000, JOR 2000, 193, LJN: AG3841 (*EMO groep*); Enterprise Court 21 Dec. 2001, JOR 2002, 57, LJN: AG8076 (*Egbouw Holding*).
416. Enterprise Court 7 May 2008, JOR 2008, 195, LJN: BD4679 (*Vialle*), Enterprise Court 17 Dec. 2007, JOR 2008, 35, LJN: BC4587 (*De Hasker Appelhof*); Enterprise Court 3 May 2006, JOR 2006, 211, LJN: BD5633 (*Bonne Route*); Enterprise Court 8 Oct. 1998, NJ 1999, 348, LJN: AC0562 and 30 Nov. 2000, JOR 2001, 4, LJN: AG3944 (*Zwagerman I*).
417. Enterprise Court 5 Aug. 2009, JOR 2009, 254, LJN: BJ4688 (*ASMI*).

practice, the Enterprise Court often orders an enquiry on the basis of a combination of circumstances.

If the Enterprise Court finds that there are sufficient grounds to doubt as to whether the company is pursuing a proper policy or a proper course of affairs it can order an enquiry but it is under no obligation to do so. The Enterprise Court may find that an enquiry should not take place because this would be disproportionately harmful to the interests of the company and/or because the facts are already sufficiently clear without an enquiry. The court order imposing an investigation is a final judgment[418] and can be declared provisionally enforceable.[419]

If a request for an enquiry is denied and the Enterprise Court finds that the request was made on unreasonable grounds, the company can ask the Enterprise Court to order the petitioner to pay for the damages incurred by the company as a result of the request.[420] The mere fact that a request for an enquiry is denied does not mean that it was made on unreasonable grounds. There must be additional circumstances to conclude that the request was unreasonable and, as long as the petitioner proceeds with care, he has little to fear. Up until this date there have not been any cases in which the Enterprise Court has awarded such a damages claim.

7.2.7 Second Stage: Enquiry

The actual enquiry forms the core of the enquiry proceedings and is conducted by investigators that are appointed by the Enterprise Court.[421] If the request for an enquiry is granted, the Enterprise Court will in its decision describe the subject of the enquiry, as well as the time period in which it must be investigated. The Enterprise Court can order an enquiry that is wider in scope than that requested, both in terms of subject and time period, if it finds this is in the interests of the company.

The duration of enquiries varies considerably. Much will depend on the complexity of the case, the number of investigators appointed, the number of persons to be heard, and the extent to which the company and other parties involved are willing to cooperate. One month seems to be a practical minimum for even the smallest enquiry, but some investigations may very well take up to a year.[422]

418. Supreme Court, 17 Dec. 2010, JOR 2011, 42, LJN: BO3356 (*KPNQwest*).
419. Supreme Court 10 Sep. 2010, JOR 2010, 337, LJN: BM6077 (*Butôt*) and Supreme Court 17 Dec. 2010, JOR 2011, 42, LJN: BO3356 (*KPNQwest*).
420. Art. 2:350(2) BW.
421. Supreme Court 27 Sep. 2000, NJ 2000, 653, LJN: AA7245 (*Gucci*); Supreme Court 18 Apr. 2003, NJ 2003, 286, LJN: AF2161 (*RNA*).
422. Such as happened in the Ahold case, Enterprise Court 30 Mar. 2006, JOR 2006, 152, LJN: AV7799 (*Ahold*).

7.2.7.1 Duties and Powers of the Investigators

The Enterprise Court will appoint one or more investigators, depending on the size and complexity of the case. The investigators appointed by the Enterprise Court are usually experts with a considerable track record in their field of expertise. The Enterprise Court has a (non-public) shortlist with (former) auditors, business consultants, attorneys and entrepreneurs who can be appointed as investigators.

Simultaneously with the appointment of the investigators the Enterprise Court will appoint an examining magistrate (*raadsheer-commisaris*).[423] At the request of the applicants or interested parties the examining magistrate may give instructions on the manner in which the enquiry will be conducted. The examining magistrate shall not decide before he has given the investigators an opportunity to present their views on the request.

The examining magistrate may also give instructions to the investigators upon their request. The examining magistrate shall not decide before he has given the company, ifit appeared in the proceedings, an opportunity to present its views on the request.

The examining magistrate may also give other parties an opportunity to present their views.

No appeal to the Supreme Court is possible against decisions made by an examining magistrate.

Investigators appointed by the Enterprise Court have far-reaching powers of investigation. They are entitled to examine all books and records of the company and they must be shown all assets and properties of the company at their request. Directors, supervisory directors and employees of the company must provide all such information and assistance as the investigators deem necessary for the proper performance of their task. This duty also applies to persons who were directors, supervisory directors or employees of the company during the time period to which the enquiry relates.

The Enterprise Court may authorise the investigators, at their request, to examine relevant books, records and other sources of information of other companies that are closely connected with the company under enquiry, if this is necessary for the proper performance of their task.[424] If such authorisation is given, the directors, supervisory directors and employees of the closely connected company are under the same obligations vis-à-vis the investigators as the directors, supervisory directors and employees of the company under enquiry. The authorisation does not mean, however, that the affairs and policies of the closely connected company become the subject of the enquiry too. It is merely an instrument for the investigators

423. Art. 2:350(4) BW.
424. Art. 2:351(2) BW.

to obtain additional information that may be relevant to their investigation into the affairs and policies of the company under enquiry.[425]

7.2.7.2 *Witnesses*

The investigators may request the Enterprise Court to hear one or more persons as witnesses.[426] The investigators may attend the hearing and question the witnesses.

A witness hearing is a potentially useful instrument vis-à-vis persons who are not subject to the aforementioned statutory obligations of (former) directors, supervisory directors and employees of the company to cooperate with the investigators, such as the external auditors, suppliers and customers of the company or directors, supervisory directors and employees of subsidiaries of the company or of a joint venture in which the company participates. It must be said that in practice many of them cooperate voluntarily with the investigators.

A party before the Enterprise Court may also offer to produce evidence by means of witnesses or otherwise. However, in view of (i) the inherently urgent nature of enquiry proceedings and (ii) the fact that evidence determined by the Enterprise Court in the enquiry proceedings is not binding in subsequent civil liability proceedings before the ordinary courts, the Enterprise Court may reject an offer by one of the parties to produce (counter) evidence.[427] This is an exception to the main rule that an offer to produce evidence should in principle be granted.[428]

7.2.7.3 *Investigator's Report*

The investigators must write a report on their findings, which must be filed with the court registry of the Enterprise Court.[429] In the report it must be stated clearly whether persons who are mentioned in the report have been given the opportunity to comment on essential findings pertaining to them.[430] The Attorney-general, the company and the petitioners and their attorneys receive a copy of the report. The Enterprise Court may decide that the report is also available for inspection, either in full or in part, to other designated persons or to the general public.[431] The report is not automatically a public document. However, the Enterprise Court has developed

425. Supreme Court 6 Jun. 2003, NJ 2003, 486, LJN: AF9440 (*Scheipar*); Enterprise Court 12 Nov. 1998, NJ 1999, 375, LJN: AC2735 (*Zuider Ster*).
426. Art. 2:352a BW.
427. Supreme Court 8 Apr. 2005, NJ 2006, 443, LJN: AS5010 (*Laurus*).
428. Art. 284(1) Rv provides that the rules of evidence that are applicable to proceedings commenced by writ also apply to petition proceedings, unless the nature of the relevant petition proceedings dictates otherwise.
429. Art. 2:353(1) BW.
430. Art. 2:351(4) BW in conjunction with Art. 2:353(1) BW.
431. Art. 2:353(2) BW and Enterprise Court 16 Jun. 2010, ARO 2010, 97, LJN: BM8183 (*Fortis*).

a practice that makes reports concerning the affairs and policies of publicly listed companies available for inspection to the general public.

If and to the extent that the report is not made available for inspection to the general public, no one other than the company itself is allowed to disclose information from the report to third parties, unless with authorisation from the chairman of the Enterprise Court.[432]

The investigators' report is a presentation of facts. It should not include a conclusion as to whether there has been mismanagement but must enable the Enterprise Court to determine, in the third stage of the enquiry proceedings, whether mismanagement has taken place.[433]

7.2.7.4 Costs of the Investigation

The company must bear the costs of the investigation, as well as, if applicable, the reasonable costs that were incurred for the defence of the investigators against liability claims based on the enquiry or the investigators' report.[434] Investigators shall not be liable for any damage ensuing from the report on the outcome of the enquiry, unless they have intentionally acted improperly or have grossly failed to understand what the proper performance of duties entails.[435]

The Enterprise Court often decides that the company shall provide security in advance for payment of the costs of the investigation. If no security has been provided for the complete budget, any party involved can request the Enterprise Court to terminate the enquiry proceedings.[436] At the request of the investigators, the Enterprise Court can increase the budget for the investigation. If such a request is made, the petitioners and other interested parties will be given the opportunity to present their views.

If the company and the appointed investigators cannot reach agreement on the remuneration of the investigators, the Enterprise Court will determine the amount of the remuneration.

After examination of the report, the Enterprise Court may, at the request of the company, decide that the company may recover the costs of the enquiry in full or in part from the petitioner, if it follows from the report that the request for an enquiry was made on unreasonable grounds.[437] This will only be the case if the petitioner used arguments in his petition that in the report turned out to be false, or actively misled the Enterprise Court in ordering an enquiry. Although in a number of cases

432. Art. 2:353(3) BW.
433. Supreme Court 19 Jun. 1997, NJ 1997, 673, LJN: AD2749 (*Bobel*); Supreme Court 27 Sep. 2000, NJ 2000, 653, LJN: AA7245 (*Gucci*).
434. Art. 2:350(3) BW and Enterprise Court 14 Oct. 2011, JOR 2012,10, LJN: BU4856 (*Mei*).
435. Art 2:351(5) BW.
436. Supreme Court 26 Jun. 2009, JOR 2009, 193, LJN: BH6537 (*KPN Qwest*).
437. Art. 2:354 BW.

requests to recover the costs of enquiry from the petitioner have been made, to date the Enterprise Court has never granted such a request.[438]

Alternatively, if it follows from the report that a managing director, supervisory director or employee of the company is responsible for an incorrect policy or an unsatisfactory course of events, the company may ask the Enterprise Court to decide that the company may recover the costs of the enquiry in full or in part from such director, supervisory director or employee.[439] An incorrect policy or an unsatisfactory course of events is not the same as mismanagement. The Enterprise Court will only award a claim for recovery of costs against a director, supervisory director or employee if it finds that serious personal blame can be attributed to that particular person.[440]

7.2.8 Third Stage: Decision

7.2.8.1 Determination of Mismanagement

If it follows from the report that there has been mismanagement, the Enterprise Court may take certain measures to remedy such mismanagement. It can do so solely at the request of: (i) the original petitioner, (ii) a party that has the right to initiate enquiry proceedings and has received a copy of the report; or (iii) the Attorney-general, if matters of public interest are involved.[441] Consequently, it depends on the aforementioned parties whether or not the enquiry proceedings proceed to the third stage.

The petition must be submitted to the Enterprise Court within two months after the report has been deposited at the court registry of the Enterprise Court.[442]

Just as at the first stage of the proceedings, at the third stage all interested parties can submit a written statement to present their views. The Enterprise Court will also organise a court session during which all parties can plead their case orally.

The Enterprise Court can only impose measures if it finds that there has been mismanagement. Such mismanagement must follow from the facts presented in the enquiry report but may also be based on other facts and circumstances that have been presented to the Enterprise Court during the third stage, as long as they relate

438. See for example Enterprise Court 20 Jun. 2007, JOR 2007, 203, LJN: BB3207 (*Cordial*); Enterprise Court 21 Jun. 1979, NJ 1980, 71, LJN: AC6621 (*Batco*); Enterprise Court 26 May 1983, NJ 1984, 481, LJN: AC8007 (*Linders/Hofstee*), and Enterprise Court 28 Oct. 1993, NJ 1994, 566, LJN: AD1980 (*RLA*).
439. Art. 2:354 BW.
440. Supreme Court 16 Aug. 1996, NJ 1997, 37, LJN: AD2594 (*VHS*); Supreme Court 4 Jun. 1997, NJ 1997, 671, LJN: AG7240 (*Text Lite*).
441. Art. 2:355(1) BW.
442. Art. 2:355(2) BW.

to the subject of the enquiry.[443] The Enterprise Court may take civil-law standards, criminal-law standards and administrative-law standards into consideration in order to determine whether there has been mismanagement. More importantly, the type of business the company is running and the position the company has within society (e.g. a systemic bank) may also be taken into account.[444]

Mismanagement is not a legally defined term. The Dutch legislature intentionally left it up to the Enterprise Court to decide in each individual case whether a certain action, mistake or behaviour is serious enough to qualify as mismanagement. In this respect, the Supreme Court has decided that 'elementary principles of sound entrepreneurship' need to have been violated.[445] This cannot be assumed too quickly. Since a company has a certain discretion as to the policies and decisions it chooses and the manner in which they are executed, the Enterprise Court must only assess whether the company could have reasonably decided or acted as it did.

The concept of mismanagement is not limited to mismanagement by the managing board but may also relate to acts or omissions by other corporate bodies, such as the general meeting of shareholders or the supervisory board, and even to acts or omissions by members of a corporate body, such as an individual shareholder.

Findings of mismanagement by the Enterprise Court vary widely in nature. Many cases in which the Enterprise Court has determined that there was mismanagement involved situations in which the company was unable to function properly as a result of a deadlock in the decision-making process.[446] Other examples that may constitute mismanagement include: acting contrary to Dutch law principles of reasonableness and fairness,[447] taking irresponsible business decisions,[448] acting in violation of the law or the articles of association,[449] improper dealing with conflicts of interest,[450] insufficient or unequal disclosure of information,[451] and shortcom-

443. Supreme Court 18 Apr. 2003, NJ 2003, 286, LJN: AF2161 (*RNA*). See also Enterprise Court 16 Oct. 2003, NJ 2003, 727, LJN: AM1448 and Enterprise Court 9 Jan. 2004, NJ 2004, 168, LJN: AO1717 (*Laurus*).

444. Enterprise Court 5 Apr. 2012, ARO 2012, 54, LJN: BW0991 (*Fortis*).

445. Supreme Court 10 Jan. 1990, NJ 1990, 446, LJN: AD0936 (*Ogem*).

446. For example, Enterprise Court 8 Oct. 1998, JOR 1998, 166, LJN: AG3231 (*Hoffmann Beheer*); Enterprise Court 27 Apr. 2005, JOR 2005, 181, LJN: AU0633 (*Dolphin Watercompany*); and Enterprise Court 18 Oct. 2004, JOR 2004, 328, LJN: AR7318 (*NIBO*).

447. Supreme Court 1 Mar. 2002, NJ 2002, 296, LJN: AD9857 (*Zwagerman I*).

448. Supreme Court 10 Jan. 1990, NJ 1990, 466, LJN: AC1234 (*Ogem*); Enterprise Court 7 Mar. 1996, NJ 1997, 674, LJN: AB9708 (*Verto*) and Enterprise Court 3 Aug. 1995, De NV 1995, p. 203 (*Vie d'Or*).

449. For example, Enterprise Court 22 Mar. 2005, JOR 2005, 176, LJN: AU0623 (*Van Doorn*) and Enterprise Court 13 Jul 2011, JOR 2011, 290, LJN: BR2929 (*Meepo Holding*).

450. For example, Enterprise Court 17 Mar. 1983, NJ 1984, 462, LJN: AC7893 and Enterprise Court 8 Oct. 1987, NJ 1989, 270, LJN: AC0548 (*Van der Klis*).

451. For example, Enterprise Court 7 Dec. 1989, NJ 1990, 242, LJN: AC0093 (*Bredero*); Supreme Court 10 Jan. 1990, NJ 1990, 466, LJN: AC1234 (*Ogem*).

ings in the annual accounts of the company.[452] Much will depend on the facts and circumstances of the case. The Enterprise Court may also take into account the manner in which the company has responded to complaints made by the petitioner or petitioners prior to the enquiry proceedings.

7.2.8.2 Types of Measures

If the Enterprise Court finds that there has been mismanagement, it can impose one or more of the following measures:[453] (i) the suspension or nullification of a resolution of the management board, the shareholders' meeting or any other corporate body; (ii) the suspension or removal of one or more managing or supervisory directors; (iii) the temporary appointment of one or more managing or supervisory directors; (iv) a temporary deviation from such provisions of the articles of association as shall be specified by the Enterprise Court;[454] (v) the temporary transfer of shares to a trustee; (vi) the dissolution of the company.

The Enterprise Court is not compelled to take any of the above-mentioned measures. It can also limit itself to a determination that there has been mismanagement.[455] It is free to take measures other than those requested by the petitioner, although it cannot take any measures other than those listed above.[456]

When the Enterprise Court orders a measure it will also determine the duration of such a measure. At the request of the petitioner who has asked for such a measure, of the company or of the Attorney-general, the Enterprise Court can extend or shorten its duration.[457] A measure taken by the Enterprise Court cannot be undone by the company. Any decision to that end is invalid as a matter of law.[458]

The Enterprise Court can declare that its decision to impose a measure is provisionally enforceable, which means that an appeal to the Supreme Court against that decision does not stay the operation of the decision.[459] But this is not possible for a measure ordering the liquidation of a company, as this is a far-reaching measure and cannot by its nature be imposed temporarily. It is quite common for the Enter-

---

452. For example, Supreme Court 4 Jun. 1997, NJ 1997, 671, LJN: AG7240 (*Text Lite*), Enterprise Court 17 Apr. 1997, NJ 1997, 672, LJN: AD2721 (*Bobel*) and Enterprise Court 9 Jul. 1998, NJ 1998, 882, LJN: AC0975 (*Vie d'Or*).
453. Art. 2:356 BW.
454. A temporary deviation from the articles of association must be in accordance with mandatory law. For example, the Enterprise Court cannot temporarily appoint a member of the supervisory board and give that member powers or rights which the law does not provide for. See Supreme Court 1 Mar. 2002, NJ 2002, 296, LJN: AD9857 (*Zwagerman I*).
455. Supreme Court 10 Jan. 1990, NJ 1990, 466, LJN: AC1234 (*Ogem*).
456. Supreme Court 4 Oct. 2002, NJ 2002, 556, LJN: AE8338 (*Zwagerman II*). If the Enterprise Court orders the dissolution of the company, it must also appoint a liquidator (Art. 2:23 BW).
457. Art. 2:357(1) BW.
458. Art. 2:357(3) BW.
459. Art. 2:358 BW.

prise Court to declare its decision to impose a measure at the third stage of enquiry proceedings to be provisionally enforceable notwithstanding an appeal.[460]

7.2.9 Provisional Measures

7.2.9.1 General

The success and importance of the Enterprise Court is to a large extent the result of an amendment to the law made in 1994, when the Enterprise Court was given the power to impose provisional measures at any stage of the enquiry procedure. This power is by far the most important tool of the Enterprise Court and has allowed it to become a highly specialised preliminary relief judge in matters concerning Dutch company law and corporate governance. Contrary to the measures that can be imposed during the third stage of the enquiry proceedings, the provisional measures are not limited by law. This gives the Enterprise Court the opportunity to impose a virtually unlimited variety of provisional measures, which allows it to act effectively and decisively in cases brought before it.

The power of the Enterprise Court to impose provisional measures is not an exclusive one. The preliminary relief judge of the District Court remains competent to impose such measures too (see § 9.1).[461] Nonetheless, the preliminary relief judge must exercise restraint in imposing provisional measures if the petitioner is also allowed to address the Enterprise Court for preliminary relief.[462] The preliminary relief judge will have to limit the duration of a provisional measure to the point the Enterprise Court will have decided on a request for provisional measures, in order to prevent contradictory judgments.[463]

7.2.9.2 The Proceedings

Provisional measures can be imposed at every stage of the proceedings, even before the Enterprise Court has ordered an enquiry. It is enough that a request for an enquiry has been submitted.[464] The Supreme Court has ruled that the Enterprise Court should only impose provisional measures in advance of ordering an enquiry, after having weighed the interests of the parties concerned and if sufficiently compelling

460. For example, Enterprise Court 9 Jul. 1998, NJ 1998, 882, LJN: AC0975 (*Vie d'Or*) and Enterprise Court 20 Jun. 2007, JOR 2007, 203, LJN: BB3207 (*Cordial*).
461. Court of Appeal 's-Hertogenbosch 22 Jan. 1996, JOR 1996, 22, LJN: AH5505 (*Van der Staak*).
462. Court of Appeal Amsterdam 7 Nov. 1996, KG 1997, 3 (*Gaus/Dijkshoorn*).
463. MvT, TK 22 400, No. 3, p. 14.
464. Arts 2:349a(2) and 2:355(3) BW which provides that Art. 2:349a BW applies equally during the third stage of the enquiry proceedings. It is also possible for provisional measures to be imposed during the enquiry, even if the Enterprise Court has initially refused to impose such measures.

reasons exist.[465] In addition the Enterprise Court will need to hold the provisional opinion that there are well-founded grounds to doubt as to whether there is a proper policy or proper course of affairs, and the decision on the enquiry itself must then be taken within a reasonable time period.[466]

The Enterprise Court must, when making its decision on imposing a provisional measure, determine whether it is likely that the request for an enquiry will be granted. If it is clear from the outset that the petitioner is not entitled to ask for an enquiry or if there is no indication whatsoever that there are grounds to doubt as to whether there is a proper policy or a proper course of affairs, the Enterprise Court cannot impose provisional measures. In that case, if a need for provisional measures remains, the petitioner should address the preliminary relief judge of the District Court, rather than the Enterprise Court.[467]

The Enterprise Court cannot impose provisional measures on its own initiative. A request is necessary. Not only the petitioner for an enquiry, but also all other parties that meet the criteria for applying for an enquiry (such as fellow shareholders) can ask for provisional relief. Moreover, once an interested party has been admitted to the enquiry proceedings, such interested party can apply for provisional measures as well.[468]

7.2.9.3 Types of Provisional Measures

When imposing provisional measures, the Enterprise Court is not restricted by the measures asked for by the petitioner. It can impose such provisional measures as it deems necessary in view of the situation of the company or in the interests of the enquiry.[469] The Enterprise Court regularly imposes provisional measures that are different from those that are asked for. Such measures can also be more far-reaching than those requested, or aimed at persons or corporate bodies other than those intended by the petitioner.

The freedom of the Enterprise Court to impose provisional measures is not unlimited, however. Firstly, the Enterprise Court can only impose temporary measures. This follows from the fact that measures must be provisional in nature. The duration of the measures can in any event not exceed the duration of the enquiry

465. Supreme Court 14 Dec. 2007, JOR 2008, 11, LJN: BB3523 (*DSM*).
466. Art. 2:349a(3) BW.
467. Supreme Court 27 Sep. 2000, NJ 2000, 653, LJN: AA7245 (*Gucci*).
468. Enterprise Court 24 Nov. 2008, JOR 2009, 9, LJN: BG5150 (*Fortis*) and Supreme Court 23 Mar. 2012, JOR 2012, 141, LJN: BV1056 (*e-Traction*).
469. Supreme Court 19 Oct. 2001, NJ 2002, 92, LJN: AD5138 (*Sky Gate*); Supreme Court 4 Oct. 2002, NJ 2002, 556, LJN: AE8338 (*Zwagerman II*).

proceedings.[470] On the other hand, the fact that a provisional measure must be temporary does not mean that it cannot have consequences that are irreversible.[471]

A second limitation on the freedom of the Enterprise Court to impose provisional measures is that it must respect the division of powers between the various corporate bodies, as prescribed by mandatory law. By way of illustration, the Enterprise Court cannot temporarily appoint a supervisory director and give that supervisory director powers which under Dutch company law typically belong to the shareholders' meeting.[472]

A third limitation is that the Enterprise Court must not take decisions in lieu of the company. The task of the Enterprise Court is to impose provisional measures that create room for the parties involved to reach a compromise or to find a solution for the dispute that has arisen between them.

Case law from the Enterprise Court shows a wide variety of provisional measures, tailored to the circumstances of the case. Examples are: prohibition on shareholders to exercise their voting rights,[473] the appointment of a supervisory director with the power to approve decisions of the board in the case of conflicts of interest,[474] a prohibition on the management board to take actions that could change the status quo of the company,[475] a prohibition on shareholders to take decisions on agenda items concerning, among other things, the dismissal of members of the management and supervisory board,[476] temporarily putting aside anti-dilution protection[477] and the appointment of a director under the articles of association to the exclusion of the representative authority of the sitting director.[478]

Decisions from the Enterprise Court in which provisional measures are imposed can also be declared provisionally enforceable notwithstanding an appeal.

7.2.10 Appeal to the Supreme Court

The Enterprise Court is the first and only factual court to deal with requests for an enquiry. Decisions of the Enterprise Court can be appealed to the Supreme Court, but the Supreme Court does not have the power to review assessments of facts. Its review is limited to questions of law and to questions of proper reasoning (see

470. Art. 2:349a(2) BW.
471. Supreme Court 19 Oct. 2001, JOR 2002, 5, LJN: AD5138 (*Sky Gate*).
472. Supreme Court 1 Mar. 2002, NJ 2002, 296, LJN: AD9857 (*Zwagerman I*).
473. Enterprise Court 16 Jun. 1994, NJ 1995, 455, LJN: AD2118 (*Betacom*).
474. Enterprise Court 31 Oct. 2002, JOR 2003, 59, LJN: AG8246 (*ZDS Trading*).
475. Enterprise Court 4 Jul. 2001, NJ 2001, 469, LJN: AB2476 (*HBG*); Enterprise Court 3 May 2007, JOR 2007, 143, LJN: BA4395 (*ABN AMRO*).
476. Enterprise Court 20 May 2008, JOR 2008, 158, LJN: BD2197 (*ASM International*).
477. Enterprise Court 29 May 2009, JOR 2009, 319, LJN: BJ1452 (*Triple E*) and Enterprise Court 31 Dec. 2009, JOR 2010, 60, LJN: BL3680 (*Inter Access*).
478. Enterprise Court 19 Jun. 2009, JOR 2009, 287, LJN: BJ2736 (*Bosman & Sorée*).

§ 6.4.2.3). The capital requirements of article 2:346 BW do not apply in order to determine the admissibility of an appeal to the Supreme Court.[479]

A decision of the Enterprise Court that there are sufficient grounds to doubt whether a company is pursuing a proper policy or proper course of affairs is to a very large degree based on a determination of the facts. This means that it is very difficult to appeal such a decision to the Supreme Court. The same is true for a decision by the Enterprise Court, to the effect that there has (not) been mismanagement.

7.2.11 Effect of a Finding of Mismanagement

The assessment by the Enterprise Court that there has been mismanagement is binding in other legal proceedings on all parties that have appeared at the third stage of the proceedings and have either asked for a finding of mismanagement or put forward a defence against such a request.

However, an assessment of mismanagement by the Enterprise Court only means that there has been mismanagement of the company, not mismanagement by individual members of its corporate bodies, such as directors or supervisory directors. A determination of mismanagement by the Enterprise Court does not therefore imply the personal liability of such individuals vis-à-vis third parties[480] or vis-à-vis the company.[481] Consequently, if third parties, such as banks or suppliers of a company, initiate legal proceedings against the directors and supervisory directors of a company, those third parties will have to assert and prove that the directors and supervisory directors are personally liable for the damages they have incurred as a result of the mismanagement of the company.

The Supreme Court has also ruled, however, that when hearing a claim for civil liability, the District Court may, on the basis of a decision by the Enterprise Court that there has been mismanagement, and on the basis of the report of the investigator and the debate conducted at the third stage of the enquiry proceedings, reach the preliminary conclusion that the managing or supervisory director against whom the liability claim is directed, did not properly fulfil his duties vis-à-vis the company. On the basis of this assumption, the District Court may subsequently conclude that that managing or supervisory director is liable vis-à-vis the company, subject to proof to the contrary.[482] This decision by the Supreme Court is especially helpful to a trustee in bankruptcy who wishes to claim damages suffered by the company from directors or supervisory directors as a result of the mismanagement.

479. Supreme Court 30 Mar. 2012, JOR 2012, 142, LJN: BV1435 (*ASMI*).
480. Supreme Court 10 Jan. 1990, NJ 1990, 466, LJN: AC1234 (*Ogem*).
481. Supreme Court 4 Apr. 2003, NJ 2003, 538, LJN: AF 3419 (*Jaarsma*).
482. Supreme Court 8 Apr. 2005, NJ 2006, 443, LJN: AS5010 (*Laurus*).

7.3 Forced Exit Proceedings

7.3.1 General

Dutch company law provides a shareholder with the right, in certain circumstances, to force out another shareholder or, alternatively, to force other shareholders or the company to acquire his shares. Translated literally, these proceedings are called dispute resolution proceedings (*geschillenregeling*) but this rather general term will be replaced here by 'forced exit proceedings'. Forced exit proceedings are available only for B.V.s and for closely held N.V.s (of which the articles of association provide for registered shares only, contain a blocking clause and do not permit the issuance of bearer depository receipts).[483] The law on forced exit proceedings has recently been amended, entering into force on 1 October 2012.[484]

One or more shareholders representing at least one-third of the issued share capital of a company may require another shareholder to transfer his shares to him or them, if the other shareholder by his conduct prejudices or has prejudiced the interests of the company to such an extent that his continued shareholding cannot reasonably be tolerated.[485]

A comparable remedy exists vis-à-vis a pledgee or holder of a right of usufruct who has been granted the voting rights on the shares. If such a pledgee or holder of a right of usufruct by his actions prejudices the interests of the company to such an extent that his continued exercising of the voting rights cannot reasonably be tolerated, one or more of the shareholders representing at least one-third of the issued share capital can claim that the voting rights will revert to the pledgor and legal owner of the shares.[486]

Conversely, a shareholder may require that his fellow shareholders buy him out if one or more of the other shareholders have prejudiced his (rather than the company's) rights or interests to such an extent that his own continued shareholding cannot reasonably be expected of him.[487] A claim to be bought out may also be made against the company if the company itself has prejudiced a shareholder's rights or interests to the same extent. A claim cannot be made against the company, however, if the buy-back of the shares by the company would violate statutory rules of capital protection.[488]

A shareholder defendant who feels that an action should not or not only be directed against him but rather, or also, against other shareholder(s) and/or the

483. Art. 2:335(2) BW.
484. Stb. 2012, 299.
485. Art. 2:336(1) BW.
486. Art. 2:342 BW.
487. Art. 2:343(1) BW.
488. Art. 2:343(1) BW and Art. 2:98/207 BW.

company, may force such other shareholder(s) and/or the company to join the proceedings as a co-defendant.[489]

Forced exit proceedings are not available if a procedure for the resolution of shareholder conflicts is already provided for in the articles of association of the company or in a shareholders' agreement, unless it has become apparent that the procedure provided for 'cannot be applied'.[490] The procedure in the articles of association or in the contract should provide the claimant with a remedy comparable to the forced exit proceedings.

7.3.2 The Proceedings

7.3.2.1 Jurisdiction

A claim in forced exit proceedings is brought against the defendant shareholder (and/or the company) in the District Court in the district where the company has its seat. A copy of the writ is served on the company, which then notifies in writing the shareholders who have not been summoned, so that the company and the other shareholders can join the proceedings, if they wish to do so.[491] An appeal against a decision from the District Court must be brought before the Enterprise Court.[492]

The articles of association or a shareholders' agreement may deviate from this jurisdiction, for instance by providing that forced exit claims will immediately be brought in the Enterprise Court (appealable only to the Supreme Court, on limited grounds) or will be decided in arbitration.[493]

The court adjudicating a forced exit claim automatically has jurisdiction with respect to other claims (such as claims for damages) between the same parties (and/or the company) relating to the same actions on which the forced exit claim is based.[494] It may also grant injunctive relief (such as an order suspending the voting rights of the defendant) for the duration of the proceedings and even beyond that until the forced exit, ordered by the court, has actually been effected.[495]

Although statutory law does not in so many words provide for this, forced exit claims have occasionally been pursued in preliminary relief proceedings, but this has seldom been successful.[496] In case of shareholder disputes requiring immediate relief, other remedies are more commonly being sought in enquiry proceedings (see § 7.2).

489. Art. 2:343(3) BW.
490. Art. 2:337 BW.
491. Art. 997a Rv.
492. Art. 2:336(3) BW.
493. Art. 2:337(2) BW.
494. Art. 2:336(5) BW.
495. Art. 2:338(3) BW.
496. One example of successful forced exit proceedings in preliminary relief proceedings can be found in Court of Appeal 's-Hertogenbosch 14 Jan. 1999, NJ 1999, 743, LJN: AD2984 (*Wichgers/De Jong*).

The proceedings in the court of first instance progress through two stages.

7.3.2.2 *First Stage: Conditions for Forced Exit*

First, the District Court will have to determine whether the conditions for the forced exit have been proven by the claimant. The District Court can stay its decision in the first stage if it becomes apparent that the company itself or one or more shareholders are taking measures to remedy as much as possible the grievances that form the basis of the claim.[497]

After the writ of summons has been served on the defendant, he can no longer transfer or encumber his shares without the claimant's permission. In view of the risk that a claimant is misusing forced exit proceedings as a means of blocking share transfers, the Civil Code provides that the District Court may give the defendant permission to transfer or encumber the shares, if he has a reasonable interest to do so (so that the claimant does not have a reasonable interest in withholding his permission). Such a decision cannot be appealed.[498]

If the court awards the forced exit claim it will appoint one or more experts to determine the price of the shares. The experts are bound by the rules described above at § 5.2.3.1.

However, if the litigating parties agree on the price, or if the articles of association or a shareholders' agreement provide such a clear mechanism for determining the price that the appointment of experts is not necessary, the court can skip the second stage altogether, and order the transfer of the shares against payment of the relevant price immediately at the end of the first stage.[499]

The court's decision to award the forced exit claim and appoint (an) expert(s) is an interim judgment. To avoid delay tactics, this decision cannot be appealed separately, but only together with the final judgment ordering the transfer of the shares in the second stage.[500]

7.3.2.3 *Second Stage: Price Determination and Judgment*

After the experts have given their opinion and the parties have been allowed to comment on the opinion, the court will determine the price of the shares to be transferred in a judgment.

The Civil Code gives much flexibility for determining the price of the shares. It does not prescribe how the experts are to determine the price; it is up to them to identify the appropriate valuation method and relevant facts and circumstances and

497. Art. 2:336(4) BW, Art. 2:343(6) BW.
498. Art. 2:338(1) BW.
499. Art. 2:339(3) and 2:340(2) BW.
500. Art. 2:339(1) BW.

it is up to the court to review their findings. However, if the articles of association or a shareholders' agreement indicate how the value of the shares is to be assessed, the experts will have to take that into account. The court is also bound by such provisions, but in establishing the price it may nevertheless deviate from them if they were to lead to an obviously unreasonable price.[501]

A shareholder claiming to be bought out may suffer a disadvantage if the actions of his fellow shareholders or of the company underlying his claim have caused a decrease in value of his shares, which is then reflected in a lower price for his shares in the forced exit proceedings. Dutch law does not provide for derivative actions or other means for a shareholder to claim a decrease in value of his shares, resulting from any wrongdoings to the company; such a claim can in principle only be made by the company itself[502] and after having transferred his shares, the exiting shareholder will no longer benefit from any such claims by the company. The Civil Code therefore provides that, in determining the price to be paid to a shareholder claiming an exit from the company, the court can increase the price with a reasonable amount in connection with actions of the defendants or of others, if it is likely that those actions have decreased the value of the claimant's shares and if it is not reasonable that this decrease in value remains for the account of the claimant.[503]

The judgment at the end of the second stage will also allocate the costs of the experts to one or more of the parties or to the company. The judgment will contain an enforceable order against one party to transfer the shares and an order against the other party to pay the price for those shares within two weeks.[504]

In the case of a defendant being forced out, where there is more than one claimant, the shares will be transferred to the claimants in proportion to their existing shareholdings. If the articles of association provide for pre-emptive rights of other parties, then the shares must first be offered to the relevant parties in accordance with such pre-emptive rights. If the defendant fails to transfer his shares, the company can and must do so on his behalf. If one of the claimants fails to pay the purchase price, the other claimants will be obliged to acquire and pay for the shares allocated to this claimant.[505]

If, on the other hand, the defendants are being ordered to take over the claimant's shares, these will be allocated to the defendants in a way the court, considering all the circumstances, deems appropriate. However, existing pre-emptive rights of other shareholders or third parties will have to be respected. If one of the defendants fails to take delivery of the shares allocated to him and/or pay the purchase price,

501. Art. 2:340(3) BW.
502. Supreme Court 2 Dec. 1994, NJ 1995, 288, LJN: ZC1564 (*Poot/ABP*).
503. Art. 2:343(4) BW.
504. Art. 2:340 (1) and (4) BW.
505. Art. 2:341 BW.

the other defendants will be obliged to acquire and pay for the shares allocated to this defendant (pro rata to the number of shares originally allocated to them).[506]

7.3.2.4 Consequences of a Judgment being Overturned on Appeal

After the shares have been transferred pursuant to a judgment in forced exit proceedings, that judgment may be overturned on appeal. The Civil Code sets out the consequences of that situation. It provides that the original transfer of shares does not automatically become invalid, but rather that an obligation comes into existence to transfer the shares back to its original owner (against repayment of the purchase price). This prevents any corporate resolutions adopted in the meantime from retroactively becoming invalid.[507]

The Court of Appeal will also have the option not to order that the shares be transferred back to their original owner(s) if that would prove impractical or unfair, but to order that the party against whom the forced exit claim was awarded will only be entitled to damages.[508]

7.3.3 Alternative Proceedings

If the parties are in agreement that one or more shareholders should exit the company and their disagreement merely relates to the price, they can (instead of going through the entire forced exit proceedings), petition the court to determine the price of the shares and appoint experts for that purpose. In connection therewith they can request the court to take into account certain agreed valuation principles.[509]

Alternatively, they can request the court to appoint experts whose findings will have the force of an expert determination[510] without, therefore, the court itself giving a judgment on the price of the shares.[511]

7.4 Squeeze-Out Proceedings

7.4.1 General

A shareholder who owns, either alone or with one of its group companies,[512] 95% or more of the company's issued share capital may initiate squeeze-out proceedings

506. Art. 2:343a BW.
507. Art. 2:341a(1) BW.
508. Art. 2:341a(2) BW.
509. Art. 2:343c BW.
510. See Chapter 2, § 7.
511. Art. 2:343c (4) BW
512. Art. 2:24b BW defines a 'group' as an economic unit within which legal entities and partnerships are united in one organisation. Group companies are legal entities and partnerships which are united in

to require all minority shareholders to transfer their shares to him.[513] Squeeze-out proceedings can be commenced both with respect to minority shareholders of N.V.s and B.V.s.

If the minority shareholders do not appear in the proceedings, if no experts are appointed and if there are no appeals to the Supreme Court, squeeze-out proceedings usually take six to 12 months. In other cases, it may take considerably longer.

7.4.2 The Proceedings

A squeeze-out action is brought in the Enterprise Court by a writ of summons against all minority shareholders collectively. The manner in which the minority shareholders need to be summoned depends on whether the majority shareholder knows their identity. This is an objective test that is linked to the kind of shares held by the minority shareholders. For example, in the case where a minority shareholder owns registered shares and is registered with an address in the shareholder's register, he must be summoned in person. In the case where the minority shareholders own bearer shares, they can be summoned collectively by serving a writ at the office of the public prosecutor and by publishing an abstract of the writ in a Dutch national newspaper.[514] If depositary receipts for shares (*certificaten van aandelen*) have been issued, it is the trust office and not the owners of such depositary receipts that needs to be summoned. The court will usually spend some time reviewing whether all shareholders have been properly summoned before declaring them to be in default of the order to appear and continue the proceedings (see § 6.1.3). In practice, the majority of squeeze-out judgments are default judgments due to the fact that only limited objections can be brought against a squeeze-out claim.

In the proceedings the majority shareholder must prove ownership of at least 95% of the issued share capital of the company. In the event that none of the minority shareholders appear, the court must examine whether the 95% ownership threshold has been met.[515]

If the 95% threshold is met, the Enterprise Court will allow the squeeze-out unless (i) the compulsory transfer of the shares will cause serious material damage to one or more minority shareholders which would not be compensated by the squeeze-out price to be determined by the court; (ii) one or more minority shareholders hold one or more priority shares (*prioriteitsaandelen*); or (iii) the majority

---

one group.

513. Arts 2:92a BW (N.V.) and 2:201a BW (B.V.).

514. Art. 54(2) Rv and Enterprise Court 15 May 2008, JOR 2008, 198, LJN: BD1687 (*Valcon/VEB*).

515. Art. 2:92a(3) BW.

shareholder has waived his right to initiate squeeze-out proceedings.[516] In practice, this list of grounds for denying a squeeze-out claim is interpreted restrictively.[517]

7.4.3 Squeeze-Out Price

If the Enterprise Court decides that the majority shareholder has an admissible claim (i.e. because he owns at least 95% of the shares and none of the grounds for refusal applies), it will determine the purchase price to be paid by the majority shareholder to the minority shareholders. This squeeze-out price should reflect the value of the shares per the date of transfer (which is shortly after the squeeze-out judgment) or a date close to it. The law does not stipulate what valuation method should be used. Depending on the circumstances of the case, relevant criteria are the stock exchange price, the offer price in a public bid (see § 7.4.4. below), the net asset value, the net assets and the profit per share.

Typically, the majority shareholder will often have proposed a squeeze-out price in the proceedings by relying on a statement from an accountant or investment bank, or explaining how the squeeze-out price was otherwise established. The Enterprise Court may, however, determine the squeeze-out price at a different price than that proposed by the majority shareholder. In practice, the court will only do this if minority shareholders object to the price proposed by the majority shareholder. In such a case, the Enterprise Court usually appoints either one or three experts at its discretion to provide it with advice on the value of the shares.[518] The experts have wide-ranging powers to review the books of the company and to interview the managing and supervisory directors. The Enterprise Court is not bound by the experts' advice but will usually follow it. If the experts advise that the value of the shares is lower than the price offered by the majority shareholder, the Enterprise Court usually determines the squeeze out price to be the higher price.

7.4.4 Squeeze-Out Proceedings after a Public Bid

Squeeze-out proceedings are often initiated soon after a public takeover bid, in which a large number but not all of the shareholders have tendered their shares. It has been common practice in such cases that the squeeze-out price is equal to the offer price in the public offer, provided that no circumstances have arisen since the public offer which should lead to a higher price. Obviously, the majority shareholder may propose a different price than the price in the public offer. However, if the proposed squeeze-out price is lower than the price in the public offer, the majority

---

516. Arts 2:92a(4) (N.V.) and 2:201a(4) (B.V.) BW.
517. For example, Supreme Court 16 Jan. 2004, NJ 2004, 184, LJN: AO1777 (*Goglio*).
518. Arts 2:92a(5) (N.V.) and 2:201a(5) (B.V.) BW.

shareholder should explain the difference. In the absence of a suitable explanation it is likely that the court will appoint experts to advise it on the value of the shares.

In October 2007, legislation was enacted on the basis of an EC Directive, introducing a specific provision for squeeze-out proceedings following a public offer.[519] An important difference compared to the general squeeze out proceedings is that it includes a valuation method. Provided that the proceedings are initiated by the company which has made the public offer within three months after the time-period for acceptance of the offer has lapsed, and at least 90% of the shares have been acquired as a result of the offer, the public offer price is presumed to be a reasonable squeeze-out price.[520] Case law has clarified that for the 90% threshold only the shares that have been accepted under the public bid count; shares that the majority shareholder bought otherwise, for example on the stock exchange, do not count for the 90% threshold.[521]

The new legislation also introduces the reverse right, namely a right for the minority shareholders to be squeezed-out by the majority shareholder. Again, such proceedings must be initiated within three months after the public offer and the public offer price is presumed to be a reasonable squeeze-out price if at least 90% of the shares have been acquired as a result of the public offer.[522] In both situations, the course of proceedings is similar to the normal squeeze-out proceedings.

7.4.5 Judgment

If the claim of the majority shareholder is allowed, the Enterprise Court will give a judgment which includes the squeeze-out price. In this judgment, the majority shareholder is ordered to pay the squeeze-out price to the minority shareholders, to be increased with statutory interest as of, usually, the date of the judgment, and the minority shareholders are ordered to transfer their shares. Payment must be made in money, payment in shares is not allowed. The Enterprise Court may also give an order for costs as appropriate, but a defendant who has not appeared in court cannot be ordered to pay costs. In practice, the majority shareholder is usually also liable for the costs of the experts, if appointed.

If the minority shareholders do not offer their shares voluntarily after the squeeze-out is permitted by the Enterprise Court, the majority shareholder can enforce the judgment on them. This is done by serving the judgment on them in

519. Art. 2:359c BW entered into force as of 28 Oct. 2007. This provision is based on EC Council Directive of 21 Apr. 2004 on takeover bids (the 'Takeover Directive'), No. 2004/25, O.J. EUR. COMM. (No. L 142) 12 (2004).
520. Art. 2:359c(6) BW.
521. Enterprise Court 28 Oct. 2008, JOR 2008, 335, LJN: BG3438 (*Numico*), Enterprise Court 11 Nov. 2008, JOR 2008, 336, LJN: BG5033 (*Grolsch*) and most recently Enterprise Court 21 Feb. 2012, JOR 2012, 144, LJN: BV7343 (*Crucell*).
522. Art. 2:359d BW.

the formal way (see § 6.1.2), and informing them where and when the squeeze-out price will be payable. In respect of minority shareholders who do not respond, the majority shareholder can pay the transfer price into an escrow account of the State of the Netherlands. As a result of such payment into escrow (*consignatie*), title to the shares automatically transfers to the majority shareholder. After payment into escrow, minority shareholders can claim the price for their shares from the State of the Netherlands.

The decision of the Enterprise Court can be appealed only to the Supreme Court, which reviews it only on grounds of insufficient or unclear reasoning or violation of the law (see § 6.4.2.3).

7.5 Proceedings to Challenge Annual Accounts

7.5.1 General

Any interested party or, in the public interest, the Attorney-general at the Amsterdam Court of Appeal, can apply to the Enterprise Court to have a company or other private law legal entity amend its annual accounts (including the annual report and other ancillary information) if these do not comply with the provisions regarding annual accounts in the Civil Code or with other legal provisions.[523] The request may not relate to the statement of the auditor who has certified the annual accounts.[524] All shareholders are interested parties by definition, other interested parties include holders of depositary receipts, the works council, and other parties that duly demonstrate their interest. As far as listed companies are concerned, the Netherlands Authority for the Financial Markets (*Stichting Autoriteit Financiële Markten*) (the 'AFM') can also submit a request, but only after having first contacted the company.[525]

7.5.2 The Proceedings

Since 31 December 2006 proceedings must be commenced by a petition instead of a writ of summons (see § 6.5).

For non-listed companies, the proceedings must in principle be commenced within two months and for listed companies within nine months after the day that the annual accounts have been adopted.[526] The term is extended, however, if the

523. Such as the provisions in the Act on the Supervision of Financial Reporting (*Wet Toezicht Financiële Verslaglegging*) and EC Council Regulation of 19 July 2002 on the Application of International Accounting Standards, No. 1606/2002, O.J. EUR. COMM. (No. L 243) 1 (2002).
524. Art. 2:447(3) BW.
525. Art. 2:448(2) BW.
526. Art. 2:449(1) BW.

shortcomings in the annual accounts were not apparent from the accounts themselves, in which case the cut-off date is the earlier of (i) two months – or nine months for listed companies – after the interested party could no longer reasonably be unaware of the shortcomings and (ii) two years after the adoption, resolution, publication (as the case may be) of the annual accounts.[527]

In view of the fact that the proceedings may require disclosure of confidential and price-sensitive information, these will take place behind closed doors, i.e. with only the parties and their counsel present. The Enterprise Court's decision, however, is public.[528] The court may order disclosure of books and documents the company is obliged to keep, on pain of a penalty.[529] Before issuing its decision, the Enterprise Court will provide the auditors that have examined the annual accounts with the opportunity to present their views. Likewise, if the claim is directed against a credit institution, an insurance company or investment institution, the relevant supervisory authorities will be requested to present their views.[530] Unlike in general petition proceedings, no other interested party will be heard or allowed to submit statements or briefs.[531]

7.5.3 Decision

If the Enterprise Court finds shortcomings in the annual accounts, it will give a detailed order on the way in which the annual accounts (and/or the ancillary documents) should be made up. This order is also binding on the corporate bodies that must adopt and approve the accounts. The decision declares the adoption and approval of the annual accounts null and void, but the Enterprise Court can limit the effects of such nullification. For example, it may uphold the obligation to pay dividends based on the annual accounts that should have been adopted.[532]

The Enterprise Court can, on the basis of a claim but even on its own initiative, extend or limit its order to future annual accounts. However, in the event that circumstances change, it can, at the request of the company, later withdraw such an order for future accounts.[533]

7.5.4 The Netherlands Authority for the Financial Markets

Pursuant to the Act on the Supervision of Financial Reporting (the 'WTFV') the AFM sees to it that the financial reporting of Dutch listed companies complies with

527. Art. 2:449(4) BW.
528. Art. 2:450(1) BW.
529. Art. 162(3) Rv.
530. Arts 2:450(4)-(8) BW.
531. Art. 2:450(3) BW.
532. Art. 2:451(4) BW.
533. Arts 2:451(3) and 2:451(5) BW.

applicable standards of reporting. The supervision is retrospective, after the annual accounts have been adopted. If the AFM is of the opinion that the annual accounts of the company (not being an investment institution) do not comply with any legal requirement regarding financial reporting, it may ask the company for additional information.[534] If the company refuses to comply with a request for information by the AFM, the AFM can ask the Enterprise Court to issue an order for information.[535] If the AFM is of the opinion that the information given is not sufficient, it may inform the company that it still doubts whether all legal requirements have been met. It may recommend that the company publish a notice explaining the incompatibility of the annual accounts with the legal requirements, the consequences of such discrepancy as regards its financial reporting, and the way in which in the future the legal requirements will be applied.[536] If the listed company does not follow up on this recommendation, the AFM can initiate the above-mentioned proceedings to challenge the annual accounts. Even without such a recommendation, it can commence the proceedings on the condition that this is required for a good functioning of the stock market and for the position of shareholders on this market.[537]

7.6 Other Proceedings in the Enterprise Court

The Enterprise Court resolves a number of other disputes, which will be referred to only briefly. It decides on objections by the supervisory boards of large companies (*structuurvennootschappen*) and private limited liability companies against the appointment of supervisory directors specifically recommended by the works council[538] or, in the case of large cooperative associations (*grote coöperaties en onderlinge waarborgmaatschappijen*), on the objections by the works council against a nomination of a supervisory director by the supervisory board.[539] The Enterprise Court can also decide on the removal of a supervisory director at the request of a company, the general meeting of shareholders or the works council.[540] Furthermore, it can decide on the approval of the nomination of a single accountant to examine the merger or demerger proposal for two companies,[541] on appeals by the works council from decisions of the employer to deviate from the works

534. Art. 2(1) WTFV.
535. Art. 2:452(1) BW.
536. Arts 3(1)-(2) WTFV.
537. Art. 4(2) WTFV.
538. Arts 2:158(7) and 2:159 BW (large company) and Arts 2:268(7) and 2:269 BW (B.V.).
539. Arts 2:63f(8) and 2:63g BW.
540. Arts 2:161(2) (N.V.) and 2:271(2) (B.V.) BW.
541. Arts 2:328(3) (N.V.) and 2:334aa(4) (B.V.) BW.

council's advice,[542] on requests to comply with the European Works Council Act[543] and on certain measures relating to pension funds.[544]

The Enterprise Court furthermore sits as the appellate court dealing with appeals from District Court decisions regarding objections by creditors against capital decreases,[545] against legal merger or demerger proposals[546] and against the intention by parent companies to withdraw joint and several liability for their subsidiaries.[547] These proceedings are conducted in an expedited fashion in the District Court and appeals must be filed with the Enterprise Court within three weeks after the final decision.[548]

8. DERIVATIVE ACTIONS, CLASS ACTIONS AND CLASS SETTLEMENTS

8.1 Derivative Actions

Derivative actions, where a shareholder is entitled to bring an action against directors or other third parties on behalf of a company, do not exist under Dutch law. Similarly, a shareholder cannot sue directors or third parties in his own name for a tort or breach of duties vis-à-vis the company which has led to a decrease in the value of his shares.[549] A shareholder is therefore dependent on a company to recuperate damages from its (former) directors or other third parties. An exception to this latter rule applies if the third party's actions also constitute a tort or breach of duty towards the shareholder, independent of the tort or breach against the company. This could be the case where there is a specific intention to harm the individual shareholder.[550] There is, however, some uncertainty as to whether such a claim can be made as long as the company is still in a position to claim compensation for the same damage, as this would create a risk of 'double compensation'. If it is established that the defendant has committed a tort towards a shareholder, that

542. Art. 26 (in conjunction with Art. 25) Works Councils Act (*Wet op de Ondernemingsraden*), Stb. 1971, 54, as amended.
543. Art. 5 European Works Councils Act (*Wet op de Europese Ondernemingsraden*), Stb. 1997, 32, as amended.
544. Arts 217, 218 and 219 Pension Act (*Pensioenwet*), Stb. 2006, 705, as amended.
545. Arts 2:100(3) (N.V.) and 2:209(3) (B.V.) BW.
546. Arts 2:316(2) and 2:334l BW.
547. Art. 2:404(5) BW.
548. Art. 997 Rv.
549. Supreme Court 2 Dec. 1994, NJ 1995, 288, LJN: ZC1564 (*Poot/ABP*); Supreme Court 16 Feb. 2007, NJ 2007, 256, LJN: AZ0419 (*Tuin Beheer*).
550. Supreme Court 16 Feb. 2007, NJ 2007, 256, LJN: AZ0419 (*Tuin Beheer*).

shareholder may in any event claim his own direct damages that are not also the company's damages, resulting for example from the forced sale of his shares.[551]

8.2 Class Actions

Class actions within the meaning that that concept has in common law jurisdictions, i.e. one or more members of a class claiming damages for an entire class of persons that have suffered damages as a result of a defendant's actions, do not exist in Dutch procedural law either. The Civil Code does, however, allow for some form of collective litigation. Under Article 3:305a BW, a foundation or association established for the purpose of protecting the interests of a certain group of persons – whether this be before or after the dispute arises – can commence an action in court for the protection of these interests, provided that these interests are of a similar nature.

The foundation or association may apply for an injunction, ordering the defendant to do or to refrain from doing something. An injured party for whose protection a judgment has been given can, however, declare that he does not want to be bound by the judgment, unless the nature of that judgment is such that its effect cannot be excluded vis-à-vis just this injured party.[552]

A foundation or association can also ask for a declaration of law that the defendant has breached his duties or committed a tort towards the persons that are part of the group (see § 6.3.5). However, the foundation or association cannot claim damages on behalf of the persons it represents,[553] although case law allows it to claim a large part of its expenses.[554] Therefore, damages will have to be claimed by the individuals themselves. Sometimes they assign their damages claims to the association or foundation which then brings these claims in bundled form. Even though a collective action decision does not have legally binding force on individuals, the decision will play an important role in follow up proceedings of individuals claiming damages.[555] It will be very difficult for a defendant to deny a breach of contract or tort in such damages proceedings, if this has previously been established in a collective action, unless the position of the individual materially differs from the group of injured parties presented in the collective action.

A bill proposing some changes to this kind of class actions is currently pending before the Lower House.[556] If the bill is implemented in its current form, a foundation or association in a collective action will have to prove that the interests of the injured parties are sufficiently safeguarded by it. If not, the representative

551. Supreme Court 2 May 1997, NJ 1997, 662, LJN: ZC2365 (*Kip en Sloetjes/Rabo*).
552. Art. 3:305a(5) BW.
553. Art. 3:305a(3) BW.
554. Supreme Court 13 Oct. 2006, NJ 2008, 527-529, LJN: AW2077, AW2080, AW2082 (*Vie d'Or*).
555. MvT, TK 22 486, No. 3, p. 26.
556. Amendment of the Act on Collective Settlement of Mass Damage (*Wijziging van de Wet collectieve afwikkeling massaschade*), TK 33 126, No. 2.

will have no cause of action. The reason for this proposed amendment is a strong emergence of representing organisations during the past years, while not all of these organisations prioritised the interests of the injured parties over their own profitability. Another amendment suggested in the bill is that if multiple collective action proceedings are pending simultaneously before different courts, the court can consolidate these proceedings on its own initiative.

A special form of collective action exists in bankruptcy proceedings. In certain circumstances, the bankruptcy trustee can claim damages from the former managing and supervisory directors of a bankrupt company on behalf of all creditors.[557] According to case law, the bankruptcy trustee can also claim damages from other third parties for the benefit of the collective creditors, provided that they have been damaged in equal manner by actions of the bankrupt company in which that third party was tortiously involved.[558] The proceeds from such an action, however, will become part of the bankruptcy estate and will be distributed in accordance with each individual creditor's ranking or preference. The bankruptcy trustee is not entitled to file a claim based on tort on behalf of just a specific category of creditors, where the proceeds only accrue to these creditors.[559]

8.3 Class Settlements

8.3.1 General

In 2005, the Act on the Collective Settlement of Mass Damage (*Wet Collectieve Afwikkeling Massaschade*, 'WCAM') was enacted, which allows for court-approved mass settlements that are binding on an entire class of injured parties, unless they opt out.[560] The WCAM creates a system strongly resembling United States-style class action settlements. As part of the preparation for the WCAM, the Dutch government and relevant interest groups in fact debated whether the Netherlands should go one step further and enact a class action system comparable to that of the United States. It was eventually decided, however, that this was not desirable in view of the complications to which such proceedings give rise (such as the process of class certification) and that the Netherlands should confine itself to legislation on class settlements only.

Under the WCAM, mass settlements have meanwhile been concluded in relation to mass tort and contract claims for defective pharmaceutical products (the

557. Arts 2:138 (N.V.) and 2:248 (B.V.) BW.
558. Supreme Court 14 Jan. 1983, NJ 1983, 597, LJN: AG 4521 (*Peeters/Gatzen*); Supreme Court 8 Nov. 1991, NJ 1992, 174, LJN: ZC0401 (*Nimox/Van den End*); Supreme Court 23 Dec. 1994 and Supreme Court 15 Sep. 1995, NJ 1996, 628-629, LJN: ZC1590, LJN: ZC1801 (*Curatoren THB*).
559. Supreme Court 16 Sep. 2005, NJ 2006, 311, LJN: AT7997 (*De Bont/Bannenberg qq*).
560. Stb. 2005, 340. The WCAM entered into force on 27 Jul. 2005 (Stb. 2005, 380).

DES case[561]), mis-selling of securities lease products (the *Dexia* case[562]), misleading financial information of a listed company (the *Shell* case[563] and the *Converium* case[564]), claims against the auditors and the public supervisory authorities of a bankrupt life insurance company (the *Vie d'Or* case[565]) and damage suffered by shareholders as a result of late disclosure of merger talks (the *Vedior* case[566]). The proceedings to render a settlement binding for an entire class develop through four stages, which will be described below.

8.3.2 The Proceedings

8.3.2.1 First Stage: Settlement Agreement

In the first stage, a foundation or association which is representative of the injured class concludes a settlement agreement with the defendant, pursuant to which the defendant agrees to make certain settlement payments to the injured parties.

The WCAM prescribes that, unless the settlement agreement provides otherwise, the injured parties are automatically deemed to waive their rights vis-à-vis other parties that could be jointly and severally liable with the defendant, for those amounts for which such other liable parties could otherwise take recourse against the defendant.[567] This provision was included in the WCAM to ensure that the settlement really guarantees that no further claims are made against the defendant. The injured parties should thus be aware that by failing to opt out of the settlement, they not only settle their claims against the defendant but also lose part of their rights against other jointly liable parties.

8.3.2.2 Second Stage: Petition

In the second stage, the agreement is submitted by both parties through a petition to a special chamber of the Amsterdam Court of Appeal.[568] This chamber must determine whether the settlement is reasonable, taking into account the magnitude of the damages, the ease and speed with which the settlement payment is obtainable from the defendant, the costs and efforts which the injured parties would otherwise have to make to litigate the matter, the potential causes of the damage, and other

561. Court of Appeal Amsterdam 1 Jun. 2006, NJ 2006, 461, LJN: AX6440 (*Des*).
562. Court of Appeal Amsterdam 25 Jan. 2007, JOR 2007, 71, LJN: AZ7033 (*Dexia*).
563. Court of Appeal Amsterdam 29 May 2009, JOR 2009, 197, LJN: BI5744 (*Shell*).
564. Court of Appeal Amsterdam 17 Jan. 2012, NJ 2012, 355, LJN: BV1026 (*Converium*).
565. Court of Appeal Amsterdam 29 Apr. 2009, JOR 2009, 196, LJN: BI2717 (*Vie d'Or*).
566. Court of Appeal Amsterdam 15 Jul. 2009, JOR 2009, 325, LJN: BJ2691 (*Vedior*).
567. Art. 7:910 BW.
568. Art. 1013 Rv.

relevant circumstances.[569] The filing of the petition stays all pending proceedings and enforcements of judgments commenced by individual injured parties.[570] It also interrupts any running limitation period and triggers a new limitation period which, under Dutch law, is five years for known tort claims and for claims for breach of contract.[571]

The proceedings are conducted as petition proceedings (see § 6.5) and all interested parties can present their views to the court. If the court declares the settlement binding, there are only very limited possibilities for an appeal to the Supreme Court.[572]

8.3.2.3 *Third Stage: Opting Out*

During the third stage, after the judgment, the individual injured parties have a period of at least three months during which they can choose to opt out of the settlement. If they do not do so, the settlement becomes binding on them. The agreement may provide that the defendant can withdraw from the settlement if too many injured parties opt out.[573]

8.3.2.4 *Fourth Stage: Distribution of Funds*

After the opt out period, the fourth stage commences, in which the settlement payments are distributed to the injured parties, who must be given a period of at least one year to collect their settlement funds.[574] Any settlement funds not collected by injured parties are repaid to the defendant or allocated to other recipients as agreed between the foundation or association and the defendant.

8.3.3 International settlements

The Netherlands is the only European jurisdiction offering a procedure to declare a collective settlement binding on all class members on an 'opt out' basis. On two occasions, the Amsterdam Court of Appeal declared an international settlement binding. In the *Shell* case, relating to a claim from investors for misleading statements about Shell's oil and gas reserves, only part of the claimants were residing in the Netherlands. The court assumed jurisdiction on the basis of the Brussels Regulation and the Lugano Convention (see §§ 4.2.1 and 4.2.2).[575] In the *Converium* case,

569. Art. 7:907 BW.
570. Art. 1015 Rv.
571. Art. 7:907(5) BW.
572. Art. 1018 Rv.
573. Art. 7:908(4) BW.
574. Art. 7:907(6) BW.
575. Court of Appeal Amsterdam 29 May 2009, JOR 2009, 197, LJN: BI5744 (*Shell*). See footnote 563.

the court even went a step further as it assumed jurisdiction where none of the potentially liable parties and only some of the potential claimants were domiciled in the Netherlands.[576] Jurisdiction was again founded on the Brussels Regulation and the Lugano Convention.

Whether settlements under the WCAM will be recognised by foreign courts and affect the rights of injured parties residing abroad who failed to opt out of the settlement, depends on local law. As there is no case law, the question remains as yet unanswered. However, compliance with the EU rules on service of process (see § 6.1.2) at least provides a convincing argument for recognition of this type of class settlement all over Europe.

The *Converium* decision confirms that the Netherlands is Europe's most attractive venue for facilitating international settlements.

8.3.4 Evaluation of the WCAM

The WCAM was evaluated in 2008. While the WCAM was found to be an effective and efficient method to deal with cases of mass damage and other kinds of class actions, one thought it could also help to enlarge the parties' willingness to negotiate and conclude a settlement agreement. As a result, a new act, the Preliminary Questions Act,[577] was introduced and a bill proposing changes to the WCAM was presented to the Lower House.[578] Under the Preliminary Questions Act a court may refer a preliminary question to the Supreme Court if the answer to this question is necessary to come to a decision, and if the answer to the question is of direct importance (i) for a significant number of other claims based on the same or similar facts and cause of action (i.e. mass action claims) , or (ii) the resolution of a significant number of other proceedings that have arisen from similar facts.[579] A preliminary ruling will thus likely act as an instrument to get parties at the negotiating table. The changes to the WCAM include among others: a clear rule on how to notify the WCAM proceedings and subsequent decision to injured parties residing abroad, the introduction of a preprocedural hearing and the application of the WCAM in winding-up proceedings.

576. Court of Appeal Amsterdam 17 Jan. 2012, NJ 2012, 355, LJN: BV1026 (*Converium*). See footnote 564.
577. Stb. 2012, 65.
578. TK 33 126, No. 2, see footnote 556.
579. Art. 392(1) Rv.

9. PROVISIONAL REMEDIES

9.1 Preliminary Relief Proceedings

9.1.1 General

In all matters requiring immediate court intervention, a party may address the preliminary relief judge (*voorzieningenrechter*), also referred to as the 'President', of the competent District Court.[580] Such proceedings are quite frequent in the Netherlands and are referred to as preliminary relief proceedings (*kort geding*). Preliminary relief proceedings are meant to provide specific provisional remedies in urgent matters only and not to finally decide a dispute between the parties. The decision of the preliminary relief judge is provisional in the sense that it does not prejudice the rights of the parties in the proceedings on the merits.[581] In practice, however, the consequences of a provisional measure can be quite decisive. It should be noted that there is no obligation for the parties in preliminary relief proceedings to commence proceedings on the merits and that quite often they will not do so, abiding by the judgment in preliminary relief proceedings.

A claimant who has been denied preliminary relief may initiate new preliminary relief proceedings on the same subject matter, even if he has not appealed the first judgment. This is only different if the circumstances of the case lead the President to conclude that by starting new proceedings, he is abusing a procedural right.[582]

9.1.2 Requirements

The most important requirement for requesting preliminary relief is that the matter requires an immediate remedy. Secondly, only provisional measures can be requested. Therefore the President cannot, for example, deliver a declaratory judgment. Finally, the facts of the matter must qualify for preliminary relief proceedings.[583] This will not be the case where there is too much uncertainty surrounding the facts or where the legal issues at stake require too complex an assessment of the facts or the hearing of witnesses. If the matter does not meet these requirements, the preliminary relief judge will deny the relief. If the criteria for preliminary relief are met, the judge's decision on whether the claim will be granted or rejected will depend on a provisional assessment of the case, and on the weighing up of the interests of both parties.

580. Art. 254 Rv.
581. Art. 257 Rv.
582. Supreme Court 16 Dec. 1994, NJ 1995, 213, LJN: ZC1583 (*Kloes/Fransman*).
583. Art. 256 Rv.

9.1.3 Available Remedies

The most significant provisional remedies are the preliminary mandatory injunction (*gebod in kort geding*) and the preliminary prohibitory injunction (*verbod in kort geding*). Often such a remedy carries with it, at the claimant's request, a penalty for each day, or other time or period, that the defendant fails to comply with the ordered measure or injunction. The fact that the requested remedies may have irrevocable consequences in practice does not preclude the preliminary relief judge from granting them, though in weighing up the interests of both parties, he will take into account all the possible repercussions that may flow from his decision. A Dutch preliminary relief judge may even in certain circumstances grant extraterritorial measures[584] although in the European context, the possibilities have been greatly limited by the case law of the CJEU.[585]

Provisional remedies may also be granted in relation to monetary claims such as claims for advance payment of damages, or payment of an outstanding debt. In such a situation, it is established case law for a preliminary relief judge to investigate (i) whether a claim is likely; and (ii) whether there are urgent facts or circumstances requiring immediate action. In conducting this assessment, the interests of the parties must also be weighed up, including the risk that repayment may not take place (e.g. because of the financial situation of the claimant) if in the proceedings on the merits the claim were to be denied. If there is a strong risk of this, the claim may be refused.[586] Provisional measures may also be given in relation to international monetary claims. If a court of another Member State of the EU has jurisdiction with regard to the merits, additional requirements must be met, such as the provision of security for the claimed amount.[587]

9.1.4 The Proceedings

The preliminary relief proceedings start with a request to the preliminary relief judge to set a date for the oral hearing. Together with such a request, which is made by filing a standard form, a draft writ of summons has to be provided. Depending on the workload of the court, the date for the oral hearing can, in general, be scheduled over a one to four week period. In very urgent matters, this period can be

584. Supreme Court 24 Nov. 1989, NJ 1992, 404, LJN: AD0964 (*Interlas/Lincoln*) and Supreme Court 19 Mar. 2004, NJ 2007, 585, LJN: AO0903 (*Philips/Postech*).
585. CJEU 17 Nov. 1998, C-391/95, ECR 1998 I-7091, NJ 1999, 339, LJN: AD2958 (*Van Uden/DecoLine*) and CJEU 13 Jul. 2006, C-539/03, ECR 2006 I-6535, NJ 2008, 76, LJN: AY6817 (*Roche/Primus*). The recent CJEU decision 12 Jul. 2012, C-616/10 (*Solvay/Honeywell*), widens the possibilities again for specific situations.
586. Supreme Court 29 Mar. 1985, NJ 1986, 84, LJN: AG4992 (*M'Barek/Van der Vloodt*); Supreme Court 14 Apr. 2000, NJ 2000, 489, LJN: AA5519 (*HBS/Danestyle*).
587. CJEU 17 Nov. 1998, C-391/95, ECR 1998 I-7091, NJ 1999, 339, LJN: AD2958 (*Van Uden/DecoLine*).

even shorter, sometimes just one day. The preliminary relief judge may then also be found willing to hear the case in the evening or at the weekend.

After a date for an oral hearing has been set, the writ of summons has to be served. This should state the claim, the grounds on which it is based, and why the matter requires immediate resolution. The urgent nature of the preliminary relief proceedings removes the duty to specify the evidence for the claim in the writ. The requirement to list the arguments of the defendant in the writ only applies if such arguments have been communicated to the claimant (see § 6.1.4.2), and in preliminary relief proceedings this will seldom be the case. The defendant is not obliged to submit a written statement of defence before the oral hearing takes place and it is rare for him to do so. Generally, the defendant will not want the claimant to be informed of his arguments before the oral hearing. However, if the defendant wishes to rely on documents as evidence for his position, he will have to submit these documents to the court at least one day before the hearing. The same applies to the claimant.[588] Only in exceptional circumstances will a document be admissible if it is submitted at the hearing itself.

Unlike the claimant, the defendant in preliminary relief proceedings may represent himself rather than engaging an attorney, but in practice this is not common.[589] The oral hearing itself is informal. Both the claimant and the defendant are allowed to present their cases and often the preliminary relief judge asks questions of counsel and of the clients attending the hearing. Theoretically, the rules of evidence in the CCP do not apply, but in practice the preliminary relief judge often applies them. Preliminary relief proceedings, however, are not designed for extensive submission of evidence or for examination of witnesses.

9.1.5 Judgment

In general, the preliminary relief judge will deliver his judgment within 14 days, unless a more urgent decision is clearly required. Owing to the nature of preliminary relief proceedings, declaratory judgments cannot be rendered (see § 6.3.5) and the judge will be reluctant to award an advance on a claim for damages.[590] The judgment does not prejudice the rights of the parties in the proceedings on the merits.[591] A penalty that is forfeited because the defendant did not live up to the decision in preliminary relief proceedings will remain forfeited, even if in the proceedings on the merits later on the defendant does prevail. This will be different, of course, if the judgment in the preliminary relief proceedings is overturned on appeal.

588. Art. 6.2 Docket rules for preliminary relief proceedings (*Procesreglement kort gedingen rechtbanken sector civiel/familie*), version 1 January 2012, <www.rechtspraak.nl>.
589. Art. 255(1) Rv.
590. Supreme Court 14 Apr. 2000, NJ 2000, 489, LJN: AA5519 (*HBS/Danestyle*).
591. Art. 257 Rv.

9.1.6 Appeal

Appeal can be made to the Court of Appeal within four weeks of the judgment.[592] In appeal proceedings, both parties are obliged to submit written statements, as in principle the procedure is not different from the procedure in the proceedings on the merits. There is an opportunity, however, to speed up the appeal proceedings by asking the court at appeal for an urgent appeal (*spoedappel*) on the basis of the docket rules. If certain conditions are met, some Courts of Appeal provide the opportunity for even more expedited proceedings, for very urgent cases such as appeals from eviction orders (*turbo appel*). The appeal judgment can be appealed to the Supreme Court within a time period of eight weeks.[593]

9.2 Pre-judgment Attachment

9.2.1 General

The purpose of a pre-judgment attachment (*conservatoir beslag*) is to prevent a debtor from frustrating recovery by his creditor, for example by alienating, removing or hiding assets.

A direct result of the attachment, and quite often an end in itself, is to put pressure on the debtor. Once the attachment is made, the debtor is not allowed to dispose of any attached property and may not transfer or encumber it, even if such disposal were in the usual course of the debtor's business.[594] Although the debtor may be hindered in his business or personal life, or may suffer detriment as a result, this does not, in general, constitute a compelling reason for denying or lifting the attachment. If the creditor fears that the debtor, despite the pre-judgment attachment, will embezzle the attached goods, he may also request sequestration of those goods.

9.2.2 Types of Attachment

A distinction can be made between an attachment of specific goods for the purpose of surrender or delivery of the goods (*beslag tot afgifte*; *beslag tot levering*), and an attachment for the purpose of recovery of a financial claim through sale of the goods or collection of the receivables (*verhaalsbeslag*). The latter form of attachment is the most common one.

In principle, all assets of the debtor in the Netherlands are subject to attachment, such as real estate, shares in a Dutch company and moveable goods. An attachment often made is a third party attachment, meaning that the creditor attaches all

---

592. Art. 339(2) Rv.
593. Arts 402(2) and 339(2) Rv.
594. Art. 453a Rv.

amounts and goods due by the third party to the debtor. Within four weeks of the attachment, the third party must declare what he owes to the debtor.[595] A common third party attachment is that by which funds in the bank accounts of the debtor are attached. The amount attached is equal to the funds in the bank account per the date of the attachment, irrespective of the amount of the creditor's claim. Credit facilities of the debtor are, however, not subject to attachment.[596] Amounts credited to the bank account after the attachment are not covered. To freeze these amounts, a new attachment will be necessary.

An interesting question is whether attachment of funds held with a Dutch bank also covers funds held by the debtor in accounts of the bank's branches (not being separate legal entities) outside the Netherlands. Likewise, does attachment of an account with a foreign bank's branch in the Netherlands cover funds at the bank's headquarters abroad?

The general opinion is that the scope of an attachment is territorial and that therefore only funds which are 'payable' in the Netherlands can be attached.[597]

The European Parliament is currently considering a proposal by the European Commission for a regulation creating a 'European Account Preservation Order' (EAPO) to facilitate cross-border debt recovery in the EU.[598] This proposal introduces harmonised European proceedings through which a claimant may request the court of a member state to issue an EAPO in order to preserve and attach bank accounts of his debtor held anywhere in the EU. The regime has been set up on an optional basis, as an alternative to existing protective measures in the Member States. The proposal has generated a lot of discussion; banks have especially been critical of the proposal as they fear a substantial increase of their financial and administrative burden. It is as yet unclear what the outcome of the discussion will be.

Specific procedural rules apply to attachments of assets in possession of the debtor, attachments of shares in a company, attachments of real estate and ships, and attachments of assets transferred by the debtor to third parties, if those transfers could be rescinded pursuant to the so-called *actio pauliana*. As a result of the incorporation into Dutch law of Article 7 of the EC Directive 2004/48 on the enforcement of intellectual property rights[599] on 1 May 2007, it is now possible in the case of

595. Arts 720 and 476a Rv.
596. Supreme Court 29 Oct. 2004, NJ 2006, 203, LJN: AP4504 (*Van den Bergh/Van der Walle*).
597. However, in 1954 the Supreme Court issued a decision which held that in specific circumstances, an attachment with a third party domiciled in the Netherlands may also cover funds payable abroad. One important condition is that such attachment is recognised in the foreign country so that the third party cannot be compelled to pay twice (once to the creditor and once to the debtor in the foreign country): Supreme Court 26 Nov. 1954, NJ 1955, 698 (*Lindeteves/Meijlink*). See also District Court The Hague 21 Feb. 2007, JBPr 2008/12, LJN: BA5155 (*Tulip/Shell*) and Court of Appeal Amsterdam 10 April 2012, JOR 2012/190, LJN: BW3378 (*Llanos Oil/The Royal Bank of Scotland*).
598. COM (2011) 0455 final.
599. EC Council Directive of 29 April 2004 on the enforcement of intellectual property rights, O.J. EUR. COMM. (No. L 157) 45 (2004).

alleged infringement of intellectual property rights to request an attachment for the purpose of preserving evidence (*bewijsbeslag*).[600] Whether such attachment for the preservation of evidence is also possible outside the scope of intellectual property disputes is still the subject of debate but is more and more accepted.[601]

9.2.3 The Proceedings

9.2.3.1 Petition to the Court

A pre-judgment attachment can only be made with the permission of the preliminary relief judge. In order to obtain such permission, the creditor must file a petition with the court where the debtor or (one of) the third parties is domiciled or where the assets are located.[602] The petition must contain the basis for the creditor's claim and the type of attachment that is requested. If the claim is for money, the creditor must give an estimate of his claim.[603] For specific kinds of attachment, such as the attachment of movable and immovable property and the attachment of registered shares, the creditor must prove fear of embezzlement.[604] If attachment is made on goods of a debtor non-domiciled in the Netherlands, fear of embezzlement need not be proven.[605]

In view of the territorial scope of attachment (i.e. the formal attachment needs to be made by government officials, who are unable to operate outside their own country), the petition may in principle only relate to goods that are located in the Netherlands or to receivables that are payable in the Netherlands, irrespective of the domicile of the parties.[606] In case of third party attachment, it is necessary that the third party (often a bank) is domiciled in the Netherlands, or has its offices or at least a branch in the Netherlands, as the third party needs to declare what funds it holds for the debtor before the Dutch court.[607]

Until recently, it was not necessary to submit any exhibits with the petition. Any party with a claim which appeared on the face of it to be justified could ask the preliminary relief judge within the District Court to grant the pre-judgment

---

600. Arts 1019b and 1019c Rv.
601. See Court of Appeal The Hague 29 Mar. 2011, LJN: BQ1725 (*IIZII Holding/Eagle Feather Investments*) and other case law mentioned in the Attachment syllabus (*beslagsyllabus*) of August 2012 on <www.rechtspraak.nl>, page 29. Also the government seems to be of the opinion that attachment for the preservation of evidence is possible, see Explanatory Memorandum of the Proposal for a revision of the duty to produce documents, MvT TK 33 079, No. 2, p. 7, see § 5.4. Usually, such a request is founded on Art. 843a Rv in connection with Art. 730 Rv.
602. Art. 700(1) Rv.
603. Art. 700(2) Rv.
604. Arts 711, 714 and 725 Rv. See also Court of Appeal Amsterdam 10 Jan. 2012, LJN: BV0477 (*X/Y*).
605. Art. 765 Rv.
606. Case law by the Supreme Court allows for a possible exception, see footnote 597.
607. Attachment syllabus, version August 2012, page 14, see footnote 601.

attachment, and in practice this was almost always granted. Since 2011, after an advice by the Council for the Administration of Justice (*Raad voor de Rechtspraak*) to strengthen the position of debtors, the requirements for obtaining a leave for attachment have become stricter.[608] First of all, the creditor should properly inform the court of the merits of the claim and must substantiate it with documents. For example, for an attachment relating to a claim for unpaid sums, it is necessary to submit all the invoices. Moreover, the creditor will have to reason in the petition why the attachment is necessary, and why it needs to be levied on the specific assets mentioned in the petition (for example, he will need to explain why it is necessary to attach the bank account of the debtor instead of his real property, as this would – usually – be less far-reaching).[609] Finally, a creditor is required to inform the court if he has submitted previous requests for attachment (with the same or another court).

Although in specific situations the debtor can and will be heard, the petition in the great majority of cases is decided *ex parte*, usually within one or two days of the filing of the petition. If the judge has 'reasonable doubts' as to whether the claim is founded, he may decide to grant a preliminary leave for attachment, and only give a final decision once he has heard both parties.[610] The judge can also grant leave for attachment on the condition that security is provided for potential damage caused by the attachment.[611] Although in practice this condition has not been imposed often, this may change in future.[612]

If the request for leave for attachment is denied, appeal is possible. If the request is granted, the decision cannot be appealed.[613] The debtor has, however, other means to challenge the attachment (see §§ 9.2.4 and 9.2.5).

After the judge's consent has been obtained, the creditor instructs a court bailiff to effect the attachment. The bailiff's official report, one copy of which is deposited at the place of the attachment and one of which is sent to the creditor, serves as proof of the attachment.

If the creditor wishes to sequestrate goods of the debtor in addition to the pre-judgment attachment, he must specifically make such a request.[614] Unless special circumstances require that the sequestration be made immediately, the judge will allow the debtor to respond to such request.[615] In practice, therefore, to prevent the debtor from embezzling the goods, the petition for sequestration is generally filed after the pre-judgment attachment.

---

608. These requirements are laid down in the Attachment syllabus, version August 2012, see footnote 601.
609. Attachment syllabus, version August 2012, p. 5.
610. Attachment syllabus, version August 2012, p. 9.
611. Art. 701 Rv.
612. The Attachment syllabus, version August 2012, p. 12, explicitly points at the ability of the courts to ask for security (www.rechtspraak.nl).
613. Art. 700(2) Rv and Supreme Court 25 Sep. 2009, NJ 2009, 460, LJN: BI8517 (*Hagemeyer/Bekkers*).
614. Art. 709 Rv.
615. Art. 709(3) Rv.

9.2.3.2 Instituting Main Proceedings

Unless main proceedings are already pending at the time of the order granting the permission, the approval for the pre-judgment attachment is given under the condition that the main proceedings relating to the underlying claim are instituted within a certain time period. This time period cannot be less than eight days[616] and is generally set at 14 days. Generally, the fact that the proceedings will be started abroad is a sound reason to obtain a longer term, for example 30 days. Following a legitimate request, and depending on the reason of the request, the time period can be extended. Generally, the fact that the parties are considering a settlement is a sound reason to obtain an extension.[617]

In principle, the attachment of goods or receivables in the Netherlands does not give jurisdiction to the Dutch courts to hear the claim on the merits. The competent court in the main proceedings should be established in accordance with the applicable jurisdiction rules and could therefore be a non-Dutch court, or an arbitral tribunal. However, the attachment does give jurisdiction to the court that granted the attachment if the following conditions are met: the debtor is domiciled outside the Netherlands, the claimant cannot obtain a judgment in another country which is directly enforceable in the Netherlands, and no other rule of law confers jurisdiction on a Dutch court (see also § 4.2.3.2).[618] Attachment does not create jurisdiction if the parties have agreed a jurisdiction clause in favour of a non-Dutch court.[619] If the attachment is made for the sole purpose of creating jurisdiction, the court may decide that the claimant is abusing his rights and decline jurisdiction.[620]

If the main proceedings are not instituted within the time frame set by the court, the attachment automatically lapses.[621] Preliminary relief proceedings may qualify as main proceedings,[622] as well as the joining in criminal proceedings to claim damages within or outside the Netherlands.[623] An expert determination (*bindend advies*) would probably also qualify as main proceedings, but a mediation would probably not do so.[624] In the case of a third party attachment, the writ or other document by which the main proceedings are instituted must be served on the third party within eight days under penalty of nullity of the attachment.[625]

---

616. Art. 700(3) Rv.
617. Attachment syllabus, version August 2012, p. 11.
618. Art. 767 Rv.
619. Supreme Court 16 Jun. 1995, NJ 1996, 256, LJN: ZC1761 (*SCI/SEC*).
620. Art. 3:13 BW. See § 3.4. See also Court of Appeal Amsterdam 20 Dec. 2011, LJN: BU9485 (*Gécamines/Dongray Industrial*).
621. Art. 700(3) Rv.
622. Supreme Court 26 Feb. 1999, NJ 1999, 717, LJN: ZC2861 (*Ajax/Reule*).
623. Supreme Court 21 Oct. 2011, NJ 2011. 493 LJN: BQ8780.
624. Supreme Court 3 Oct. 2003, NJ 2004, 557, LJN: AI0347 (*Ontvanger/Heemhorst*) and Court of Appeal Amsterdam 31 Jan. 2008, JBPr 2008, 21, LJN: BC9785 (*Beerschoten/Hoeksema*).
625. Art. 721 Rv.

9.2.4 Lifting the Attachment

In view of the sometimes severe consequences of the (*ex parte*) attachment order, the CCP provides for the possibility of having the attachment lifted at short notice. To that end, the debtor can ask the preliminary relief judge who granted the attachment to lift it in preliminary relief proceedings. These proceedings are similar to standard preliminary relief proceedings (see § 9.1), but the requirement of urgency does not have to be substantiated. The attachment will be lifted if it was made without taking formal requirements into account, if the claim for which the attachment was made is *prima facie* without merit or if the attachment is considered disproportionate (e.g. in the case of attachment of stock-in-trade where the creditor could also attach funds in a bank account). The attachment must also be lifted if the debtor provides sufficient security (e.g. a bank guarantee) for the underlying claim.[626] Provision of a bank guarantee is the most common reason for lifting an attachment. In practice, it is not easy to convince the courts that the claim is *prima facie* without merit, and therefore it is difficult to oppose the attachment, even if the attachment debtor is a bona fide company with good reasons to contest the alleged claim. The Netherlands is therefore, in comparison to many other countries, and even after the tightening of the criteria in 2011, an attachment-friendly country.

9.2.5 Liability for Wrongful Attachment

If the underlying claim in the main proceedings is fully denied, the party which was granted the attachment is strictly liable for all damages suffered by the party against which the attachment was made. The fact that the preliminary relief judge granted the pre-judgment attachment is not a valid defence. There is in principle no liability if the claim has only been partially denied. In that case liability will only be assumed if the creditor may be considered to have abused his right to attach the property of his debtor (see § 3.4).[627]

9.2.6 Conversion into Executory Attachment

Once the claim underlying the attachment is awarded in the main proceedings, and the creditor has obtained an enforceable judgment against the debtor, the pre-judgment attachment can be converted into an executory attachment (see § 10.2).

626. Art. 705(2) Rv.
627. Supreme Court 11 Apr. 2003, NJ 2003, 440, LJN: AF2841 (*Hoda/Mondie*).

10. ENFORCEMENT AND RECOGNITION OF JUDGMENTS

10.1 General

In principle a judgment delivered by a Dutch court can be immediately enforced in the Netherlands after a specially certified copy of the judgment (*grosse*) has been served by a bailiff on the losing party.[628] The judgment does not have to be final and conclusive (*kracht van gewijsde*) in order to be enforceable. However, if the losing party takes action to obtain a legal remedy – such as lodging an appeal – the enforceability of the judgment is suspended until the action is concluded. To exclude the effect of this suspension, parties usually request the court to declare the judgment enforceable notwithstanding an appeal (see § 6.1.8.6).

Judgments delivered by a non-Dutch court cannot be enforced directly in the Netherlands unless specifically provided for in, or pursuant to, a Treaty or EC Regulation.

10.2 Enforcement of Dutch Judgments

10.2.1 Enforcement of Monetary Judgments

The enforcement of monetary judgments (judgments on the basis of which a party is ordered to pay a certain amount of money to the prevailing party) is usually effected by a post-judgment, or 'executory' attachment (*executoriaal beslag*), on the assets of the losing party. An executory attachment can be made on all the assets of the losing party, including property which is in the actual possession of third parties, or on receivables and other claims on third parties. The executory attachment ultimately leads to a public sale of the attached goods or to the collection of receivables. If, prior to the proceedings, a pre-judgment attachment has been made, that attachment will be converted into an executory attachment on service of the judgment on the losing party. Service of a judgment is subject to the same rules as service of a writ of summons (see §§ 6.1.2.2 and 6.1.2.3). If the prevailing party cannot locate the assets of the losing party, little can be done. Although the CCP provides that the debtor is obliged to inform the court bailiff charged with the enforcement of the location of his assets, there is no penalty if he refuses to do so.[629] The bailiff can request third parties whom he suspects of making regular payments to the debtor (such as employers and insurance companies) to inform him accordingly.[630] As the costs of enforcement are the responsibility of the debtor, a solvent debtor will usually pay the amount awarded to the creditor, thus avoiding

628. Art. 430 Rv.
629. Art. 475g(1) Rv.
630. Art. 475g(3) Rv.

the need for the creditor to take enforcement measures. The limitation period for enforcing a (monetary) judgment is 20 years.[631]

10.2.2 Enforcement of Other Judgments

If the judgment relates to the delivery of movable goods, the bailiff is entitled to seize the goods and to deliver them to the judgment creditor.[632] If the goods are legally required to be transferred other than by means of handing over (e.g. by a deed by a civil law notary in the case of real estate or registered shares), the court can order that its judgment has the same force as the legal deed required. Another option is for the court to appoint a third party to act on behalf of the losing party.[633] If the losing party is required to do something which cannot be performed by anybody else, the court can order it to do so on pain of a penalty or commitment to prison. In order to forfeit a penalty, the judgment must first be served on the losing party.[634] When penalties are due, they can be enforced in the same way as a monetary judgment. Unlike the 20 year limitation period for the enforcement of judgments, the limitation period for a claim to penalties is only six months.[635] Commitment to prison is a remedy of last resort and rarely used in practice.[636]

10.2.3 Disputes Regarding Enforcement

If the losing party wishes to prevent the enforcement of the judgment, he should start proceedings before the competent District Court.[637] As prevention is often an urgent matter, in practice these proceedings usually take the form of preliminary relief proceedings. The proceedings may not be used as a form of appeal against the judgment. The court will therefore only prohibit the enforcement of the judgment if the party enforcing the judgment is seen to abuse its right to do so.[638] The right to enforce is abused if, for example, there is an obvious error in the judgment (such as a calculation mistake) or if the judgment creditor wishes to enforce a monetary judgment when it is clear that the losing party has already paid the amount awarded.[639]

---

631. Art. 3:324(1) BW.
632. Arts 491-500 Rv.
633. Art. 3:300 BW.
634. Art. 611a(3) Rv.
635. Art. 611g(1) BW.
636. Art. 587 Rv.
637. Art. 438 Rv.
638. Art. 3:13 BW. See § 3.4.
639. Supreme Court 22 Apr. 1983, NJ 1984, 145, LJN: AG4575 (*Ritzen/Hoekstra*); Supreme Court 22 Dec. 2006, NJ 2007, 173, LJN: AY9224 (*Schmidt/Thunnissen*).

10.3 Enforcement of Foreign Judgments

10.3.1 General

Although a distinction must be made between recognition and enforcement of a foreign judgment, recognition will generally lead to enforcement. In practice foreign judgments will be recognised by a Dutch court if the following three conditions are met. First, the judgment must be a result of proceedings compatible with Dutch concepts of due process. Secondly, the judgment should not contravene public policy. Thirdly, the non-domestic court must have assumed jurisdiction on grounds which are internationally accepted.[640] One example of such internationally accepted grounds is a forum chosen by the parties.

As regards enforcement, judgments delivered outside the Netherlands can only be directly enforced within the Netherlands on the basis of an enforcement Treaty or EU instrument.[641] Foreign judgments to which no such Treaties apply must in principle be enforced by commencing a new cause of action before the Dutch courts, but if the above-mentioned three criteria for recognition are met, no litigation on the merits will be required (see § 10.3.4).

10.3.2 Enforcement and Recognition Treaty Applicable

For commercial litigation, the most important enforcement and recognition 'Treaties' are the EC Regulation and the Lugano Convention (see § 4.2.1).[642] They provide that judgments delivered in the 27 Member States of the EU, and in Norway, Switzerland and Iceland, are enforceable in the Netherlands once leave to do so has been obtained from the preliminary relief judge of the competent District Court. That will be the court in whose area of jurisdiction the party against whom enforcement is sought or the place of enforcement is located.[643] Leave will automatically be granted, provided that certain formal requirements are met.[644]

---

640. See e.g. Supreme Court 27 Jun. 2003, NJ 2004, 615, LJN: AF7005 (*B./H.*).
641. Art. 431 Rv. Under Art. 40 Act on the Kingdom of the Netherlands (*Statuut voor het Koninkrijk der Nederlanden*) as revised, Stb. 2010, 775, judgments of Curaçao, St. Maarten, Aruba and the Netherlands can be directly enforced in the Kingdom of the Netherlands as a whole.
642. The Netherlands has concluded bilateral Treaties regarding recognition and enforcement with Belgium, Germany, Italy, Austria and the United Kingdom, which Treaties however have for the greatest part been superseded by the EC Regulation. The Treaty between the Netherlands and the United Kingdom of 17 Nov. 1967 (Trb. 1967, 197) continues to be relevant in relations with Guernsey, Jersey and the Isle of Man and in relations between Curaçao, St. Maarten and Aruba on the one hand and the United Kingdom on the other hand. Regarding countries outside Europe, the Netherlands has entered into a bilateral Treaty on recognition and enforcement with Surinam. In relation to the United States, there exists a bilateral Treaty only as regards maintenance obligations.
643. Art. 39 and Annex II EC Regulation and Lugano Convention.
644. Art. 41 EC Regulation and Lugano Convention.

The limited grounds on which an application for enforcement can be denied will not be looked into by the court on its own initiative but will only be reviewed once the party against whom the judgment is entered lodges an appeal against the declaration of enforceability with the District Court.[645] A declaration of enforceability (*exequatur*) may only be refused or revoked on one of the grounds specified in Articles 34 and 35 of the EC Regulation and the Lugano Convention.[646] A judgment will not be recognised and therefore not be declared enforceable, for example, if such recognition is manifestly contrary to public policy in the State where recognition is sought, or if the judgment is given in default of appearance and the defendant has not been properly served with the document in order to enable him to arrange for his defence.[647] Neither the EC Regulation nor the Lugano Convention allows for a review on the merits of a case.

Under the EC Regulation, in principle preliminary relief judgments rendered in other EU countries are also recognised and enforceable in the Netherlands. However, if the judgment is rendered by a court that does not have jurisdiction as to the proceedings on the merits, additional criteria come into play for its recognition.[648]

The question may arise whether an (*ex parte*) foreign freezing order against a debtor holding an account with the branch of a Dutch bank in another EU country will be recognised in the Netherlands, so that not only the debtor's account at the foreign branch is blocked, but also his account in the Netherlands. The CJEU held that judicial decisions authorising provisional or protective measures, which are rendered *ex parte* and which are intended to be enforced without prior service, do not fall within the system of recognition and enforcement provided for by the EC Regulation.[649]

On 14 December 2010 the European Commission published a proposal for a revision of the EC Regulation.[650] At the time of writing of this book it is not yet

645. Art. 43 EC Regulation and Lugano Convention.

646. These do not include the defense that the defendant has already complied with the judgment in the country of origin (CJEU 13 Oct. 2011, C-139/10, NJ 2012, 18, LJN: BU1234 (*Prism/Van der Meer*)).

647. Arts 34(1) and 34(2) EC Regulation and Lugano Convention.

648. Recognition will be withheld if the judgment cannot qualify as a provisional measure under Article 31 EC Regulation. If the judgment concerns the award of a claim for payment, it will only be regarded as a provisional measure under Article 31 if, firstly, repayment to the defendant is guaranteed if the claimant is unsuccessful in the proceedings on the merits and, secondly, the defendant has assets within the territorial jurisdiction of the court awarding the claim (CJEU 17 Nov. 1998, C-391/95, ECR 1998 I-07091, NJ 1999, 339, LJN: AD2958 (*Van Uden/Deco-Line*), CJEU 27 Apr. 1999, C-99/96, ECR 1999 I-02277, NJ 2001, 90, LJN: AD3042 (*Mietz/Intership*)).

649. CJEU 21 May 1980, C-125/79, ECR 1980, p. 1553, NJ 1981, 184, LJN: AC6892 (*Denilauler/Couchet*). Contrary to many scholars, the Dutch Supreme Court has interpreted this decision restrictively, in the sense that decisions which are taken *ex parte* but which are later served on the defendant (so that he has an opportunity to defend himself) do fall within the scope of the Regulation and can therefore be recognised and enforced.

650. COM (2010) 748.

certain how the new Regulation will read. It is however very likely that the requirement of a declaration of enforceability (*exequatur*) will be abolished, so that under the new rules it will be even easier to enforce European judgments within the EU. Furthermore, the new Regulation will stipulate explicitly that provisional, including protective, measures which are ordered without the defendant having been summoned to appear (such as *ex parte* attachment orders), can be enforced if the court ordering the measure had jurisdiction as to the substance of the matter and if the judgment was served on the defendant prior to enforcement.

10.3.3 Specific European Regulations

Apart from the EC Regulation, which relates to recognition and enforcement of judgments in general, there are three other European Regulations regarding enforcement of specific judgments delivered in a EU Member State.

EC Regulation 805/2004 was adopted on 21 April 2004, creating a European Enforcement Order for uncontested claims. This Regulation applies from 21 October 2005 in all Member States except Denmark.[651] Its purpose is to ensure that a judgment which has been certified as a European Enforcement Order in the Member State of origin will be recognised and enforced in the other Member States without the need for a declaration of enforceability and without any scope for opposing its recognition. A judgment can be classified as a European Enforcement Order if it concerns a claim that is 'uncontested' within the meaning of the Regulation and if the court proceedings in the Member State of origin meet several procedural requirements. Only on the ground of irreconcilability with an earlier judgment and upon application by the defendant can enforcement be refused by the competent court in the Member State of enforcement.

EC Regulation 1896/2006, creating a European order for payment procedure, was adopted on 12 December 2006. This Regulation applies from 12 December 2008 in all Member States except Denmark.[652] Its purpose is to simplify, speed up and reduce the costs of litigation in cross-border cases concerning uncontested monetary claims, by creating a single, uniform European procedure for such claims. This is one step further than the previously mentioned European Enforcement Order, as there the underlying proceedings still vary according to national laws. On application of the claimant, and if certain requirements are fulfilled, a court of a Member State may issue a European order for payment and ensure that the order is served on the defendant. If the defendant lodges a statement of opposition against the order, the proceedings continue before the competent

651. EC Council Regulation of 21 April 2004 creating a European Enforcement Order for uncontested claims, No. 805/2004, O.J. EUR. COMM. (No. L 143) 15 (2004).

652. EC Council Regulation of 12 December 2006 creating a European order for payment procedure, No. 1896/2006, O.J. EUR. COMM. (No. L 399) 1 (2006).

courts of the Member State of origin in accordance with the rules of ordinary civil procedure, unless the claimant requests that the proceedings be terminated in that event. If the defendant does not lodge a statement of opposition, the European order for payment can be enforced in all Member States without prior recognition or enforcement procedure. Enforcement of a European order can only be refused by the competent court in the Member State of enforcement, upon application of the defendant, on the ground that the order is irreconcilable with an earlier judgment or that the defendant has paid the amount awarded.

Finally, EC Regulation 861/2007 establishing a European Small Claims Procedure was adopted on 11 July 2007.[653] The aim of this Regulation, which applies from 1 January 2009 in all Member States except Denmark, is to establish a uniform procedure in the Member States for so-called small claims. As an alternative to proceedings existing under national laws, the Regulation establishes a procedure for claims where the value does not exceed EUR 2,000 in cases where at least one of the parties is domiciled or habitually resident in a Member State other than the Member State of the court or tribunal seised. A judgment given in a Member State in the European Small Claims Procedure will be recognised and enforced in another Member State without the need for a declaration of enforceability and without any scope for opposing its recognition. Again, only on the ground of irreconcilability with an earlier judgment and upon application by the defendant, can enforcement be refused by the competent court in the Member State of enforcement. Appeals against a judgment given in the European Small Claims Procedure are governed by the procedural rules of the Member State where the judgment was given.

10.3.4 Absence of an Enforcement and Recognition Treaty

For commercial litigation, the Netherlands has not entered into enforcement and recognition Treaties with most countries outside Europe, including the United States. Judgments delivered in these jurisdictions cannot be enforced directly in the Netherlands, but need to be enforced by commencing a new cause of action before the Dutch courts. In practice, however, if a foreign judgment meets the criteria mentioned in § 10.3.1 and will therefore be recognised in the Netherlands, the Dutch court will generally grant the same judgment as the foreign court without

653. EC Council Regulation of 11 July 2007 establishing a European Small Claims Procedure, No. 861/2007, O.J. EUR. COMM. (No. L 199) 1 (2007). A report by the European Consumer Centres Network dated 21 September 2012 shows the procedure is rarely used (<www://ec.europa.eu/consumers/ecc/docs/small_claims_210992012_en.pdf>).

a new debate on the merits of the case.[654] Even if the non-domestic judgment does not meet these requirements fully, the court may nevertheless recognise some aspects of such judgment as evidence of certain issues before the Dutch courts.

654. Supreme Court 17 Dec. 1993, NJ 1994, 348, LJN: ZC1183 (*Esmil/Enka*). On 23 June 2010, the Amsterdam District Court was the first Dutch court ever to recognise and enforce a US final judgment in a class action. The court ruled there were insufficient grounds to conclude that the rights of the Dutch shareholders were not sufficiently safeguarded (JOR 2010, 225, LJN: BM9324 (*SOBI/ Deloitte Accountants*)).

Chapter 2
Arbitration

1. INTRODUCTION

1.1 General

There are several alternatives to the resolution of disputes through the courts. Expert determination and mediation will be discussed briefly at the end of this chapter, but the main focus will be on arbitration as this is the most important form of out-of-court settlement of a case. Unlike court litigation, arbitration is a private, consensual process. The similarity is that both result in a binding and enforceable award. The main advantages of arbitration are generally considered to be neutrality, confidentiality, procedural flexibility, the option to select expert arbitrators, the option to exclude appeal (which also saves time and costs) and the fact that arbitral awards are generally enforceable in more countries than court judgments. The disadvantages of arbitration are the lack of an appeals mechanism (although this can be agreed upon), the higher costs of arbitration as compared to court proceedings and arguably the tendency of arbitral tribunals to make awards which reflect a compromise between the parties rather than an outright decision in favour of one or other of the parties.

The Netherlands is considered an arbitration-friendly jurisdiction, and as a result it is quite common for (Dutch) commercial contracts to contain an arbitration clause. For example, in respect of large mergers and acquisitions and joint venture contracts, it is more the rule rather than the exception for parties to refer their disputes to arbitration.

Dutch arbitration law is contained in Articles 1020 to 1076 CCP. This part of the CCP is often referred to as the Arbitration Act (*Arbitragewet*). The Arbitration Act came into force on 1 December 1986 and is influenced by foreign arbitration laws, especially by the Model Law of UNCITRAL 1985 (the 'Model Law').[1] The Netherlands, however, has not actually adopted the Model Law.

Over recent years, there have been discussions about a revision of Dutch arbitration law. On 13 March 2012, the Ministry of Justice presented a proposal

1. Act of 2 Jul. 1986, Stb. 1986, 372.

for a new bill (the 'Arbitration Amendment Act').[2] The consultation phase for the Arbitration Amendment Act was closed on 1 June 2012,[3] and the proposal is currently under revision by the Ministry of Justice. Although the main principles of the Arbitration Act remain unchanged, the Arbitration Amendment Act contains many amendments, partly to modernise the Act and bring it even more in line with 'best practices' in (international) arbitration. To the extent that the Arbitration Amendment Act deviates significantly from the current Arbitration Act this is indicated below.

A recent example confirming the recognition of the Netherlands as an arbitration friendly jurisdiction, is the establishment of P.R.I.M.E. Finance (Panel of Recognised International Market Experts in Finance) in 2012, which deals with the settlement of disputes on complex financial transactions under the P.R.I.M.E. Finance Arbitration Rules.[4]

1.2 Applicable Rules

The provisions of the Arbitration Act are quite detailed in order to provide adequate procedural rules for ad hoc arbitration. This is the case when parties enter into an arbitration agreement without referring to the specific rules of an arbitration institute. The Arbitration Act therefore provides a specific set of rules on, for example, the appointment of arbitrators and the course of proceedings. At the same time, the frequently used wording 'unless the parties have agreed otherwise' indicates that the parties have considerable freedom to deviate from the Arbitration Act.

The majority of commercial arbitrations in the Netherlands are institutional arbitrations which are governed by their own set of procedural rules. The Netherlands Arbitration Institute (the 'NAI'), based in Rotterdam, is the only general Dutch arbitration institute (for domestic and international arbitrations). The latest version of the NAI's arbitration rules is dated 1 January 2010. There are also many institutional arbitrations in specific industries such as construction, sports and consumer affairs. A well-known international arbitration institute is the International Court of Arbitration of the International Chamber of Commerce.

The Arbitration Act is applicable to ad hoc arbitrations where the place of arbitration is situated in the Netherlands (see § 2.2).[5] The nationality of the parties is not relevant in this respect. If the parties do not agree on the place of arbitration, the appointment or challenging of arbitrators may nevertheless be governed by the

2. Proposed bill '*Wijziging van boek 6 en boek 10 van het burgerlijk wetboek en het vierde boek van het wetboek van burgerlijke rechtsvordering in verband met de herziening van het arbitragerecht*', published at <www.rijksoverheid.nl>.
3. See <www.internetconsultatie.nl/herzieningarbitragerecht>.
4. See <www.primefinancedisputes.org>.
5. Art. 1073(1) Rv.

Arbitration Act if at least one of the parties is domiciled or has actual residence in the Netherlands.[6]

2. ARBITRATION AGREEMENT

2.1 Requirements of an Arbitration Agreement

Arbitration is possible for disputes which have arisen or which may arise between the parties out of a defined legal relationship, whether contractual or not.[7] The arbitration agreement may not serve to determine legal consequences which the parties cannot freely dispose of.[8] Such matters include those that, pursuant to a statutory provision, are the exclusive province of the national courts and those that are considered to form part of public policy. This will be the case if an award is likely to have legal consequences not only for the parties to the arbitral proceedings but also for third parties.[9] For example, the parties may not arbitrate certain corporate law issues (e.g., the dissolution of legal entities, the amendment of articles of association or the legal validity of board resolutions), bankruptcy petitions or the legal status of persons.

Even though the parties may orally agree to submit their existing or future disputes to arbitration, an arbitration agreement can only be proven by written evidence. A reference to general conditions containing an arbitration clause may suffice if the other party expressly or implicitly accepts those conditions.[10]

The validity of an arbitration agreement is considered as a separate agreement, even if that agreement has been laid down in an arbitration clause included in a more extensive contract. This means that even if the contract is terminated, annulled or void, this will not impact the arbitration clause in that contract.[11]

Although not mandatory, it is recommended that the following elements are included in an arbitration agreement: the applicable arbitration rules, the number of arbitrators, the method of appointment of the arbitrators, the place of arbitration, the language of arbitration, whether the arbitral tribunal is to make its decisions as amiable compositeur (see § 4.2) or in accordance with the rules of law and – if not yet agreed upon – the law applicable to the dispute.

---

6. Art. 1073(2) Rv.
7. Art. 1020(1) Rv.
8. Art. 1020(3) Rv.
9. Supreme Court 10 Nov. 2006, NJ 2006, 561, LJN: AY4033 (*Groenselect/Van den Boogaard*) and Supreme Court 26 Nov. 2010, NJ 2011, 55, LJN: BN8533 (*Silver Lining/Perstorp Waspik*).
10. Art. 1021 Rv. Please note, however, that under the Arbitration Amendment Act, an arbitration clause in general conditions would be considered unreasonably onerous (*onredelijk bezwarend*) and therefore subject to annulment (*vernietigbaar*) if invoked against a consumer. Under current law, the circumstances of the case are decisive (Supreme Court 21 Sep. 2012, RvdW 2012, 1132, LJN BW6135 (*Van Marrum/Wolff*).
11. Art. 1053 Rv.

2.2 Place of Arbitration

The place of arbitration will be determined by the agreement of the parties, or, failing such agreement, by the arbitral tribunal.[12] If neither the parties nor the tribunal determine the place of arbitration, the place where the award is rendered will be the place of arbitration.[13] The determination of the place of arbitration is important, as it also decides the 'nationality' of the arbitral award. If the place of arbitration is in the Netherlands, the Arbitration Act will be applicable.[14] This also means that the Dutch courts will decide whether the award can be enforced or set aside.[15] The place of arbitration also determines which procedural arbitration law applies and is often also decisive for the conflict of law rules.

The place of arbitration does not prevent the arbitral tribunal from holding hearings or from deliberating or examining witnesses or experts elsewhere within or outside the Netherlands.[16]

2.3 Jurisdiction of the Civil Courts

If the parties have entered into an arbitration agreement, a court shall declare that it has no jurisdiction to hear the dispute if one of the parties relies on the arbitration agreement, unless the arbitration agreement is invalid.[17] However, an arbitration agreement does not preclude a party from requesting preliminary relief measures before the preliminary relief judge of the District Court. In this case, the preliminary relief judge must decide whether he has jurisdiction or whether the matter should be referred to arbitral preliminary relief proceedings (see § 3.4). The court also has jurisdiction to grant interim protection measures such as a pre-judgment attachment or to order preliminary witness or expert hearings.[18]

The competence of state courts *versus* arbitration tribunals, especially in the situation where one of the parties disputes that there is a valid arbitration agreement, has been a topic of interest in a European context over the past years – especially given the fact that arbitration is excluded under the EC Regulation. The CJEU has found in its 'West Tankers' decision of 2009[19] that a court of a Member State, designated under an arbitration agreement as the jurisdiction of choice, may not

12. Art. 1037(1) Rv.
13. Art. 1037(2) Rv.
14. Art. 1073(1) Rv. However, the Dutch Arbitration Act may also apply if the parties have not determined the place of arbitration, see § 1.2.
15. Arts 1058(1) and 1064(2) Rv.
16. Art. 1037(3) Rv.
17. Art. 1022(1) Rv.
18. Arts 1022(2) and 1022(3) Rv.
19. CJEU 10 Feb. 2009, C-185/07, ECR 2009 I-00663, RvdW 2009, 546, LJN: BH3000 (*Allianz SpA/West Tankers*).

restrain a person from commencing court proceedings in another Member State on the basis that such proceedings are in breach of the agreement. So-called 'anti-suit' injunctions, even if they are in support of arbitration agreements, are deemed incompatible with the EC Regulation and can not be used to counter a torpedo action before a court of a Member State (see also Chapter 1 § 6.3.6). Parties can thus try to avoid or delay arbitration proceedings by initiating state court proceedings before the other side can start arbitration. This issue is also being debated in the context of a proposed revision of the EC Regulation.[20]

3. ARBITRATION PROCEEDINGS UNDER THE ARBITRATION ACT

3.1 The Arbitral Tribunal

3.1.1 Appointment of Arbitrators

For a person to be appointed as an arbitrator he must be impartial and independent. This also applies to party-appointed arbitrators. Unless the parties have agreed otherwise, no person is precluded from appointment by reason of his nationality.[21]

The parties are free to agree on the method of appointing the arbitrators. The arbitrators can be appointed by the parties or by a third party. If the parties have not agreed on a method of appointment, the arbitrators will be appointed by the parties jointly.[22] The arbitral tribunal must comprise an odd number of arbitrators and may also consist of just one arbitrator.[23] If the arbitration agreement gives one of the parties an advantageous position with respect to the appointment of the arbitrators, the other party may make an application to the preliminary relief judge to appoint the arbitrator(s).[24]

If the parties have not appointed the arbitrator(s) within two months of the notice of arbitration (see § 3.2.1), either party can apply to the preliminary relief judge to appoint the arbitrator(s).[25] The time limit is three months if one of the parties is domiciled or has its actual place of residence outside the Netherlands.[26]

20. See the European Commission's Greenbook COM (2009) 175 and the Proposal for a revised EC Regulation, COM (2010) 748 final (see also Chapter 1 § 4.2.2).
21. Art. 1023 Rv. The Arbitration Amendment Act provides, in addition, that unless the parties decide otherwise at least one of the arbitrators (or the secretary to the arbitral tribunal) shall have a law degree or the equivalent thereof.
22. Art. 1027(1) Rv.
23. Art. 1026(1) Rv.
24. Art. 1028 Rv.
25. Art. 1027(3) Rv.
26. Under the Arbitration Amendment Act the time limit is three months in both cases, regardless of the parties' domiciles.

The preliminary relief judge shall in principle not investigate whether or not there is a valid arbitration agreement; however, to the extent that the preliminary relief judge can immediately and without further investigation determine that there is no arbitration agreement, he may deny the application for the court to appoint the arbitrator(s).[27]

3.1.2 Jurisdiction

The arbitral tribunal may rule on its own jurisdiction (also known as the principle of '*Kompetenz-Kompetenz*').[28] Jurisdiction may be contested by a party on several grounds, such as the lack of a valid arbitration agreement or that the constitution of the tribunal is in violation of the applicable rules.[29] These grounds must be raised by a party before it submits its defence on the merits, meaning that they should be included in the first written statement or oral defence. If a party fails to do so, it is barred from raising the issue of lack of jurisdiction either in the arbitral proceedings or before a court. A party may not raise the argument that the constitution of the arbitral tribunal is invalid if it participated in the constitution of the arbitral tribunal.[30] The only jurisdictional ground that can also be raised at a later stage of the arbitral proceedings or before a court is that the dispute is not capable of settlement by arbitration (see § 2.1).[31] The parties must await the outcome of the jurisdictional issue before they can continue on the merits. If the arbitral tribunal declares that it has jurisdiction, the arbitral proceedings must be continued. The parties can then only raise the jurisdiction issue again in proceedings to set aside the final award (see § 4.7).[32] Unless the parties have agreed otherwise, the court will have jurisdiction to hear the case if the arbitral tribunal declares that it lacks jurisdiction.[33]

3.1.3 Challenge of Arbitrators

If circumstances exist that give rise to justifiable doubts as to an arbitrator's impartiality or independence, a party may challenge that arbitrator.[34]

An arbitrator can only be challenged on grounds which a party became aware of after that arbitrator's appointment.[35] If an arbitrator is challenged by one of the

27. Supreme Court 21 Oct. 2011, JBPr 2001, 53, LJN: BQ8777 (*Hasfeld/Cohen*).
28. Art. 1052(1) Rv.
29. Arts 1052(2) and 1052(3) Rv.
30. Art. 1052(3) Rv.
31. Arts 1052(2) and 1020(3) Rv.
32. Art. 1052(4) Rv.
33. Art. 1052(5) Rv. Under the Arbitration Amendment Act, however, the court shall only have jurisdiction if the arbitral tribunal lacks jurisdiction on the ground that there is no valid arbitration agreement.
34. Art. 1033(1) Rv.
35. Art. 1033(2) Rv.

parties and the arbitrator does not resign within a certain time period (two or six weeks, depending on whether the challenged arbitrator or one of the parties is domiciled or has its actual place of residence outside the Netherlands), the preliminary relief judge will decide whether or not the challenge is valid.[36] In this respect, the IBA Guidelines on Conflicts of Interest and the Judicial Impartiality Guidelines (*Leidraad Onpartijdigheid van de Rechter*) may be used as a point of reference.[37]

If an arbitrator is challenged, the arbitral tribunal may suspend the arbitral proceedings, but is not obliged to do so.[38] However, the tribunal may not make an award before the preliminary relief judge has ruled on whether the challenge is valid. This may not apply if the challenge is an obvious abuse of power and the interests of the other party are unreasonably damaged by postponing the arbitral award.[39]

3.2 The Arbitration Proceedings

3.2.1 Commencement of the Proceedings

Unless otherwise agreed by the parties, arbitration proceedings shall be deemed to have commenced on the date of receipt of a written notice in which one party informs the other party that it is commencing arbitration. In this notice, the party commencing the arbitration must give a description of the matter it wishes to submit to arbitration.[40] If the parties have agreed that arbitrators will be appointed by a third party, a copy of this notice should also be sent to that third party.[41] The date of commencement of the arbitration is important in connection with possible statutes of limitation or contractual limitation periods. In addition, the time limits for appointing arbitrators run from the date on which the arbitration is commenced (see § 3.1.1).[42]

3.2.2 The Proceedings

The arbitral proceedings shall be conducted in such a manner as agreed between the parties or, if the parties have not so agreed, as determined by the arbitral tribunal.[43]

---

36. Art. 1035 Rv. The Arbitration Amendment Act provides that the term shall be two weeks from the date that the arbitrator confirms that he will not resign or six weeks from the date of the challenge if he does not respond, regardless of the parties' domiciles.
37. IBA Guidelines on Conflicts of Interest in International Arbitration 2010 which are published at <www.ibanet.org> and Judicial Impartiality Guidelines 2004 which are published at <www.nvvr.org>.
38. Art. 1035(1) Rv.
39. Supreme Court 29 Jun. 2007, NJ 2008, 177, LJN: AV7405 (*N./AEGON Verzekeringen*).
40. Arts 1025(1) and 1025(3) Rv.
41. Art. 1025(2) Rv. This provision is deleted in the Arbitration Amendment Act.
42. Art. 1027(2) Rv.
43. Art. 1036 Rv.

During the proceedings, arbitrators must treat the parties equally and each party should be given the opportunity to substantiate its claims and present its case.[44] Violation of this rule may lead to the setting aside of the arbitral award (see § 4.7).[45] The parties have a right to an oral hearing, which can be held at the request of one of the parties, or at the initiative of the arbitrators.[46] At any stage of the proceedings, the arbitral tribunal may order the parties to appear in person for the purposes of providing information or attempting to arrive at a settlement.[47]

3.2.3 Evidence

The arbitral tribunal is free to determine the rules regarding evidence, including its admissibility and its weight, unless the parties agree otherwise.[48] The rules of evidence as laid down in the CCP are not applicable in principle.

3.2.3.1 Documents

The arbitral tribunal has the power to order the parties to disclose documents.[49] It may do so on its own initiative or at the request of one of the parties. An order by the arbitral tribunal requiring the disclosure of certain documents cannot be enforced by a court. If a party refuses to disclose certain documents, the arbitral tribunal can in principle do no more than draw its own conclusions from such a refusal (e.g., that the relevant documents sustain the other party's position). It is unclear whether the arbitral tribunal can impose a penalty payment upon a party which has failed to comply with its order to disclose documents. The disclosure of documents in the hands of third parties can only be ordered by a court (see Chapter 1 § 5.4). In practice, arbitrators tend not to use their power to order disclosure very often, as the common law concept of document disclosure or discovery as known in Anglo Saxon jurisdictions is not recognised within the Dutch legal system (see Chapter 1 § 2.2.5).

3.2.3.2 Witnesses and Experts

Although the law stipulates that witnesses can only be examined at the request of one of the parties, it is generally presumed that an arbitral tribunal may also request

44. Art. 1039(1) Rv.
45. Art. 1065(1)(e) Rv.
46. Art. 1039(2) Rv.
47. Art. 1043 Rv.
48. Art. 1039(5) Rv. For instance, the parties can agree to the application of the IBA Rules on the Taking of Evidence in International Commercial Arbitration, published at <www.iba.org>.
49. Art. 1039(4) Rv.

the hearing of witnesses.[50] If necessary, the arbitrators may decide that witnesses are to be sworn in before the arbitral tribunal,[51] which may also appoint one or more experts to give advice.[52]

The manner in which witness hearings are conducted is determined by the arbitrators, unless specifically agreed otherwise by the parties. Cross-examination is allowed, but generally only agreed to between the parties in international arbitrations. If cross-examination has not been agreed between the parties, the arbitral tribunal will generally take the lead in hearing the witnesses. Counsel to the parties will only be allowed to pose additional questions after the witnesses have been heard by the tribunal. Unless the parties agree otherwise, testimonies will generally not be recorded verbatim.

Prior to the appointment of arbitrators, the parties may request a court to conduct preliminary hearings of witnesses or experts.[53] Once arbitrators are appointed, the court may only intervene in witness hearings in the event that a witness does not appear before the tribunal or, after his appearance, is unwilling to testify.[54]

Arbitrators may only undertake expert investigations themselves if the parties to the arbitral proceedings expressly agree that the arbitral tribunal, in assessing the evidence, can also take into account the results of its own investigations.[55]

3.2.3.3 Joinder of Third Parties

Upon the written request of a third party with an interest in the outcome of the arbitral proceedings, the arbitral tribunal may permit such a party to join the proceedings or to intervene therein.[56] A party which claims indemnification by a third party may also request the joinder of that third party.[57] Such joining or intervention will only be permitted by the arbitral tribunal if the third party enters into a written agreement with the other parties to accede to the arbitration agreement.[58]

---

50. Art. 1039(3) Rv. The Arbitration Amendment Act explicitly provides that the arbitral tribunal itself may also request the hearing of witnesses.
51. Art. 1041(1) Rv.
52. Art. 1042 Rv.
53. Art. 1022(3) Rv.
54. Art. 1041(2) Rv.
55. Supreme Court 29 Jun. 2007, NJ 2008, 177, LJN: AV7405 (*N./AEGON Verzekeringen*).
56. Art. 1045(1) Rv.
57. Art. 1045(2) Rv.
58. Art. 1045(3) Rv. The Arbitration Amendment Act allows joining or intervention by a third party if the same arbitration agreement that is applicable between the original parties 'is or becomes applicable' between (all) the original parties and that third party. However, if a party wants to bring a claim for indemnification against a third party, the original arbitration agreement only has to be or become applicable between the party claiming indemnification and that third party.

3.2.3.4 Consolidation

If two or more connected disputes have been brought before arbitral tribunals established in the Netherlands, either party may apply to the preliminary relief judge of the District Court in Amsterdam to order full or partial consolidation.[59] The preliminary relief judge may wholly or partially grant or refuse the request after he has given all parties and the arbitrators an opportunity to be heard.[60] In the event of full consolidation, the parties will appoint the arbitral tribunal in consultation with each other and will determine the procedural rules applicable to the consolidated proceedings. If the parties cannot reach agreement on the appointment of the arbitral tribunal or on the procedural rules within the period of time prescribed by the preliminary relief judge, the preliminary relief judge will rule upon these matters. If by reason of the full consolidation the mandate of one or more of the arbitrators is terminated, the preliminary relief judge will determine the remuneration for the work already carried out by them.[61]

The consolidation of connected arbitral proceedings cannot be ordered if previously excluded by the parties.[62] As consolidation proceedings may result in the removal of arbitrators and in the delay of arbitration proceedings, consolidation is often excluded in (Dutch) arbitration agreements.

3.3 Confidentiality

Unlike court litigation, the principle of the public nature of proceedings and decision making does not apply to arbitration. However, the Arbitration Act contains no specific provisions on confidentiality. Although arbitration is generally considered to be confidential, the parties should explicitly agree to this if they want to ensure full confidentiality. Proceedings before the national courts which arise in connection with arbitration (enforcement, revocation, etc.) are public in principle. Information disclosed in arbitral proceedings can be referred to in subsequent or parallel court proceedings unless the parties provide otherwise in their arbitration agreement.

3.4 Preliminary Relief

The arbitral tribunal is only permitted to award preliminary or interim relief if the parties agree that it has such competence.[63] If this is agreed, the tribunal may take

---

59. Art. 1046(1) Rv.
60. Art. 1046(2) Rv.
61. Art. 1046(3) Rv.
62. Art. 1046(1) Rv.
63. Art. 1051 Rv. Conversely, the Arbitration Amendment Act provides that the arbitration tribunal shall be permitted to award preliminary or interim relief unless the parties agree otherwise.

provisional measures, such as the granting of a preliminary (mandatory or prohibitory) injunction. A provisional remedy can also comprise monetary awards, such as a claim for advance payment of damages or payment of an outstanding debt. The protective measure of attaching goods can, however, only be ordered by a court. A decision rendered in arbitral preliminary relief proceedings is regarded as an arbitral award, which can consequently be enforced in accordance with the normal rules (see § 4.6).[64]

If the parties fail to agree on giving the arbitral tribunal the power to grant preliminary or interim relief, the preliminary relief judge has jurisdiction to grant such relief.[65] If the parties do give the arbitral tribunal such power, the preliminary relief judge still has jurisdiction to grant relief at the request of one of the parties (see § 2.3). However, if the opposing party then relies on a valid arbitration agreement, the preliminary relief judge is required to take into account all circumstances in deciding whether or not he has jurisdiction,[66] and is required to make his decision considering the interests of both parties.[67] The preliminary relief judge will usually declare that he does not have jurisdiction in circumstances where the time frame for preliminary relief proceedings before the civil courts is similar to the time frame for such proceedings before the arbitral tribunal. This is often not the case if arbitrators have not yet been appointed. If the parties have agreed to arbitration by specialised arbitrators (e.g. on technical issues or trade practices), there is an increased likelihood that the preliminary relief judge will decide he has no jurisdiction to hear disputes on specific issues in which the arbitrators are specialised.

3.5 Costs

Dutch arbitration law does not deal with the recovery of fees or costs. The parties may provide for the allocation of costs (including legal fees) in their arbitration agreement. If there is no such agreement, arbitrators may decide on the issue of costs. In practice, arbitrators will often decide that the losing party should bear the costs of arbitration, including the legal fees of the other party. Arbitrators can, however, limit the costs to an amount they consider reasonable. This is often the case in national arbitrations, as a result of which the prevailing party will not be able to recover all or at any rate a substantial part of his legal fees from the losing party. If a party's claim is only partially allowed, costs are usually divided between the parties.

---

64. Art. 1051(3) Rv.
65. Art. 1022(2) Rv.
66. Art. 1051(2) Rv.
67. The Arbitration Amendment Act provides that in such cases the preliminary relief judge will declare that he has no jurisdiction, unless the relief requested cannot be obtained timely in arbitration or the arbitration agreement is invalid.

4. ARBITRAL AWARD

4.1 General

The arbitral tribunal may declare a final, partial or interim award.[68] The nature of the award may have an effect on such issues as enforcement and whether the award may be set aside or revoked.[69] The arbitral tribunal is free to determine when the award shall be made and has the power to impose penalties for non-compliance in cases where the court also has such power.[70]

4.2 Laws and Rules Applicable to the Merits of the Dispute

The arbitral tribunal must make its award in accordance with the law chosen by the parties or, failing such a choice of law, in accordance with the rules of law which it considers appropriate.[71] Although the tribunal is not obliged to apply the conflict of law rules of the place of the arbitration, in practice it often follows them. The arbitral tribunal will only make a decision as amiable compositeur (on the basis of principles of equity, disregarding legal technicalities) if the parties so agree.[72] It should, however, be noted that many writers argue that, if Dutch substantive law applies, the difference is in practice very small. The reason for this is that standards of reasonableness and fairness play an important role in Dutch law. For example, it is a rule of law that a contractual obligation can be disregarded to the extent that it would be unacceptable to rely on it by the standards of reasonableness and fairness.[73] In all cases, the arbitral tribunal shall take into account any applicable trade practices.[74]

4.3 Requirements of an Arbitral Award

Unless otherwise agreed by the parties, an arbitral award is made by majority vote.[75] An arbitral award should be in writing and signed by each of the arbitrators.[76] A refusal by a minority of the arbitrators to sign an award must be mentioned in the

68. Art. 1049 Rv.
69. Arts 1062(1) and 1064(1) Rv.
70. Art. 1056 Rv.
71. Art. 1054(2) Rv.
72. Art. 1054(3) Rv. It should be noted that this is different under the NAI Rules, see § 6.5.
73. Art. 6:248(2) BW.
74. Art. 1054(4) Rv.
75. Art. 1057(1) Rv. In addition, the Arbitration Amendment Act provides that if there are more arbitrators than one, procedural issues of minor importance may also be decided upon by the chairman of the tribunal unless the parties agree otherwise.
76. Art. 1057(2) Rv.

award.[77] A dissenting opinion given by an arbitrator does not become part of the award and is not sufficient to constitute signature.[78] An award must contain the following information: (i) name(s) and domicile(s) of the arbitrator(s); (ii) names and domiciles of the parties; (iii) the date of the award; (iv) the place of the award (which is the same place as the place of arbitration, where such place exists) (see § 2.2); (v) the decision; and (vi) the reasons for the decision (unless the award only relates to the determination of the quality of goods or is simply the record of a settlement).[79]

As soon as the award is made, a copy must be sent to the parties. The original award is deposited with the Registry of the District Court in the same district as the place of arbitration.[80]

4.4 Binding Force and Appeal

In principle, a (partial) final award has binding force as from the date on which it is rendered.[81] An appeal against an arbitral award to an arbitral appeals tribunal is only possible if the parties have agreed to this (in the arbitration agreement or separately).[82] Unless the parties have agreed otherwise, such appeal should be lodged within three months of the date of deposit of the award with the Registry of the District Court.[83] If an appeal is possible, the award shall only have binding force from the date on which the time limit for lodging an appeal has lapsed. If an appeal is lodged and the original award is confirmed on appeal, the appeal award has binding force as of the date on which it is rendered.[84] In the event that an arbitral award can be appealed, the arbitral tribunal may declare its award provisionally enforceable notwithstanding an appeal. In that case, it may also determine that the award is only provisionally enforceable subject to the giving of security.[85]

4.5 Rectification, Correction and Supplementation of Award

If the award contains a manifest computing or clerical error, rectification or correction of the award can be requested by either of the parties or be made at the initia-

77. Art. 1057(3) Rv.
78. Supreme Court 5 Dec. 2008, NJ 2009, 6, LJN: BF3799 (*Güris/Bursa*).
79. Art. 1057(4) Rv. The Arbitration Amendment Act provides that the parties may agree (in writing) that no reasons for the decision have to be given in the award.
80. Art. 1058(1) Rv. Under the Arbitration Amendment Act, the parties can agree that the award shall not be deposited with the Registry of the District Court.
81. Art. 1059(1) Rv.
82. Art. 1050(1) Rv.
83. Art. 1050(4) Rv. The Arbitration Amendment Act allows the parties to agree on a different term for lodging the appeal.
84. Art. 1059(2) Rv.
85. Art. 1055 Rv.

tive of the arbitral tribunal within 30 days of deposit of the award.[86] If the tribunal has failed to decide on one or more matters which have been submitted to it, either party may within 30 days of deposit of the award ask it to make a supplementary award.[87] Before deciding on such requests, the arbitral tribunal must give the parties the opportunity to be heard. If a supplementary award is made, it will be regarded as a regular arbitral award.

4.6 Enforcement

Enforcement of an arbitral award can take place only after the preliminary relief judge (from the District Court with which Registry the original award must be deposited) has granted leave to enforce it.[88] Leave to enforce must be recorded on the original arbitral award if already deposited or, failing such deposit, in a separate decision by the preliminary relief judge.[89] If the award is not declared provisionally enforceable, leave to enforce the award may only be granted after the time limit for lodging the appeal has lapsed.[90]

Enforcement of an arbitral award may only be refused by the preliminary relief judge if (i) the award or the manner in which it was made is manifestly contrary to public policy or good morals; or (ii) the award is unjustly declared enforceable notwithstanding an appeal; or (iii) a penalty for non-compliance is unjustly imposed.[91] The first ground represents by far the most common reason for refusal to grant enforcement. It should, however, be noted that the preliminary relief judge may only refuse leave to enforce if the award is prima facie contrary to public policy.

If the preliminary relief judge refuses leave to enforce, the petitioning party may lodge an appeal with the Court of Appeal within two months after the date on which the preliminary relief judge's appeal decision is given.[92] If the refusal to grant leave to enforce is confirmed on appeal, the time limit for review by the Supreme Court is two months after the date on which the appeal decision is given.[93]

---

86. Art. 1060 Rv. In the Arbitration Amendment Act this term is extended to three months from deposit of the award, or any other term agreed between the parties.
87. Art. 1061 Rv.
88. Art. 1062(1) Rv. The Arbitration Amendment Act provides that such leave to enforce shall be granted by the preliminary relief judge from the Court of Appeal (rather than the District Court) that has jurisdiction over the place of arbitration.
89. Art. 1062(2) Rv.
90. Art. 1062(3) Rv.
91. Art. 1063(1) Rv. A refusal on the basis of (iii) is limited to the enforcement of the penalty. The wording of this clause is slightly amended under the Arbitration Amendment Act, which refers to an award that is likely to be set aside or revoked rather than an award which is contrary to public policy or good morals, but that is meant as a stylistic rather than a substantive change of the grounds for a refusal.
92. Art. 1063(3) Rv.
93. Art. 1063(4) Rv. As set out above, the Arbitration Amendment Act provides that leave to enforce shall be granted by the Court of Appeal rather than the District Court. This means that there will only be one instance of appeal to a refusal (the Supreme Court) rather than two.

If leave to enforce is granted, that decision is not open to appeal and the only legal remedies left available to the other party are the setting aside or revocation of the arbitral award itself.[94]

The enforcement in the Netherlands of foreign arbitral awards is discussed in § 5.2 below.

4.7 Setting Aside and Revocation

4.7.1 General

In the great majority of cases, the preliminary relief judge will grant leave to enforce. If this is granted, the only recourse available to the party against whom enforcement is sought is to apply to have the award set aside or revoked.[95]

4.7.2 Setting Aside

The grounds for setting aside an award are (i) the absence of a valid arbitration agreement; (ii) the arbitral tribunal being constituted in violation of the applicable rules; (iii) the arbitral tribunal not complying with its mandate; (iv) the award not being signed or not containing the reasons for the arbitration decision (see § 4.3); and (v) the award, or the manner in which it was made, being in violation of public policy or good morals.[96]

Grounds (i), (ii) and (iii) cannot lead to the award being set aside if the party that wishes to set aside the award did not bring these issues to the attention of the tribunal during the course of the arbitration proceedings.[97][98] However, this does not preclude that new factual or legal propositions may be introduced, provided that this does not violate the requirements of due process or the (procedural) rules of appeal.[99]

With respect to ground (iv), the Supreme Court has ruled that an award may also be set aside in the event that, although some reasoning may have been given,

---

94. Art. 1062(4) Rv; with the understanding that setting aside or revoking the arbitral award will by operation of law also cause annulment of the leave to enforce. Under the Arbitration Amendment Act, if leave to enforce is granted that decision is open to appeal (with the Supreme Court), unless the parties have agreed otherwise.
95. Arts 1062(4) and 1064(1) Rv.
96. Art. 1065(1) Rv.
97. The court will, however, not investigate this at its own initiative; it is up to the party who is against the setting aside of the award to raise this defence (Supreme Court 23 Apr. 2010, NJ 2011, 475, LJN: BK8097 (*Areb/Ameg*)).
98. Under the Arbitration Amendment Act ground (iii) can also not lead to the award being set aside if the non-compliance with the mandate was not serious.
99. Supreme Court 27 Mar. 2009, NJ 2010, 169, LJN: BG4003 (*Hendrix Poultry Breeders/Burshan*) and Supreme Court 27 Mar. 2009, NJ 2010, 170, LJN: BG6443 (*Smit Bloembollen/Ruwa Bulbs*).

it lacked any well-founded argument.[100] On the basis of this judgment, it has been argued that the courts have more discretion to examine the reasoning of the arbitrators. However, the Supreme Court has made it clear that setting aside an arbitration decision on the basis that it does not contain the reasons for the decision should be applied restrictively by the national courts, who may only intervene in an arbitral award in clear-cut cases.[101] This restrictive approach has generally been followed by lower courts.

With respect to ground (v), the Supreme Court has ruled that an award may be set aside in the event that the fundamental principle of hearing both sides of the argument was violated during the arbitral proceedings.[102] Again, this ground should be applied restrictively; not every breach of procedural rules during the arbitral proceedings will be a ground for setting aside the award, even if the breach amounts to a violation of the principles of due process.

An award may also be set aside partially, on the condition that it contains several decisions which are not inextricably linked to each other, so that it can be set aside with respect to one decision but upheld with respect to the other decisions.[103]

An application to have an award set aside may be made as soon as the award has binding force (see § 4.4). The time limit for such an application expires three months after the date of deposit of the award. However, there is a further three-month period in which such application can be made if the award, together with leave to enforce, is officially served on the other party.[104] Unlike the enforcement procedure, a writ of summons is required to initiate an application to set aside an arbitral award. All grounds for setting aside an award must be mentioned in the writ of summons or they will not be able to be argued before the court.[105] The competent court is the District Court in the same district as the place of arbitration.[106]

4.7.3 Revocation

Revocation is an extraordinary legal remedy to redress misrepresentations of the parties rather than mistakes or errors of the arbitrators. The grounds for revocation are (i) fraud; (ii) the forgery of documents; and (iii) the withholding of documents.[107]

100. Supreme Court 9 Jan. 2004, NJ 2005, 190, LJN: AK8380 (*Nannini/SFT Bank*).
101. Supreme Court 22 Dec. 2006, NJ 2008, 4, LJN: AZ1593 (*Kers/Rijpma*).
102. Supreme Court 25 May 2007, NJ 2007, 294, LJN: BA2495 (*Spaanderman/Anova*) and Supreme Court 24 Apr. 2009, NJ 2010, 171, LJN: BH3137 (*IMS/Modsaf*).
103. Supreme Court 20 Jan. 2006, NJ 2006, 77, LJN: AU4523 (*ASB Grünland/Sagro*) and Supreme Court 24 Apr. 2009, NJ 2010, 171, LJN: BH3137 (*IMS/Modsaf*).
104. Art. 1064(3) Rv.
105. Art. 1064(5) Rv.
106. Arts 1064(2) and 1058(1) Rv. The Arbitration Amendment Act provides that the competent court shall be the Court of Appeal (rather than the District Court) that has jurisdiction over the place of arbitration.
107. Art. 1068(1) Rv.

The time limit for an application to revoke an award is the same as that for setting aside an award (i.e., three months after the date of deposit of the award). However, an application to revoke an award may also be made within three months of a misrepresentation being discovered, if this would lead to a later date.[108] Like the procedure for setting aside an award, the procedure for revocation is initiated with a writ of summons. However, a key difference is that the competent court is the Court of Appeal which would have had jurisdiction to decide an appeal relating to the application for the setting aside (see § 4.7.2).[109]

4.7.4 Consequences

An award can usually be enforced notwithstanding an application for it to be set aside or revoked. However, if the award is enforced, the party challenging it may request that the court suspend enforcement.[110] If the award is set aside or revoked, the jurisdiction of the court is resumed (i.e., the court must decide on the dispute between the parties), unless the parties have agreed otherwise.[111]

5. ARBITRATION OUTSIDE THE NETHERLANDS

There are only three articles in the Arbitration Act that are applicable to arbitration proceedings taking place outside the Netherlands (i.e., where the place of arbitration is outside the Netherlands). These articles concern the jurisdiction of Dutch courts and the enforcement of awards rendered outside the Netherlands.

5.1 Jurisdiction of the Dutch Civil Courts

If the parties have agreed to arbitration outside the Netherlands, a Dutch court will decline jurisdiction if the following three conditions are met. First, there must be an arbitration agreement specifying a place of arbitration outside the Netherlands. Second, the defendant in the court proceedings must invoke the arbitration agreement before submitting its defence on the merits. Third, the arbitration agreement must not be invalid under the applicable law (due to the manner in which the agree-

---

108. Art. 1068(2) Rv. Under the Arbitration Amendment Act the only applicable term is three months after the fraud or forgery has been discovered or a party has obtained the documents that were withheld.
109. Art. 1068(2) Rv.
110. Art. 1066 Rv.
111. Arts 1067 and 1068(3) Rv. The Arbitration Amendment Act provides that the jurisdiction of the court shall only be resumed if the award is set aside on grounds of invalidity of the arbitration agreement. If the award is set aside on another ground or revoked, the arbitration agreement remains effective (and the court has no jurisdiction) unless the parties have agreed otherwise.

ment was concluded, its form or its content).[112] An agreement to arbitrate abroad does not preclude a party from requesting a Dutch court to grant interim protection measures, such as attachment, or interim measures in preliminary relief proceedings (see § 3.4).[113]

5.2 Enforcement of Foreign Arbitral Awards

The Netherlands is a party to the 1958 New York Convention on the Recognition and Enforcement of Foreign Arbitral Awards (the 'New York Convention').[114] Arbitral awards made in countries that are a party to the New York Convention are enforceable in the Netherlands in accordance with the provisions of the New York Convention.[115] Currently, approximately 147 countries are party to the New York Convention.[116]

Pursuant to Article VII of the New York Convention, a party seeking enforcement of a foreign arbitral award may also base its request on relevant national legislation. The Dutch national enforcement law[117] may be considered as slightly more favourable than the New York Convention as it appears to set less stringent formal requirements for the arbitration agreement than the 'agreement in writing' required by the New York Convention.[118] The party requesting enforcement may therefore consider basing his claim primarily on the national enforcement provisions and alternatively on the New York Convention.

If a court refuses to grant leave to enforce a Dutch arbitral award that decision is open to appeal, but if leave to enforce is granted that decision is not open to appeal (see § 4.6). The Supreme Court has confirmed that this also applies to the leave or refusal of enforcement of foreign arbitral awards that fall under the scope of the New York Convention.[119]

Foreign arbitral awards made in countries that are not party to the New York Convention can also be enforced in the Netherlands.[120] Pursuant to Dutch national enforcement law, the preliminary relief judge may only refuse to enforce an award on grounds which are exhaustively enumerated in the Arbitration Act.[121] These

112. Art. 1074(1) Rv.
113. Art. 1074(2) Rv.
114. Convention on the Recognition and Enforcement of Foreign Arbitral Awards, New York, 10 Jun. 1958, which was ratified by the Netherlands on 24 Apr. 1964. Trb. 1958, 145 (English and French versions), Trb. 1959, 58 (Dutch translation) and Trb. 1964, 96. Also <www.uncitral.org>.
115. The Netherlands has made the reservation of reciprocity in accordance with the New York Convention, Art. I(3).
116. <www.uncitral.org>.
117. Art. 1076 Rv (discussed in the next paragraph).
118. Arts II(1) and II(2) New York Convention.
119. Supreme Court 25 Jun. 2010, NJ 2012, 55, LJN: BM1679 (*Rosneft/Yukos Capital*).
120. Art. 1076(1) Rv.
121. Art. 1076 Rv.

grounds are very similar to those for setting aside an award (see § 4.7.2) (which are based on the grounds for refusing enforcement or recognition of an arbitral award set forth in the New York Convention).

6. ARBITRATION UNDER THE NAI ARBITRATION RULES

6.1 General

The NAI, established in 1949 and based in Rotterdam, is an arbitration institution of considerable prestige. The current NAI Arbitration Rules have been in force since 1 January 2010.[122] Like the Arbitration Act, the NAI Arbitration Rules do not distinguish between domestic and international arbitration. They do, however, contain a number of separate provisions for international arbitration in order to meet the special circumstances of international arbitration, such as the fact that arbitrators in international arbitrations must decide matters according to the rules of law as opposed to deciding as amiable compositeur (see § 6.6)[123] and the fact that (only) in international arbitrations it is possible for a minority of arbitrators to give a dissenting opinion.[124] Under the NAI Arbitration Rules, an arbitration qualifies as an 'international arbitration' if at least one of the parties is, at the commencement of the proceedings, domiciled or has its seat or actual residence outside the Netherlands.[125] Although the NAI Arbitration Rules are meant primarily for both domestic and international arbitration proceedings taking place in the Netherlands, they may govern arbitration proceedings held outside the Netherlands. A standard arbitration clause is recommended by the NAI.[126] The major differences between the Arbitration Act and the NAI Arbitration Rules are considered below.

6.2 Appointment of Arbitrators

If the parties do not agree on the number of arbitrators, the administrator[127] will determine whether there are to be one or three arbitrators. In doing so, the administrator will take into account the preferences of the parties, the amount of the claim and the complexity of the dispute. Generally, when the amount in dispute exceeds EUR 200,000, the administrator will determine that three arbitrators are to be ap-

122. The NAI Arbitration Rules can be found at the website of the NAI <www.nai-nl.org>.
123. Art. 45(2) NAI Arbitration Rules.
124. Art. 48(4) NAI Arbitration Rules.
125. Art. 1(g) NAI Arbitration Rules.
126. NAI Arbitration Rules, pages 6-7.
127. In principle, the administrator is the director of the NAI as provided for in the NAI Articles of Association (Art. 1(d) NAI Arbitration Rules).

pointed. Unless otherwise agreed, a list procedure is used to select the arbitrators.[128] Under the list procedure, the administrator, after receiving the claimant's request for arbitration and the respondent's short answer thereto, composes a list of names of possible arbitrators. Depending upon whether the number of arbitrators will be one or three, the list will contain at least three or nine names. Each party must then strike out the candidates to which it objects and list the remaining candidates in order of preference. The administrator reviews the list that is returned and appoints the arbitrator(s) on the basis of the parties' preferences. If it is not possible to select all of the arbitrators immediately, the administrator will send a new list of names to the parties. In general, the names on the lists are drawn from the general panel of arbitrators of the NAI. This panel presently contains approximately 350 individuals with experience and expertise in a large number of fields. Information regarding the identity of those panel members is not available to third parties.

6.3 The Proceedings

NAI arbitration proceedings generally take the following course. The arbitration commences with the filing of a request for arbitration with the NAI secretariat. The administrator forwards a copy of the request to the respondent. The respondent has 14 days to file a short answer to the request.[129] The request and the short answer serve as an introduction to the arbitration and do not prejudice the right of the claimant or the respondent to submit a statement of claim or a statement of defence.[130] In addition, the request or the short answer do not have to contain an exhaustive overview of the specific claim(s) or counterclaim(s) or their legal basis (although a clear description of the claim is required). On the basis of the request and the short answer, the administrator will start the list procedure for appointing the arbitrator(s), if applicable (see § 6.2).

After the arbitral tribunal is appointed, the claimant and the respondent have the opportunity to submit a statement of claim and a statement of defence, respectively.[131] The NAI Arbitration Rules do not provide for the drawing up of 'Terms of Reference' as known in arbitration proceedings under the Rules of Arbitration from the International Chamber of Commerce.[132]

128. Art. 14 NAI Arbitration Rules.
129. Art. 7(4) NAI Arbitration Rules.
130. Art. 8 NAI Arbitration Rules.
131. Art. 24(1) NAI Arbitration Rules.
132. Under the ICC Rules of Arbitration, Terms of Reference are drawn up on the basis of the request for arbitration and the answer to the request (Art. 23.1 ICC Rules of Arbitration). After the Terms of Reference have been signed and approved by the International Court of Arbitration, parties cannot in principle make new (counter) claims (Art. 23.4 ICC Rules of Arbitration).

The statement of claim and the statement of defence may be followed by a second exchange of written statements.[133] Thereafter, a hearing takes place unless the parties waive their right to such a hearing.[134] During the hearing, witnesses of fact or expert witnesses may be heard.[135]

In general, the arbitral tribunal shall determine the manner in which, and the periods of time within which, the proceedings shall be conducted, taking into account the provisions of the NAI Arbitration Rules, arrangements between the parties and the circumstances of the arbitration.[136]

6.4 Confidentiality

Newly introduced in the 2010 NAI Arbitration Rules is a specific provision to safeguard confidentiality. The NAI Arbitration Rules now provide that arbitration is confidential and that all individuals involved either directly or indirectly are bound to secrecy, save and insofar as disclosures are required by virtue of the law or the agreement between the parties. Whether this confidentiality obligation would also prevent a party from disclosing that arbitration is pending (without disclosing the merits of the dispute) is unclear.[137]

6.5 Provisional Measures

Like most other rules of arbitration institutes, the NAI Arbitration Rules authorise an arbitral tribunal to make a provisional order at any stage of the proceedings. This includes the authority to order the provision of security (in a form to be determined by the tribunal) regarding any claim or counterclaim, as well as costs related to the arbitration in the main proceedings.[138] If the arbitral tribunal determines that the case is not sufficiently urgent or is too complicated to be settled in a provisional decision, it may reject the claim either wholly or partially and determine that it shall be decided in the main proceedings.[139] A provisional decision of the arbitral tribunal shall in no way prejudice the final judgment of the tribunal with regard to the merits of the case.[140]

Unlike most other rules of arbitration, the NAI Arbitration Rules also provide for preliminary relief arbitral proceedings before commencement of the arbitration

133. Art. 24(2) NAI Arbitration Rules. Unless the parties have agreed otherwise, this is at the discretion of the arbitral tribunal.
134. Art. 26 NAI Arbitration Rules.
135. Arts 26, 29, 30 and 31 NAI Arbitration Rules.
136. Art. 23(2) NAI Arbitration Rules.
137. Art. 55(1) NAI Arbitration Rules.
138. Arts. 37(1) and 38(1) NAI Arbitration Rules.
139. Art. 37(4) NAI Arbitration Rules.
140. Art. 37(6) NAI Arbitration Rules.

on the merits.[141] These proceedings can only be requested if the place of arbitration is in the Netherlands.[142] As soon as possible after the receipt of a request for preliminary relief arbitration proceedings by one of the parties, the administrator shall appoint a sole arbitrator. If the parties have agreed on the method of appointment of the arbitrator(s) such method shall not apply to the appointment of the preliminary relief tribunal, unless the parties have actually agreed upon a method of appointment of such preliminary relief tribunal.[143] The NAI aims to have an arbitrator appointed within 24 hours of a request for preliminary relief being filed, and to have a first hearing within two weeks and an award within four weeks of the request being filed. As such, the arbitral preliminary relief proceedings – which need not necessarily be followed by arbitration on the merits – constitute a true alternative to preliminary relief proceedings before the preliminary relief judge of the District Court (see Chapter 1 § 9.1).

6.6 Rules Applicable to the Merits of the Dispute

Under the NAI Arbitration Rules a tribunal decides in principle as amiable compositeur unless the parties have agreed that the award should be made in accordance with the rules of law.[144] In an international arbitration under the NAI Arbitration Rules, however, this principle is reversed, i.e., the arbitral tribunal will in principle make its decisions in accordance with the rules of law.[145] If a choice of law is made between the parties, the arbitral tribunal shall make its award in accordance with the rules of law chosen by the parties. Failing such choice of law, the tribunal will make its award in accordance with the rules of law which it considers appropriate.[146]

6.7 Costs

Upon commencement of the arbitration, administration costs are due to the NAI. The administration costs due depend on the amount of the (counter)claim filed.[147] The arbitrators' fees are determined on the basis of the time spent, the amount in dispute and the complexity of the case.[148] The party bringing the claim must pay

141. Section Four A NAI Arbitration Rules.
142. Art. 42a(4) NAI Arbitration Rules.
143. Art. 42f(1) NAI Arbitration Rules.
144. Art. 45(1) NAI Arbitration Rules.
145. Art. 45(2) NAI Arbitration Rules.
146. Art. 46 NAI Arbitration Rules.
147. The administration costs for legal entities currently range from EUR 450 for claims of less than EUR 50,000 to EUR 15,000 for claims of more than EUR 10 million. For private persons, the administration costs range from EUR 340 for claims of less than EUR 50,000 to EUR 12,000 for claims of more than EUR 10 million.
148. Art. 58 NAI Arbitration Rules.

a deposit to the NAI to cover fees and other expenses of the arbitrators.[149] As a general rule, the award renders the losing party liable for payment of these costs. With respect to legal fees, arbitrators decide on the basis of the circumstances of the case whether these should be fully or partially borne by the losing party (see § 3.5).

6.8 Publication of Award

The NAI is authorised to publish the award, but without mentioning the names of the parties and subject to a duty to delete any further information that might disclose the identity of the parties. If either of the parties wishes to object to such publication, it should communicate this in writing within one month of receipt of the award.[150]

7. EXPERT DETERMINATION

Another form of alternative dispute resolution widely used in the Netherlands is dispute resolution by means of expert determination (*bindend advies*). The rules on expert determination are to a large extent developed in case law. The general provisions in the Civil Code on settlement agreements (*vaststellingsovereenkomsten*) are, however, applicable.[151]

Parties that agree to dispute resolution through expert determination request a decision from a third party (called an 'expert' (*bindend adviseur*)) with respect to specific disputes indicated by them. The determination results in a decision which binds the parties. The expert is obliged to take into account the fundamental principle of hearing both parties in coming to his decision.

The main difference between an arbitral award and expert determination is that the former results in an award that can be enforced, while the latter leads to an agreement between the parties which can only be enforced by requesting specific performance from a court (see Chapter 1 § 6.3.1). Another major difference between an arbitral award and expert determination is that a court has a wider ability to assess the contents of the expert determination and the manner in which it has been concluded. In the event that it would be unacceptable under the principles of reasonableness and fairness for a party to be bound by the decision of the expert, either based on its contents or on the manner in which it came into existence, a court may annul the expert determination and replace it with its own decision.[152] This can be the case, for example, where the parties' right to hear and be heard has

149. Art. 59 NAI Arbitration Rules.
150. Art. 55(2) NAI Arbitration Rules.
151. Arts 7:900-7:910 BW.
152. Art. 7:904 BW.

been violated.[153] The test for setting aside arbitral awards is more restrictive (see § 4.7).

Due to the lack of formal rules applicable to expert determinations, in practice they are more often applied to technical disputes, such as accountancy disputes under share purchase agreements. Expert determinations are also commonly adopted as the applicable dispute resolution method for specific industries, such as in the case of financial disputes between banks or insurers and their customers, and some consumer disputes.[154] Often, these industries' regulations on expert determinations contain guarantees from the members of those industries that the binding opinions can be enforced, which removes one of the disadvantages of expert determinations as opposed to arbitration.

8. MEDIATION

At the end of this section on arbitration we should make brief mention of another alternative to resolving disputes: mediation. Mediation is a method of alternative dispute resolution in which a neutral third party, the mediator, assists disputing parties in reaching a mutually acceptable solution. Unlike court or arbitration proceedings, the process is not aimed at imposing a decision on the parties but rather at reaching agreement voluntarily.

The main characteristic of mediation is that both parties must be willing to solve their dispute by mediation. Parties cannot be forced to mediate. In general, confidentiality is also a key element for entering into mediation. If the parties fail to reach a settlement they can pursue court or, if agreed, arbitration proceedings.

Since the 1990s, mediation has become increasingly popular in the Netherlands. In 1993, the independent Netherlands Mediation Institute (the 'NMI') was founded. The main purpose of this foundation is to promote mediation, offer a platform for consultation on mediation and improve the quality of mediation and of mediators in general.[155] In addition to the NMI, there are several specialised professional mediation organisations. One of these is the ACB Foundation (the 'ACB'). This organisation was founded by a large group of Dutch multinationals and law firms (including Allen & Overy LLP) and aims to promote business mediation in the Netherlands. The ACB Mediation Rules are available in English.[156]

---

153. Supreme Court 8 Jul. 2011, NJ 2011, 310, LJN: BQ5081 (*X/'t Sleyk*).
154. In these cases disputes will be settled by a dispute resolution committee established for the specific industry, e.g., the dispute resolution committee for financial services (<www.kifid.nl>) or one of the dispute resolution committees for consumer complaints (<www.sgc.nl>).
155. More information on the NMI and its Mediation Rules can be found at <www.nmi-mediation.nl>.
156. More information on the ACB and its Mediation Rules can be found at <www.acbmediation.nl>.

Mediation is promoted by the Dutch government. In September 1999, certain Dutch courts took part in an experiment called 'mediation besides litigation', in order to research whether a permanent need for referral to mediation exists and whether mediation during legal proceedings can achieve a successful result. The experiment proved that mediation can be a successful alternative to litigation and, as a result, on 20 January 2005, the Dutch Parliament approved the measures announced by the government to promote referral to mediation by the courts. From 1 April 2007, all courts have the ability to refer the parties to mediation. A court should consider whether a case would be suitable for mediation and, if so, inform the parties about the possibility of mediation.

Mediation is also promoted by the European Union. An EU directive on mediation was adopted on 21 May 2008.[157] The objective of this EU directive is to facilitate access to alternative dispute resolution and to promote the amicable settlement of disputes by encouraging the use of mediation and by ensuring a balanced relationship between mediation and judicial proceedings. One of the means to achieve this is to make the content of a mediation agreement enforceable upon request. A legislative proposal to implement this EU directive in Dutch civil (procedural) law for cross-border cases is currently under debate in government.[158] One of the aspects of this proposal is that it will allow the parties in a cross-border dispute to grant complete or partial legal privilege to the mediator.

Whether mediation will actually be used to resolve a dispute remains dependent on the willingness of the parties to use this form of dispute resolution. Practice shows that it has become quite successful in the area of family law. However, in commercial disputes, especially ones where there are significant financial sums at stake, mediation is still quite rare.

---

157. EC Council Directive of 21 May 2008 on certain aspects of mediation, No. 2008/52, O.J. EUR. COMM. (No. L 136) 3 (2008).
158. See also <www.officielebekendmakingen.nl/dossier/32555>.

Chapter 3
Administrative Litigation

1. GENERAL INTRODUCTION

1.1 Administrative Law and Administrative Litigation

The State of the Netherlands has, like many other Western jurisdictions, a constitution that creates governmental bodies and vests specific powers in them. These powers are exercised in the relationships between the governmental bodies themselves and in the relationships between governmental bodies and their citizens. The Dutch constitution is based on the principle of the trias politica: namely, the separation of the legislative, executive and judicial functions.

Administrative law covers all aspects of the exercise of powers by governmental bodies (i.e. the administration). Therefore, administrative law deals with, *inter alia*, (i) how governmental bodies are organised, (ii) what their powers are, (iii) which rules and principles they must obey, (iv) how they can enforce the rules that apply to citizens, and (v) what legal protection is available for citizens against acts of government. The aspects described in (i)-(iv) above relate to the government's exercise of its legislative and executive functions while the aspect described in (v) above deals with administrative litigation, the subject of Chapter 3 of this book.

The most important part of administrative litigation is the review of governmental decisions by administrative courts. This is generally referred to as judicial review, which obviously relates to the judicial function of government. Under Dutch administrative law, judicial review of a decision of an administrative authority is generally only available after the authority has been requested to reconsider and correct its own decision having reviewed the objections of a claimant. This review by the administration is generally referred to as administrative review and is part of the executive function. Administrative review is often a prerequisite for judicial review. In addition, the scope of the objections raised by the claimant in administrative review may limit the scope of the subsequent review by the administrative courts. As a result, the rules relating to administrative review are important for a proper understanding of the rules for judicial review. Chapter 3 of this book therefore deals with the procedural rules for both administrative review and judicial review, jointly referred to as administrative litigation.[1] It does not cover substantive administrative law: that is, the rules and principles governing what administrative authorities can and cannot do and how their decisions are properly implemented when issuing laws, orders and policies.

An important question in administrative law is the extent to which the administrative courts should respect the separation of powers. A court which finds that a particular governmental decision is flawed can generally not substitute its own decision for that of the government. It is confined to exercising its judicial function and should leave the exercise of the executive function to the authority in question. Only if the authority has no discretion left in the case at hand and there can be no doubts as to what decision should be taken on the basis of law, may the court include this decision in its judgment.

It should be noted that governments have rights and obligations not just under administrative law but also under civil law. Civil law is concerned with the relationships between citizens (natural persons and legal entities) and may apply to governmental bodies and agencies when they engage in civil relationships in their capacity as legal entities. These civil relationships can be subject to review by the civil courts. In addition, the civil courts are competent to review governmental acts over which the administrative courts have no jurisdiction.

1.2 Importance of Administrative Law

The extent to which government regulates the conduct of its citizens has been increasing significantly since World War II. This can be seen as a result of the developing view of the role of government in an increasingly complex society. In addition to the traditional areas of government regulation, such as land planning, public order, and security and immigration, the Netherlands has seen vast increases in administrative legislation and in regulation relating to the environment, social security, health care, social housing and education, as well as in specific economic sectors such as the current and former utilities (referred to as economic administrative law).

Several sector-specific statutes have created a new type of executive governmental power. Such powers have led to significant volumes of regulatory decisions and case law by administrative courts in disputes between parties in, for instance, the telecommunications, cable TV and electricity sectors. In these instances, the authority that is charged with the supervision of the sector in question is empowered to resolve disputes between private parties in a civil relationship that is, in part,

1. In administrative litigation, the term 'appeal' is used for the proceedings before the administrative court of first instance (usually the District Court), as the proceedings concern an appeal from the relevant order of the administrative authority. The term 'higher appeal' is used for the proceedings before the competent administrative appellate court. By contrast, in civil litigation, the term 'appeal' is used only in connection with proceedings before a Court of Appeal against a judgment of a District Court.

determined by obligations imposed by administrative laws and regulations. For instance, telecommunications network providers are under a statutory obligation to interconnect their networks in order to allow their customers to communicate with the customers of other networks. Where the relevant supervisory authority resolves a dispute, this is effected by means of an administrative order that is itself subject to review. The administrative order may contain provisions which become part of the civil law relationship between the parties to the dispute, or even amend provisions earlier agreed upon, which are enforceable in civil courts or in arbitration. These dispute resolution powers have created a new dimension in administrative law and administrative litigation.

1.3 Sources of Administrative Law

One of the cornerstones of Dutch public law is that any government act that could adversely affect a citizen requires a statutory basis: the principle of legality (*legaliteitsbeginsel*). Therefore national legislation is the most important source of administrative law. Most of the principles of Dutch administrative law are now codified in the General Administrative Law Act (the 'GALA') (*Algemene wet bestuursrecht*) ('Awb'),[2] discussed in more detail below. The GALA also contains the procedural rules for administrative litigation in the District Courts. The procedural rules for litigation in the other administrative courts are set out in various other statutes, each governing one specific administrative court.

In addition to legislation by the Dutch Parliament and central government, case law is also an invaluable source of administrative law. As no single court in the Netherlands has responsibility for unifying the interpretation of the rules of administrative law, including the GALA (see § 4.1.4), academic articles and legal scholars' annotations of published case law are also an important source of law, in that they identify ambiguities and discrepancies in the case law of the courts. Such discrepancies can often be explained by the different positions of the citizens seeking legal protection of the various courts.[3] However, due to the unifying effect of the GALA, the differences between the administrative appellate courts are diminishing, firstly because the same procedural rules now apply to all administrative appellate courts, and secondly because the courts will often – but not always – take the same line with regard to case law insofar as it relates to aspects of general administrative law. Although Dutch judicial review is not based on a system of

2. *Algemene wet bestuursrecht*, Stb. 1992, 315, as amended.
3. The Central Appeals Council (*Centrale Raad van Beroep*) deals with individuals challenging their social security or employment position, the Trade and Industrial Affairs Appeal College (*College van beroep voor het bedrijfsleven*) often deals with sophisticated companies in regulated sectors, while the Litigation Division of the Council of State (*Afdeling bestuursrechtspraak van de Raad van State*) often rules on appeals in environmental and spatial planning matters initiated by collective organisations.

binding precedents, in practice a judgment from any administrative appellate court is quite influential and generally regarded as a precedent. This being said, since the primary purpose of administrative procedures is to provide legal protection for the individual, all courts remain free to deviate from previous judgments of the administrative appellate courts if deemed necessary.

Much of the regulation in the policy areas described above is nowadays mandated by European Union legislation[4] and influenced by the interpretation of case law of the European courts. All of these sources of law not only provide substantive rules, but also provide rules that have bearing on the organisation of the legal protection of citizens. The latter is also influenced to a significant extent by the case law of the European Court of Human Rights, which interprets the European Convention on Human Rights. Article 6 of the ECHR is particularly important as it guarantees citizens of Member States a right to a fair trial (see Chapter 1 § 3.4).

1.4 General Administrative Law Act

The central piece of legislation in Dutch administrative law is the GALA. It came into force on 1 January 1994 in order to streamline the countless specific provisions on administrative law (including administrative litigation) formerly laid down in national legislation. In addition, the GALA aimed to codify developments in case law relating to administrative litigation. While it does not legislate in relation to any specific area of government policy or regulation, it contains the legal framework for nearly all government acts, including standard procedures for review. The GALA describes standard procedures that are not mandatory, but prevail where no other procedures have been provided for in specific legislation.

In addition, the GALA prescribes general principles for proper administration applicable to all government acts (including those in civil law form). These principles include criteria for the delivery of decisions, the weighing of the interests of the parties involved (proportionality) and the reasoning behind orders.

The GALA is a modular piece of legislation, meaning that new sets of rules are added over time. In mid-2009 the fourth tranche of the GALA entered into force ('Awb-IV'). This amendment introduced some important changes to the rules on administrative supervision and enforcement (discussed in more detail in § 8.), including a set of rules governing administrative fines. In addition, Awb-IV introduced (i) rules on the collection by authorities of monetary claims and (ii) rules on

4. The most common legislative instrument of the EU is the directive, which compels Member States to transpose the rules in the directive in their national legislation. In this respect the EU legal framework differs from the concept of federal legislation in the US, which directly affects citizens in areas in which the US Constitution will allow it, but by means of a legal system separate from that of the states. Although proper transposition is obviously a challenge, once this is effected the common rules will have become an integral part of the national laws, independent of the continued existence of the underlying EU legislation.

the attribution of powers to subordinates. Both subjects are beyond the scope of this work. As of 1 July 2012, around 150 amendments had been made since the GALA came into force more than 18 years earlier, while around 30 amendments have been proposed up to the time of writing.

In 2010 the Crisis and Recovery Act (*Crisis- en herstelwet*) entered into force. The main goal of this act is to speed up legal procedures for certain types of large infrastructural projects such as construction of main roads and certain types of energy projects. For projects that fall within the scope of this act different procedural rules apply. Some of these rules are discussed in more detail below.

Currently, an important bill implementing changes in procedural administrative law is pending before Parliament.[5] The most important aims of this bill concern the implementation of: (i) substantive amendments to streamline administrative proceedings and to facilitate effective and definitive dispute resolution, and (ii) a limited reallocation of the jurisdiction between the three highest administrative courts. To achieve the first aim, the following amendments are suggested: (i) an extension of the possibilities to disregard certain flaws in a decision if no interested party will be adversely affected, (ii) the creation of a so-called 'grand chamber' (*Grote Kamer*) consisting of five judges from the different divisions of a high administrative court to which an issue can be referred for a unified ruling, (iii) the power for the president of a high administrative court to request an *amicus brief* (*conclusie*) from an independent member of its court in important cases, and (iv) the introduction of the relativity requirement. To achieve the second aim, the Dutch legislature has taken a more detailed look at the field of expertise of the three highest administrative courts and decided that certain matters should be reviewed by a different highest administrative court. Some of the proposed amendments will be discussed briefly below. At the time of writing of this book, it is unclear whether and if so, when, this bill will enter into force.

2. THE SYSTEM OF DUTCH ADMINISTRATIVE LITIGATION

2.1 Introduction

Unlike civil litigation, administrative litigation cannot be commenced on the claimant's initiative merely on the basis of an asserted cause of action. Rather, an action will, subject to certain exceptions, only be admissible if (i) an administrative authority (*bestuursorgaan*) publishes (ii) an order (*besluit*), by which (iii) the claimant is directly affected so that he qualifies as an interested party (*belanghebbende*). These three key concepts of administrative litigation are discussed below in §§ 2.2-2.4.

5. *Wetsvoorstel aanpassing bestuursprocesrecht*, TK 32 450, No. 2.

The standard procedure for the review of orders consists of three phases. In principle, first, the so-called administrative pre-proceedings must be completed; these are discussed in § 3. In most cases, these pre-proceedings are initiated by means of a notice of objection (*bezwaarschrift*) from the claimant addressed to the administrative authority responsible for the order concerned. The authority will then reconsider the order and conclude the pre-proceedings by issuing a reviewed order (*beslissing op bezwaar*). The second phase consists of a judicial review of the reviewed order by a District Court. The appeal to the District Court may be initiated by the original claimant (who is then referred to as the appellant) or by another interested party. The third and last phase of the standard procedure involves a higher appeal from the judgment of the District Court to one of the higher administrative courts. This higher appeal may be initiated either by the appellant, the administrative authority, or by an interested party. In practice, this entire review takes at least two and a half years to complete.

In comparison with civil proceedings, administrative review and judicial review are designed to function quite informally. There is no requirement to engage professional legal representation and the procedural rules are such that the authorities and courts will play an active role in the proceedings. For example, there are relatively few procedural formalities to be observed by the claimant or appellant and, if they are not adhered to, the parties will be so notified and given an opportunity to correct this. Even if a notice is filed with the wrong authority or court, there is an obligation by that authority or administrative court to forward it to the correct one. The administrative authority or court will arrange for all relevant documents to be made available. In addition, it must actively investigate whether other parties should be invited to become involved in the case. Courts primarily investigate the claims of the appellant, but must also establish whether certain procedural formalities have been met (such as questions of jurisdiction (*bevoegdheidsvragen*) and admissibility issues (*ontvankelijkheidsvragen*)), even if the appellant does not raise this.

The original intention of the GALA, that citizens could conduct these proceedings without professional representation, may hold true in cases where the order at hand is sufficiently simple. However, the substantive rules in many areas of administrative practice, as well as the procedural rules, are, in practice, quite complex. Therefore, professional legal representation is often a practical necessity for cases at court level.

2.2 Admissibility (1): Order

An order is defined in the GALA as: 'a written ruling of an administrative authority constituting a public law deed'.[6] Examples include permits[7] for construction or environmental activities (*omgevingsvergunning voor bouwactiviteiten of milieuactiviteiten*), grants of subsidies, and orders designating no-parking zones.

The definition in the GALA makes clear that three characteristics distinguish an order from other administrative actions: an order (i) is in writing, (ii) intends to establish a certain legal consequence (*rechtshandeling*), and (iii) is based on a provision in public law (*publiekrechtelijk*). These three elements are discussed below. Moreover, an order should be issued by an administrative authority; this requirement is discussed in § 2.3.

First, only a written ruling constitutes an order. Oral rulings, despite their public nature, do not qualify as orders as defined in the GALA. For instance, although a civil servant charged with the enforcement of environmental permits may orally order certain systems to be turned off in order to facilitate inspection of the premises, such a ruling does not constitute an order under the GALA. Only if and when an oral ruling has been confirmed in writing can it (provided the other requirements have been met) be subject to administrative and judicial review.

Secondly, an order must aim to establish a legal consequence by granting, imposing or changing legal rights or obligations. In other words, an order creates, redefines or cancels a legal relationship. For instance, written information published by an administrative authority explaining powers under certain legislation does not constitute an order.

Thirdly, the phrase 'based on a provision in public law' implies that the administrative authority can only issue an order if exercising a power based on a particular constitutional or statutory provision. An act that is in the nature of private law, including one that can also be used by private parties, is not an order. For instance, the written decision by a city council to refuse, in violation of an earlier promise, to sell a particular piece of land, is not derived from a power attributed to the council by statute and therefore does not qualify as an order.

However, the courts have in certain circumstances accepted that, even where one of these requirements is not met, a written decision by an administrative authority may nevertheless constitute an order. A decision by an administrative authority providing financial compensation for damage caused by the exercise of a statutory power by that authority, is deemed to be an order under the GALA even though there is no statutory basis for the granting of such compensation. Similarly, a written confirmation by the competent authority that it will not exercise its powers

6. Art. 1:3(1) Awb.
7. These permits are issued under the Environmental Permitting General Provisions Act (*Wet algemene bepalingen omgevingsrecht*).

to address an illegal situation as long as certain conditions are met (see § 8.8), is deemed to be an order, despite the fact that there is no direct statutory basis for it.

As a result of such lenient interpretations of the law, legal protection (in the form of administrative review and subsequent judicial review by administrative courts) is available in these instances. In fact, the courts have welcomed such interpretations as it means that the administrative courts, with their familiarity with the framework of the exercise of executive powers, have jurisdiction rather than the civil courts.

In order to provide adequate legal protection, the review procedures that can be commenced against an order can also be used in response to an express refusal to issue an order or in response to the competent authority's failure to issue an order upon a petition.[8] Such a failure is often referred to as a fictitious refusal of an order. Hence, these refusals can be challenged, despite the fact that they are not actual orders.

2.3 Admissibility (2): Administrative Authority

Only orders issued by an administrative authority qualify as 'orders' under the GALA. The GALA defines an administrative authority as '(a) an organ of a legal entity which has been established under public law, or (b) any other person or body which is invested with any public powers'.

Part (a) of the definition in the GALA includes the traditional government bodies at the central, provincial and local government levels (such as the Ministers and State Secretaries (Under-Ministers), the Provincial and Local Councils, the Provincial Executive Board, the Court of Mayor and Aldermen and the Mayor individually), as well as other government agencies. These include a large number of independent agencies charged with specific administrative duties, usually involving the supervision of the exercise of executive functions and known under Dutch law as autonomous administrative authorities (*zelfstandige bestuursorganen*), such as the Netherlands Competition Authority (*Nederlandse Mededingingsautoriteit*). It should be noted that the administrative authority is the organ designated in the relevant statute, which is often not the legal entity of which it forms part (e.g. the Mayor, not the Municipality). While the authority will be the party in administrative litigation, the entity can become a party in civil litigation.

In addition to the legal entities established under public law, private law entities and natural persons can also be invested with public powers. For instance, the Dutch Central Bank (*De Nederlandsche Bank N.V.*) has the legal form of a public limited liability company, while the Netherlands Authority for the Finan-

8. Art. 6:2 Awb. According to Art. 4:13 Awb, the reasonable term for issuing the order will be deemed to have expired if the authority has not notified the petitioner within eight weeks after receipt of the petition of the reasonable term within which the order will be issued.

cial Markets (*Stichting Autoriteit Financiële Markten*) is a foundation. As is the case with all private law entities, these entities are subject to the general rules of corporate law, in addition to the special public law rules contained in the relevant statutes and regulations. The owner of an automobile repair shop who is licensed to perform periodic safety inspections is vested with the public power to issue the relevant official certificates. Natural persons and private law entities are considered administrative authorities when exercising their powers under public law.

Several public bodies are expressly exempted from the definition of 'administrative authority' in the GALA. They include, because of their special constitutional tasks, the legislative branch of central government, both chambers of Parliament, the Council of State (*Raad van State*) and the judiciary. This means that their decisions do not qualify as orders that can be subjected to judicial review by the administrative courts.

2.4 Admissibility (3): Interested Party

In order to be able to obtain a review of an order issued by an administrative authority, the claimant must qualify as an interested party, unless specific administrative legislation opens up the review to the public at large.[9] In addition to natural persons and legal entities, a group without separate legal personality can also qualify as an interested party, as well as an administrative authority, for instance in an appeal against an order issued by it. The GALA defines an interested party as: 'he whose interest is directly affected by an order'.[10] Therefore, third parties who are not the addressees of an order can be interested parties if they are directly affected by the order (*derdebelanghebbenden*).

Case law has established that a party can only be considered an interested party if it (i) has an individual and personal interest that is (ii) directly affected by the order involved and that is (iii) objectively determinable, meaning that a real, present interest must be identifiable, excluding future or imaginary interests. The purpose of these qualifications is to strike a balance between providing adequate legal protection and having a workable and acceptable limitation of the classes of parties who are entitled to seek review of a particular order.

9. This general right of action is sometimes referred to by the term *actio popularis*. Review of a decision for the public at large is generally limited to the pre-proceedings. For example any party can submit a view against a draft-decision on a request for a permit for environmental activities (*omgevingsvergunning voor milieuactiviteiten*).
10. Art. 1:2(1) Awb.

2.5 No Review of Legislation or of Internally Binding Policy Rules

Not all orders can be challenged. Firstly, orders containing generally binding regulations (*algemeen verbindende voorschriften*) are not subject to review.[11] These include Acts of Parliament (statutes), legislation by local governments and delegated rulemaking. However, review can be sought against an order containing an individual decision that is based on the legislation in question, binding a specific (group of) citizen(s) in a particular situation. In such a case, it is the application of the legislation that is subject to review, rather than the legislation itself: the claimant can ask the court to hold that, due to the alleged illegality of the legislation in question, it cannot be applied in the case at hand.

It should be noted that the Dutch Constitution forbids the courts from assessing whether a statute is compliant with the Dutch Constitution.[12] Therefore, the courts can only assess the legality of a statute if its application is challenged on the basis of international law. This includes Treaties or legal instruments binding under them (such as EU regulations and other provisions with direct effect) or rules promulgated in international case law. For instance, the European Convention on Human Rights and the case law of the European Court of Human Rights have proven to be formidable weapons in the hands of the courts against unlawful legislation. Specifically, this case law has had a very significant impact on the Dutch rules for judicial review.

Secondly, it is not possible to seek review of the internally binding policy rules of an administrative authority (*beleidsregels*).[13] However, the application of the policy can be subject to review if that application is in the context of an order binding a specific (group of) citizen(s) in a particular situation. Again, the appellant can ask a court to find that an unlawful internally binding policy rule is not applicable in the case at hand.

The restrictions mentioned above imply that, under Dutch administrative law, the review of orders is possible insofar as these orders contain decisions – or rejections or refusals to give decisions – binding a specific (group of) citizen(s) in particular situations. In addition, 'other' general orders, not constituting legislation or internally binding policy rules, such as plans of a binding nature, can also be challenged.

11. Art. 8:2(a) Awb.
12. Art. 120 Constitution. Local legislation and delegated rulemaking do not fall within this prohibition, so their unconstitutionality can be assessed by the courts.
13. Art. 8:2(a) Awb.

2.6 Civil Law Remedies Available

If a particular administrative decision does not qualify as an order and cannot be subject to review by the administrative courts, the claimant may initiate a civil action against the administrative authority in question (or, if the administrative authority is not an independent legal entity, against the legal entity of which the administrative authority is part; see § 2.3). Such civil action will often be based in tort. Whether such a civil action is capable of producing the desired result is of course a different matter. The most important procedural rules concerning review of an administrative act by the civil courts are discussed in § 6.

3. ADMINISTRATIVE REVIEW AND OTHER PRE-PROCEEDINGS

3.1 Three Types of Pre-proceedings at Government Level

As mentioned above, the administrative courts can generally only review an administrative order on appeal after the appellant has: (i) requested the administrative authority which issued the order to review and reconsider its order on the basis of the objections which the appellant has raised (as claimant); and (ii) obtained a decision in respect of its objections. This decision is referred to as the reviewed order (*beslissing op bezwaar*), even if the objections are held to be unfounded and the original order remains unchanged. The administrative courts will always review the reviewed order and not the initial one.

These so-called objection proceedings (*bezwaarschriftprocedure*), also referred to as administrative review, are by far the most important category of pre-proceedings (*bestuurlijke voorprocedures*) at the government level. They serve different purposes. For the administrative authority, the objection proceedings provide an opportunity to correct any mistakes and to reconsider the order in the face of the claimant's specific objections. For the administrative courts, they reduce the caseload and avoid appeals in matters that can easily be resolved at the administrative level. For the claimant, objection proceedings can provide informal, often simple and low-cost redress (see § 3.2), although there is of course the potential risk that the authority may not be willing to reconsider its original decision with an open mind. Many orders are issued by means of largely automated processes, which offer relatively little opportunity to exchange arguments and case-specific information. In these instances, the objection proceedings are a useful first step on the way to obtaining legal protection against government orders. Where the original order was prepared on the basis of an elaborate exchange of arguments and information, objection proceedings may be less useful. In such cases, the claimant can request the authority to forward his notice of objection to the competent administrative court for a so-called direct appeal (*rechtstreeks beroep*). The objection proceedings will be discussed in § 3.2, while the direct appeal is described in 4.1.3.

The second type of pre-proceedings at government level is the so-called administrative appeal (*administratief beroep*), another form of review of administrative orders at government level. Under this procedure, an authority other than the one that issued the contested order conducts the review. This can either be another body of the same government entity (such as the City council hearing an administrative appeal against an order of the Mayor), or a body of another entity (such as the Provincial Board hearing the administrative appeal against an order of the City council). The administrative appeal, which is not very common, can only be used if prescribed by specific administrative legislation. Its purposes are largely the same as those for objection proceedings, although it also contains an element of administrative supervision (*bestuurlijk toezicht op de naleving*). The procedure for administrative appeals is very similar to that for objection proceedings, and so it is not discussed separately below.

The third type of pre-proceedings at government level does not provide for review of an administrative order, but rather for a public procedure for the careful preparation of the order itself. This so-called public preparatory procedure (*uniforme openbare voorbereidingsprocedure*) is described in § 3.3.

3.2 Objection Proceedings

3.2.1 General

If an interested party wishes to challenge an order, it must as a general rule initiate objection proceedings by filing a notice of objection with the administrative authority which issued the order. To facilitate the legal protection of citizens each order must mention (in a so-called legal protection clause (*rechtsmiddelenclausule*)) who can file objections or an appeal against the order, within what period and with which authority or court. In case the Crisis and Recovery Act is applicable to a certain order, this should be included in the legal protection clause. This is important given the procedural consequences of application of the Crisis and Recovery Act.[14] However, the absence of such a clause does not compromise the legal effect of the order, nor does it in itself provide an excuse for failure to file the objections or appeal within the prescribed time scale (see § 3.2.4).

---

14. For example: in case the Crisis and Recovery Act applies, a so-called pro forma appeal is not allowed. An appeal needs to be substantiated within the regular six-weeks appeal period. However, if an administrative authority or court of first instance fails to state that the Crisis and Recovery Act is applicable, a party that submits a pro forma appeal or pro forma higher appeal will in principle be excused for exceeding the term to substantiate the grounds of (higher) appeal. (Council of State, 23 Feb. 2011, AB 2011, 79, LJN: BP5483).

There are a number of exceptions to the general rule that administrative review must take place before judicial review is possible. First, this requirement does not apply where the order in question (i) has been issued following a public preparatory procedure, or (ii) remains subject to approval or administrative appeal, or (iii) contains the approval of another order or the refusal of such an order.[15] Similarly, this requirement may be excluded (iv) by a specific statutory provision which occurs where the legislature wishes to shorten the period during which a particular order remains subject to challenge. Furthermore, parties can decide to skip the administrative review and file a direct appeal (direct appeal is discussed in more detail in § 4.1.3.).

3.2.2 Jurisdiction

Objection proceedings are initiated by filing a notice of objection with the administrative authority that issued the order. As mentioned above, the authority is the specific organ designated in the relevant statute and mentioned in the order, which is usually not the legal entity of which this organ forms part. For instance, an order may be issued by the Minister as the authority, being an organ of the legal entity the State of the Netherlands. The administrative authority, not the legal entity, has the power to decide on the admissibility of the notice and on the validity of the objection, and to review the contested order.

If a notice of objection has been sent to the wrong authority, this authority is obliged to forward it to the appropriate authority after having marked it with the date of receipt. This day will generally be deemed to be the date of receipt for determining whether the notice was filed within the limitation period.

3.2.3. Notice of Objection

A notice of objection should be in writing and meet certain elementary requirements of form. It should contain at least (i) the name, address and signature of the claimant, (ii) the date, (iii) a description of the disputed order, and (iv) the grounds for challenging the order. In the event that one or more of these requirements are not met, the administrative authority is obliged to grant the claimant a grace period in which the deficiency can be remedied. Legal practitioners often file a notice of objection which does not contain the grounds for challenging the order (a so-called pro forma notice of objection; *pro forma bezwaarschrift*) in order to prevent the notice being time-barred. Upon receipt of the pro forma notice of objection, the authority will grant an additional period (usually four weeks) for submitting a supplemental notice (*aanvullend bezwaarschrift*) containing a full description of

---

15. Art. 7:1(1) Awb.

the grounds for the objection. A notice of objection may be filed electronically where the authority has officially introduced electronic communications in relation to citizens.[16]

It should be noted that, despite the timely filing of a notice of objection, the order will remain in full force and effect, unless the relevant legislation or the order itself provide otherwise. To obtain a suspension of the order, preliminary relief has to be requested from the administrative courts (see § 5).

3.2.4 Time Allowed for Filing a Notice of Objection

Unless a specific statute provides otherwise, a notice of objection must be filed within six weeks from the day following the day of receipt of notification of the order.[17] The GALA contains specific rules for the notification of orders, depending on the type of order involved. Orders containing a decision that is binding on a specific citizen or group of citizens in a particular situation usually have to be notified to the relevant citizen(s) by post. In some cases, either in addition to or instead of notification by post, orders must be published in a free local newspaper and/or in the Official State Gazette (*Staatscourant*).

When a notice of objection is filed by means of the postal services of the incumbent postal operator PostNL, the notice is considered timely if it has been submitted to PostNL's postal services before the end of the six-week period and has been received by the administrative authority within a further week. If the notice is filed by other means, such as by a competing postal operator, by courier or by fax, the administrative authority must receive it before the end of the six-week period.[18]

It should be noted that administrative authorities and the courts are very strict in verifying the timeliness of notices. Even the slightest violation of the deadline for filing a notice invariably leads to its inadmissibility, unless the claimant or appellant cannot reasonably be held at fault,[19] e.g. if he was not informed about a particular order because it was sent by post to the addressee of the order only, and was not published elsewhere.[20]

---

16. As from 1 July 2004 the GALA has been amended by the Electronic Administrative Communications Act (*Wet elektronisch bestuurlijk verkeer*), Stb. 2004, 214. This Act introduced Articles 2:13 through 2:17, which provide for the possibility of electronic communications between citizens and authorities. Similarly, a citizen who has shown that he can be reached by electronic means may be addressed in that way by the authorities.
17. Art. 6:7 Awb.
18. Art. 6:9 Awb.
19. Art. 6:11 Awb.
20. Council of State (*Afdeling bestuursrechtspraak van de Raad van State*) 16 May 2000, AB 2000, 325, LJN: AA9532.

When the notice of objection relates to an express refusal or failure by an administrative authority to issue an order, no time limit applies. In such cases, a notice of objection will only be inadmissible if it is filed unreasonably late.[21]

3.2.5 The Proceedings

The administrative authority may appoint an advisory committee[22] to conduct the objection proceedings and to advise the authority on the validity of the objection and on the need to amend or even withdraw the original order in the reviewed order. This committee, usually referred to as the advisory committee for objection proceedings (*bezwaarschriftencommissie*), may consist of civil servants from the administrative authority itself, or of persons from outside the government, such as private legal practitioners, legal scholars or judges. Ultimately, the authority itself will remain responsible for the review of the order.

The central element of the objection proceedings is the obligation for the authority (save the exceptions described below) to provide interested parties, including the claimant, with an opportunity to be heard before it accepts or rejects the objections and issues the reviewed order.[23] The authority must actively notify the claimant and any other party that was involved in the preparation of the original order of this opportunity. There are only four situations in which a hearing is not required, namely where: (i) the notice of objection is manifestly inadmissible, (ii) the objection is manifestly unfounded, (iii) the interested parties have stated that they do not wish to exercise their right to be heard, or (iv) the administrative authority decides that the objection is valid in its entirety and therefore issues a reviewed order which fully satisfies the objection, without prejudicing the interests of other interested parties.[24] If the administrative authority has decided not to conduct a hearing, it should explain the reasons in the reviewed order.[25]

Generally, the hearing is public and conducted in the presence of all interested parties. If an advisory committee has been established, the administrative authority will also be represented at the committee's hearings. If no advisory committee is established, the hearing can be conducted by the authority itself, by one or more of its members or, as is more customary, by three of its civil servants. If three civil servants conduct the hearing, it is a requirement that a majority of them were not involved in the preparation of the original order. A record must be kept of the hearing.[26]

---

21. Art. 6:12 Awb.
22. Art. 7:13 Awb.
23. Art. 7:16 Awb.
24. Art. 7:3 Awb.
25. Art. 7:12 Awb.
26. Art. 7:7 Awb.

Unless a specific statute provides otherwise, the authority can decide whether the hearing will be open to the public.[27] An interested party can ask to be heard separately if a joint hearing would hinder the proper conduct of the proceedings or if he intends to state facts or address circumstances which need to remain confidential for reasons of secrecy.

The authority must make the objections of the claimant and all other documents in its file available to all who qualify as interested parties, except to the extent that all interested parties agree to the contrary or if confidentiality is required for reasons of secrecy. All interested parties can submit additional documents, including written arguments in support of or in opposition to the objections, up to ten days prior to the hearing.[28] There is a trend in case law that arguments and evidence that are available at the time of the pre-proceedings at government level should be submitted in a timely manner and may not be accepted if they are submitted for the first time in the appeal proceedings before the administrative court.

In practice, a party that submits documents and claims that these contain confidential information will also be allowed the opportunity to produce an amended public version to be made available to the other interested parties, provided the authority agrees with the claim of confidentiality.

3.2.6 Reviewed Order

If the notice of objection is admissible, the disputed order will be reviewed on the basis of all the objections that have been put forward.[29] This review involves a full re-assessment of all relevant facts and issues. In other words, the authority must reconsider its decision not only from the point of view of its legality, but also from the point of view of its suitability and its political desirability, all based on the situation with regard to both facts and law as at the date of the reviewed order (*ex nunc*).

Insofar as the administrative review provides grounds for doing so, the authority will amend or revoke the disputed order and, if necessary, issue a new order (the reviewed order) replacing the initial one.[30] As with any order, the reviewed order must be based on proper reasoning, which must be set out in the order itself. Obviously, the reviewed order can incorporate by reference reasoning that is set out in other decisions relevant to the case, such as official policy documents and the original order. It is the reviewed order that will be scrutinised in any appeal. To facilitate legal protection the reviewed order must mention that interested parties

27. Arts 7:5(2) and 7:6(2) Awb.
28. Art. 7:4 Awb.
29. Art. 7:11 Awb.
30. The authority's decision on the objections is referred to as the reviewed order, even if it merely dismisses the objections as unfounded.

can file an appeal, as well as identify the competent court and the applicable time limit.

The authority must issue the reviewed order within six weeks of receipt of the notice of objection, or within twelve weeks if an advisory committee has been appointed.[31] However, there are no legal consequences in the event that this time limit is not met, other than the fact that this will constitute a fictitious refusal to issue the reviewed order. Just as a notice of objection can be filed against a fictitious refusal to issue an original order (see § 2.2), an appeal to the competent administrative court can be lodged against a fictitious refusal to issue a reviewed order. The administrative authority can expressly defer the reviewed order for six weeks or for a longer period, as long as the claimant(s) involved agree(s) and the interests of other interested parties are not prejudiced by the deferral.

The reviewed order must be notified by sending or handing it to the persons to whom it is addressed (which may be an interested party other than the claimant).[32] If the original order was not addressed to the interested parties, but was published in a free local newspaper or the Official State Gazette, the reviewed order must be published in the same way. Otherwise, all interested parties who have lodged a notice of objection must receive a copy of the reviewed order.

3.2.7 Costs

There is no government charge for the objection proceedings. Interested parties are entitled to compensation from the administrative authority for the costs incurred during the pre-proceedings only if, upon review, the original order is revoked as unlawful. If compensation is granted (which rarely happens in practice), this will be effected as part of the reviewed order. The administrative authority can only award a fixed amount of compensation for the costs of legal assistance, which is usually insufficient to cover the costs that were actually incurred.

3.3 Public Preparatory Procedure

The public preparatory procedure sets out the procedure to be followed when preparing orders that have an effect on a large group of citizens or on a number of citizens who are not all known to the authority. It therefore primarily creates the basis for careful decision making in these instances.[33] Orders that were prepared on

31. Art. 7:10 Awb.
32. Art. 7:12 Awb.
33. Although this book does not cover the general standards for government decision making, the public preparatory procedure is discussed here because it is a type of pre-proceedings at the government level and, as such, has bearing on the path of legal protection against government orders that ends in the administrative courts (or beyond, if human rights claims are brought before the European Court of Human Rights).

the basis of the public preparatory procedure can be appealed to the competent administrative court directly. The objection proceedings described above are neither required nor available in those cases.

The public preparatory procedure, inserted into the GALA in mid-2005,[34] is applicable to the preparation of a particular order if (i) the relevant statute so requires or (ii) the competent authority decides to use it. The procedure requires the authority to make available for public inspection a draft of its order and all documents relating thereto. If not published on the authority's website, copies will be made available at cost. The availability must be published and notified to interested parties to whom the order will be addressed, including the party at whose request the order will be issued (if any).

Interested parties may present comments on the proposed order, either in writing (within six weeks of publication, unless the relevant statute provides otherwise) or during a hearing, of which a record will be made. The relevant statute can require that others should also be offered an opportunity to present comments. Where the public preparatory procedure is used to prepare an order which will be issued in response to a petition, the petitioner may be granted an opportunity to respond to the comments presented. In such case the order must be issued within six months after receipt of the petition, except in very complex or contested cases, where this term can be extended.

4. JUDICIAL REVIEW BY THE ADMINISTRATIVE COURTS: APPEAL AND HIGHER APPEAL

4.1 Jurisdiction

4.1.1 General

If an interested party does not agree with the outcome of objection proceedings or administrative appeal, or with the original order where no objection proceedings were available, judicial review can be sought by bringing an appeal before a court. Appeals at first instance are generally adjudicated by the administrative divisions of one of the District Courts,[35] although other courts have first instance jurisdiction in specific matters. In other matters, such other courts also have jurisdiction to hear appeals from judgments of the administrative divisions of the District Courts. Such

34. Division 3.4 Awb.
35. Art. 43 RO.

appeals are referred to as higher appeals as the term 'appeal' is reserved for appeals to the District Courts against orders from the administrative authority.[36]

An administrative court of first instance can generally only admit an appeal if the appeal is directed against an order, not against other types of administrative decision (see § 2.2). Moreover, for certain types of orders, appeal is expressly excluded;[37] those orders cannot be contested before an administrative court. They include legislation and internally binding policy rules (see § 2.5), orders in preparation of civil law acts, and numerous orders pursuant to legislation specified in a list annexed to the GALA. Some of these orders can be subjected to judicial review by administrative courts indirectly, e.g. in the context of an appeal against the application of a legislative order.

Jurisdiction of the administrative courts sometimes depends on the geographical location of the parties and sometimes on the subject matter of the contested order, i.e. the legislation on which that order is based. This is, in part, due to the fact that the transition from a system with specialised courts for different types of orders to one integrated system of general courts has not (yet) been fully completed.

4.1.2 Subject Matter Jurisdiction and Territorial Jurisdiction at First Instance

Absent any special rules on subject matter jurisdiction, the District Courts are competent to hear appeals against an order issued by an administrative authority. If an appeal is lodged against an order given by a local government,[38] the appeal must be heard by the District Court of the district of the seat of the administrative authority which issued the contested order. If an appeal is lodged against an order of another administrative authority, the appeal will generally be heard by the District Court within whose area of authority the appellant has his residence. If the appellant is not a resident of the Netherlands, then jurisdiction lies with the District Court within whose area of authority the administrative authority resides.

In some laws, specific rules in relation to subject matter jurisdiction have been created in order to allow certain courts to build up and maintain a level of expertise in the area in question. For instance, most of the orders made pursuant to the Financial Supervision Act (*Wet op het financieel toezicht*), the Competition Act (*Mededingingswet*), the Postal Services Act (*Postwet*) and the Telecommunications Act (*Telecommunicatiewet*), can only be reviewed by the District Court of Rotterdam. Some legislation vests jurisdiction at first and last instance in courts that

---

36. Although the subject of judicial review at first instance is generally the 'reviewed order', which is issued after the administrative review is completed, this chapter will refer simply to judicial review of the 'order'.
37. Arts 8:2-8:6 Awb.
38. For this purpose, the term 'local government' includes province, municipality, water control board or a public corporation or joint authority established under the Act on Communal Arrangements (*Wet gemeenschappelijke regelingen*), Stb. 1991, 242, as amended.

are primarily engaged in hearing appeal cases (see § 4.1.4). For example, District Courts generally have no jurisdiction over a permit issued under the Nature Protection Act 1998.[39] Therefore, the appeal has to be brought directly before the Litigation Division of the Council of State (*Afdeling bestuursrechtspraak van de Raad van State*, 'ABRvS'). Similarly, the Telecommunications Act has abolished both objection proceedings and appeals to the District Court for certain matters. In these matters, an order of the Board of the Independent Post and Telecommunications Authority (*Onafhankelijke Post en Telecommunicatie Autoriteit*) ('OPTA') can only be challenged by means of an appeal directly to the Trade and Industrial Affairs Appeal College (*College van Beroep voor het bedrijfsleven*).

4.1.3 Direct Appeal

Normally an appeal will be admissible only if pre-proceedings at government level have been completed. Objection proceedings generally constitute an easily accessible and relatively low-cost procedure that enables claimants to seek redress against orders. Nevertheless, in certain cases, e.g. when it is clear that the administrative authority will not substantially revise its order in objection proceedings, instituting such proceedings would create an unwanted delay, both for the claimant and the administrative authority involved. The Act on Direct Appeal (*Wet rechtstreeks beroep*),[40] incorporated in the GALA,[41] allows a claimant to request the administrative authority to decide that the case is suitable for direct appeal. If the administrative authority so decides, it will send the notice of objection to the competent court. The court may nevertheless instruct the administrative authority to apply the standard procedure for administrative review and to conduct objection proceedings at the government level, if it rules that the case is unsuitable for direct appeal. Direct appeal is sometimes precluded. If the request concerns a notice of objection which is directed at an unwritten (fictitious) refusal to issue an order on time, direct appeal is deemed unsuitable because the authority will not have included grounds for its refusal. In addition, direct appeal is impossible if another party has also filed a notice of objection against the same order without a request for direct appeal (unless that notice of objection is manifestly inadmissible), because it is impossible to conduct objection proceedings and appeal proceedings in relation to the same order simultaneously.

39. Art. 39 *Natuurbeschermingswet 1998* Stb. 1998, 403, as amended.
40. *Wet rechtstreeks beroep*, Stb. 2004, 220.
41. Art. 7:1a Awb.

4.1.4 Appellate Jurisdiction

An appeal from a judgment of the administrative division of a District Court (referred to as higher appeal) can be lodged in one of five types of appellate courts, depending on the nature of the order: (i) the Central Appeals Council (*Centrale Raad van Beroep*), which is based in Utrecht, deals with social security matters and litigation involving civil servants' employment relationships with the government (such as disputes concerning appointment, dismissal and remuneration). The Appeals Act (*Beroepswet*)[42] sets out the procedural rules of the Central Appeals Council and the exact scope of its jurisdiction; (ii) the Trade and Industrial Affairs Appeal College, based in The Hague, rules on socio-economic matters, such as orders of the Dutch Competition Authority and of numerous sector-specific regulators. The scope of its jurisdiction and the relevant procedural rules are set out in the Administrative Litigation for Trade Organisations Act (*Wet bestuursrechtspraak bedrijfsorganisatie*, 'Wbbo');[43] (iii) the Leeuwarden Court of Appeal hears higher appeals from judgments of the cantonal divisions of the District Courts concerning orders for traffic violations;[44] (iv) all ordinary Courts of Appeal (see Chapter 1 § 3.1.2) hear appeals from District Court judgments in tax matters. Judgments of the Courts of Appeal can be appealed to the Supreme Court of the Netherlands (see Chapter 1 § 3.1.3); and (v) in all other disputes, the ABRvS is the competent appellate court.[45] It deals mainly with appeal cases based on environmental law, land planning law and immigration law.

The position of the Council of State in Dutch constitutional law is subject to debate. The fact that the Legislative Division of the Council of State advises the central government on bills, while the Litigation Division of the same Council functions as the appellate court in certain administrative matters, does not seem to be entirely in line with standards set by international law guaranteeing independent administration of justice, such as those laid down in Article 6 of the ECHR. A bill amending the relevant legislation was introduced in 2006 and entered into force in September 2010.[46] However, this bill does not seem to remove the existing doubts about the non-compliance with Article 6 of the ECHR.

The procedural rules that govern appeals to the District Court generally also apply to appeals made to any of these appellate courts.[47] The remainder of this

42. Arts 17 and 18 *Beroepswet*, Stb. 1993, 650 and 690, as amended.
43. Arts 18, 19, 20 and 22 *Wet bestuursrechtspraak bedrijfsorganisatie*, Stb. 1993, 416, as amended.
44. Act on the Administrative enforcement of traffic regulations (*Wet Administratiefrechtelijke Handhaving Verkeersvoorschriften*), Stb. 1997, 275.
45. Arts 46, 47 and 49 Council of State Act (*Wet op de Raad van State,* 'WRvSt'), Stb. 1962, 88, as amended.
46. The Act on the restructuring of the Council of State (*Wet van 22 april 2010 tot wijziging van de Wet op de Raad van State in verband met de herstructurering van de Raad van State*), Stb 2010, 175.
47. The *Beroepswet*, the Wbbo and the WRvSt all refer to Chapter 8 of the GALA.

section will therefore be applicable to the appellate practice in the higher administrative courts as well, except to the extent expressly stated otherwise.

4.2 Parties

In general, an appellant must qualify as an interested party in relation to the reviewed order for his appeal to be admissible (see § 2.4). A party can qualify as such even if he was not a party to the objection proceedings: for example, the licensee who did not become involved as a party in objection proceedings initiated against the order containing his licence, can appeal the reviewed order in the event that it is less favourable than the original one. A licensee will of course always be admitted as an interested third party in an appeal lodged against his licence by someone else.

In addition to qualifying as an interested party, the appellant must also have a so-called procedural interest (*procesbelang*): the appeal should be capable of achieving the result that the appellant wants to achieve. For instance, if, pending the appeal, the authority amends its order fully in conformity with the grounds of appeal, there is in principle no more procedural interest.

The administrative authority whose order is being attacked on appeal will be invited to become involved as a party in the proceedings as the respondent. If the competent District Court finds in favour of the appellant, the authority can lodge a higher appeal against the District Court's judgment and become the appellant in the higher appeal. If the authority is not itself a legal entity, but rather the organ of a particular legal entity so designated in the statute on which the order is based (see § 2.3), the organ is the respondent.

Third parties may join appeal and higher appeal proceedings if they qualify as interested third parties in relation to the contested order but have not filed their own appeal (or higher appeal). If not already invited by the court, they may request the court in writing to be admitted at any stage of the proceedings until the end of the investigations (usually the end of the hearing; see § 4.6.4).[48]

4.3 Representation

Dutch administrative legislation provides that all parties are allowed to represent themselves. This applies not only to pre-proceedings at the administrative level, but also to appeals and higher appeals in the administrative courts. Only in proceedings before the Supreme Court is representation by an attorney compulsory. Obviously, any party admitted to administrative review or to litigation can choose to call on an attorney for representation. Others can also act as the legal representative of a party in administrative litigation, provided they have a written power-of-attorney

48. Art. 8:26 Awb.

evidencing their representative capacity for the matter at hand. Administrative authorities are often represented by their civil servants, usually including a member of their legal staff. As both substantive and procedural rules have become increasingly complex, representation by legal professionals is advisable in many matters. Subsidised legal aid is available for individuals with personal income below a certain threshold.

4.4 Filing the Appeal

Appeal proceedings are commenced by the timely filing of a notice of appeal. The basic requirements of form for lodging an appeal are similar to the requirements for lodging a notice of objection (see § 3.2.3), as are the time periods for the filing (see § 3.2.4). The notice of appeal should be sent directly to the competent court; if it is sent to another court or authority, the recipient must forward the notice to the competent court, marked with the date of receipt.

Unlike objection proceedings, a fee is due for appeal proceedings. If payment is not arranged at the time of filing,[49] the court will send the appellant an invoice. It is essential that this fee be paid on time, as failure to do so will lead to the inadmissibility of the appeal.

4.5 Scope of the Appeal

In the Dutch administrative law system, judicial review is primarily viewed as a means of protecting the individual rights of citizens. In line with this purpose, a number of limitations exist in the scope of the appeal (and the higher appeal) to the courts.

First, the scope of the appeal is generally limited by the fact that the appeal concerns only the order against which it is directed. An exception to this limitation is the opportunity to claim damages if the appeal proves to be successful (see § 4.8.3).

Secondly, the scope of the appeal is generally limited to the grounds set out by the appellant: the court cannot rule on the basis of other grounds (*ultra petita*). The only exception is that the court will investigate on its own initiative (*ex officio*) the so-called issues of public order (*kwesties van openbare orde*). These include at least the issues concerning jurisdiction and admissibility at both the government level and the court level. While the court cannot add new grounds of appeal it must, in order to assist the appellant, supplement the legal basis of the grounds brought forward by the appellant, to the extent necessary to evaluate the grounds of appeal

49. Many law firms have a current account agreement with the various courts, so that a notice of appeal may contain a request to debit the fee from this account.

fully. Moreover, unlike in civil proceedings, the court can on its own initiative supplement the facts stated by the parties.[50]

Thirdly, a party cannot lodge an admissible appeal insofar as it may reasonably be considered at fault for not coming forward in the pre-proceedings at government level.[51] If it could have attacked the order or a particular part of it in the pre-proceedings at government level,[52] but did not do so without proper justification, the appeal will not be admitted. This rule does not require that all grounds of appeal are brought forward in the pre-proceedings, but only that all parts of the original order against which the appeal is directed, were also attacked in the pre-proceedings (except if there was a valid reason for not doing so). This raises the question of what does and does not constitute a 'part' of an order. In environmental matters, the Council of State used to decide that the provisions concerning noise reduction and those concerning soil protection constitute two different parts if contained in one order. If, for example, the provisions concerning noise reduction were not attacked in the pre-proceedings, the Council of State would decide that these provisions could, in principle, not be attacked in the appeal proceedings. In a recent ruling the Council of State explicitly reversed the former case law and decided that with regard to permits issued under the Environmental Permitting General Provisions Act (*Wet algemene bepalingen omgevingsrecht*), the different parts of the permit are constituted by the different types of activities that are permitted (construction activities, environmental activities etc).[53] This implies that the different categories of environmental effects are no longer considered parts of an order and that it is sufficient to attack a single environmental effect during the pre-proceedings to safeguard the possibility to submit appeal and challenge other types of environmental effects. In other areas of administrative case law, the delineation of a 'part' is less clear.

While the second limitation on the scope prohibits the court from ruling on grounds which the appellant did not raise, this third limitation allows the court to refuse to consider grounds which the appellant did bring forward on appeal but which pertain to a part of the order which was not attacked during the pre-proceedings.

A fourth limitation of the scope of the appeal is that the appellant may not – as a result of his own appeal – end up in a situation worse than that before his appeal (generally referred to as the prohibition against *reformatio in peius*).[54] This

50. Art. 8:69 Awb.
51. Art. 6:13 Awb.
52. While the original order should have been attacked in objection proceedings or in an administrative appeal, in public preparatory proceedings the draft order must have been commented upon.
53. Council of State, 9 Mar. 2011, AB 2011, 130, LJN: BP7155.
54. This limitation does not seem to apply, at least not as strictly, during the objection proceedings. This is because the objection proceedings are a complete review of the contested order *ex nunc*, i.e. taking into account all facts, circumstances and legislation at the time the reviewed order is issued, even if they came into existence after the original order was made.

limitation does not apply in the case of an appeal lodged by an interested third party who is not the addressee of the order. In such a case, the appeal may well, if successful, lead to a deterioration in the position of the addressee of the order.

A fifth limitation is that judicial review, unlike administrative review, is a review *ex tunc*, i.e. based on the facts and legislation existing on the date the contested order was issued, not the date of the decision of the court. This difference can be explained by the different nature of the review procedures at the government and judicial levels. As mentioned above (see § 3.1), the pre-proceedings at government level aim to give administrative authorities the opportunity to reconsider their decisions fully and, if necessary, correct mistakes. In order to make a complete and useful reconsideration, administrative authorities should be able to adapt their decisions to changed circumstances, and should therefore be allowed to review their orders *ex nunc*. In a judicial review, on the other hand, only the legality of the order is at issue and this should be assessed on the basis of the facts and law as they stood at the time when the order was issued. Changes in facts and law that have taken place after the contested order has been made cannot, in principle, be taken into account by the court. However, in the interests of efficient and effective dispute resolution, the court can – and does – find ways to express how the parties should proceed after the court's decision on appeal in light of the new facts.

The sixth limitation is that the administrative courts cannot go beyond the domain of the judicial function of government. The doctrine of separation of powers dictates that courts should not exercise powers or discretion that the legislature has given to the executive branch of government. As a result, the standard by which a court reviews a particular order depends on the statutory basis of the order. If discretionary powers have been conferred on the administrative authority, the courts have to respect this discretion and limit their reviews to whether the authority in question could have reasonably decided to exercise its discretion in the way it did by issuing the contested order. If, on the other hand, the relevant statute has awarded the administrative authority very little or no discretion, judicial review can be more thorough. It should be noted that where administrative penalties are concerned, the administrative courts can – and must on the basis of applicable international law – always undertake a complete, in-depth review of the order in question.

A final note on the scope of the appeal is as follows. As mentioned above (see § 2.4), an appellant must qualify as an interested party for his appeal to be admissible. This does not mean, however, that the scope of his interest must be based on the scope and aim of the relevant legislation. For example, the car garage that qualifies as an interested third party in relation to the order granting an environmental licence enabling a competitor to set up a new shop in the vicinity, can file a notice of objection against this licence on the ground that the additional traffic generated by the competitor's new shop will exceed the prevailing environmental standards. The fact that his true interest is based on their competitive relationship, whilst the purpose of the environmental legislation (i.e. to keep the air clean) is completely unrelated, does not prevent his appeal from being admissible. Under the Crisis and Recovery Act, however, a so-called relativity requirement was introduced.[55] This means that (for projects that fall within the scope of this act) an appellant can only successfully bring forward grounds of appeal that aim to protect the interests of the appellant.

The pending bill implementing changes in procedural administrative law aims to introduce the relativity requirement in all administrative appeal proceedings.[56] According to the proposal an administrative court cannot annul a decision that is in violation of a written or unwritten rule of law or general legal principle, in the event that this rule or principle does not aim to protect the interests of the appellant.

4.6 The Proceedings

4.6.1 General

Upon receipt of the notice of appeal, the court will begin an enquiry, which consists of two phases: the pre-hearing phase in order to arrive at a proper instruction on the case, and the enquiry at the hearing. Since establishing the truth is an important part of appeal proceedings, the court has a number of investigative powers at its disposal. It can require the parties and other persons to submit documents and information in writing or to appear before it and provide testimony orally, either at the hearing or at a pre-trial conference. It can appoint experts or even organise a court inspection of the premises or site. The parties are obliged to cooperate. If a party does not cooperate or does not submit the requested information, the court may draw conclusions from that behaviour. In practice, the active role of the court is often limited to the invitation of parties who may qualify as interested third parties, or the notification that the parties can invite experts and witnesses to the hearing. In addition, courts sometimes actively investigate, ahead of the hearing, the admissibility of an appeal, either by means of questions to be answered in writing or during a hearing held for this purpose only.[57]

The District Court will assign each appeal case to a single judge, who may refer the matter to a three-member panel, depending on the complexity of the matter.[58] Preliminary relief hearings will always be conducted by a single judge. In addition, a clerk is assigned to each case, who will be involved in all of the preparations before the hearing and will generally attend the hearing to take notes. Except in preliminary relief cases, which are handled by a single judge, the appellate courts

55. Art. 1.9 Crisis and Recovery Act.
56. New Art. 8:69a GALA. EK 32 450, nr. A, p. 18.
57. Divisions 8.1.5, 8.1.6, 8.2.2 and 8.2.5 Awb.
58. Art. 8:10 Awb.

will assign each case to a three-member panel. This panel can refer the matter to a single judge, except if it concerns an appeal from a District Court judgment rendered by a three-member panel.

Recently, most of the administrative District Courts adopted a so-called 'new case handling system' (*nieuwe zaaksbehandeling*). Under this new system, the District Courts aim to schedule a hearing within three to five months after the notice of appeal is submitted. The goal of this hearing is to get a clear understanding of the issues that keep the parties divided and to find out whether alternative solutions (such as mediation or trying to settle the matter) seem achievable. In most cases this will be the only hearing and after this hearing the District Court will hand down a ruling within (normally) six to twelve weeks. In more complex cases a new hearing may be scheduled. The idea behind this new system is that early contact with the District Court, and an active approach of the judges, will enhance the chances of reaching a final solution to the problem at hand.

4.6.2 Documents and Written Submissions

Normally within one week of receiving the notice of appeal, the court will inform the administrative authority (the respondent) that an appeal has been lodged. The court will send the notice of appeal[59] to the respondent and ask him to submit (initially within four weeks) the file with all relevant documents pertaining to the matter, as well as a written statement of response to the appeal. The court will then send the appellant a copy of the file (or a notice that it is available for inspection) and the response. Although it is rare for a court to do so, it may decide to allow the appellant an opportunity to submit a written statement of reply to the statement of response, in which case the respondent may submit a statement of rejoinder. As in objection proceedings, all parties may submit additional documents and statements up to ten days before the hearing, an opportunity that is used frequently in practice.

4.6.3 Confidential Documents

If information or documents requested by the court contain confidential information, the party to whom the request is made may, if he can establish that it is required for reasons of secrecy, refuse to provide the confidential information or, more commonly, state that only the court can review this information. The court will then verify whether the confidentiality of the information in question is truly required for reasons of secrecy. If so, the parties that have no access to the information are asked to inform the court whether they will allow it to consider this information in

59. If the initial notice of appeal was a pro forma notice (see § 3.2.3), the court will also send the supplementary notice containing the grounds of appeal.

the appeal proceedings nevertheless. If they do not allow this, the court will make sure that the judges who have had access to the confidential information will not be involved in deciding the case. In the practice of economic administrative law, this procedure allows the courts to review orders issued by competition authorities or sector regulators in the context of the confidential information on which these orders were based, without this information being divulged to the other parties or to the public. One difficulty is that this procedure can only be used for information requested by the court. A party that would like to introduce confidential information on its own initiative will need to make sure that it is submitted to the administrative authority (confidentially) prior to the issue of the reviewed order, so that it will be part of the documentation that the authority must submit to the court.

4.6.4 Hearing

A hearing will be held in all appeals and higher appeals, unless the court decides to handle the case by means of simplified proceedings (see § 4.9.1) or to abstain from a hearing after all parties have waived their right to a hearing.[60] The hearing is the focal point of the appeal proceedings. The court will actively lead the enquiry at trial. Generally, the parties are allowed to argue their case first,[61] before being questioned by the court. However, since the introduction of the 'new case handling system', the hearing at the District Courts normally starts with questions of judges and it is generally no longer necessary to prepare written pleading notes (*pleitnota*). The parties can bring forward witnesses and experts, and this is being done more and more frequently. Evidence that is already documented in the file does not need to be presented again in open court. Therefore, bringing forward a witness or expert will be most useful where an oral presentation of findings or an elaboration on earlier written testimony is necessary. The hearing is public, unless the court decides otherwise on the grounds set out in the GALA, or unless a specific statute provides that the hearing should be held behind closed doors.[62] The clerk assigned to the case will generally take notes; no verbatim transcripts are made. If a higher appeal is filed against a judgment of the District Court, the clerk will draw up a report of what transpired at the hearing, to be signed by the panel chairman and the clerk.

---

60. Art. 8:57 Awb.
61. These presentations are usually based on written pleading notes, which are handed to the court and to all other parties at the beginning of the hearing.
62. For instance, the Financial Supervision Act provides that when the Rotterdam District Court hears a request to suspend an order of the AFM to publish the imposition of a fine, the hearing will be held behind closed doors.

4.6.5 Evidence

Dutch administrative law has very few substantive rules of evidence, i.e. rules concerning the burden of proof, the admissibility of evidence and the valuation of evidence. All these matters are within the discretion of the courts. As we have seen, the courts have wide-ranging investigative powers, which are often referred to as procedural rules of evidence.

There are a number of reasons for the lack of substantive rules of evidence: many facts will already be in the court's file; the respondent authority has the obligation to submit all relevant documents to the court; the contested order should, as all orders, contain a sufficient reasoning; and the appellant should underpin the grounds of his appeal with sufficient relevant facts. As in civil cases, there is generally no need to prove facts that have not been disputed by the other party. The respondent, being an administrative authority, will generally not misstate or deny the facts intentionally. Since the court actively attempts to establish the truth, it may find reasons to question certain facts even where the parties have not called these into question. In such a case, it may employ its investigative powers in order to generate additional evidence. Although the court must generally stay within the boundaries of the appeal as outlined by the appellant, it is also inclined to serve the general interest and ensure that justice is done. If there is a need for additional evidence to be presented, the court will usually look at the party with the best access to the relevant information to provide it.

4.7 Judgment

Since the District Court rules on an appeal from an order of an administrative authority, while the appellate court rules on a judgment of a District Court, some of the rules for judgments vary somewhat. Therefore this paragraph will distinguish between appeals (before District Courts) and higher appeals (before appellate courts) where necessary.

Unless a court renders its judgment orally, it should render written judgment within six weeks after formally closing its enquiry (usually at the end of the hearing).[63] Formally, this term can be extended by no more than a further six weeks in special circumstances. However, this rule is often violated in practice, as the courts are faced with significant backlogs. Given the importance of certain large infrastructural projects, the Crisis and Recovery Act requires that the administrative court should hand down its ruling within six months after the expiration of the

63. Art. 8:66 Awb.

appeal period.[64] In practice this results in District Courts and the Council of State giving priority to these types of cases, which further delays the other types of cases.

The District Court can rule that: (i) it lacks jurisdiction, (ii) the appeal is inadmissible, (iii) the appeal is ill founded, or (iv) the appeal is well founded.[65] If the District Court rules that the appeal is well founded, it will annul all or part of the contested order. If the contested order (or a part of this order) is annulled, its legal consequences (or the legal consequences of the annulled part of the order) are void, unless the District Court holds that all or some of these legal consequences will stand despite the annulment (*in stand laten van rechtsgevolgen*). In addition, the court may rule that the respondent authority has to issue a new order *ex nunc* or perform another act reflecting its judgment. Alternatively, it may hold that its judgment will replace the annulled order or the annulled part of the order (*zelf in de zaak voorzien*). Where the respondent has to issue a new order, this order will have the same status as the contested order, generally a reviewed order or an order which is not subject to administrative review. Therefore, administrative review of the new order is not available. When ordering the respondent authority to issue a new order, the court may grant temporary relief for a time period determined by the court.[66]

Before rendering a final judgement, the administrative courts can decide to give an interim judgment (*tussenuitspraak*)[67] to enable the administrative authority to remedy a shortcoming in the decision that is the subject of the appeal procedure. This procedure is called the application of the 'administrative loop' (*bestuurlijke lus*).[68] Application of this procedure prevents loss of time and the need for new decisions that could result in new legal proceedings. In order to apply the 'administrative loop' the shortcoming has to be capable of repair (*herstelbaar*) and interested parties (also those who do not participate in the appeal procedure) should not be adversely affected. Shortcomings that could be repaired are, for example: the decision lacks a proper motivation (*motiveringsgebrek*) or the decision was not prepared prudently (*zorgvuldigheidsgebrek*).

An appellate court may uphold or quash the judgment of the District Court. If the appellate court upholds the judgment, it may add or amend the legal grounds on which the judgment of the District Court was based. Where the appellate court quashes the judgment of the District Court, it may decide the appeal itself, or it may refer the case back to the competent District Court.[69] The appellate court will refer the case back to the District Court if: (i) the District Court has declared that it lacks jurisdiction or that the appeal is inadmissible, whilst the appellate court rules

---

64. Art. 1.6(4) Crisis and Recovery Act.
65. Art. 8:70 Awb.
66. Art. 8:72 Awb.
67. Art. 8:80a Awb.
68. Art. 8:51a Awb; Art. 46(6) and Art. 49(6) WRvSt; Art. 17(6) and Art. 21(6) *Beroepswet*; Art. 19(6) and 22(6) Wbbo.
69. Art. 53 WRvSt; Art. 26 Wbbo; Art. 24 *Beroepswet*.

that the District Court actually has jurisdiction or that the appeal is admissible, or (ii) the appellate court is of the opinion that the District Court should hear the appeal again on other grounds.[70]

The respondent authority is expected to comply with the court's judgment. However, if the court fears that the respondent will not comply in a timely fashion, it may set a deadline by which the new order should be issued. In addition, the court may hold that a penalty will be forfeited if the authority does not comply with the judgment on time. However, this power is rarely used. If the administrative authority, in issuing its new order, fails to observe the judgment, or if the order does not comply with the law in other respects, the interested party can appeal again to the District Court.

4.8 Court Fees, Costs and Damages

4.8.1 Court Fees

If the court annuls all or part of the contested order or, in the case of a higher appeal, the contested judgment, the legal entity of which the respondent authority is a part will be ordered to refund the court fee which the appellant paid for his appeal or higher appeal. In the event the appeal or higher appeal does not lead to an annulment, the court has discretion as to whether or not to order such a refund.[71]

4.8.2 Costs

The court can rule that a party must compensate another party for the costs it reasonably incurred in connection with the appeal proceedings and also, if so requested, in connection with the administrative pre-proceedings.[72] The court will only order a citizen to pay costs in cases of apparent abuse of procedure. Only a limited number of cost categories are eligible for this compensation; they include: costs of professional legal representation, costs of witnesses, experts and interpreters, travel expenses and lost income as a result of attending the hearing. It should be noted that only a limited fixed amount of the costs can be awarded, which will generally not even cover the actual costs of professional legal representation.

4.8.3 Damages

A party can claim damages from the respondent authority in three ways. The first and easiest is a request, to be made during the appeal or higher appeal proceedings,

---

70. Art. 55 WRvSt; Art. 28 Wbbo; Art. 26 *Beroepswet.*
71. Art. 8:74 Awb; Art. 54 WRvSt; Art. 27 Wbbo; Art. 25 *Beroepswet.*
72. Art. 8:75 Awb.

to the court to award damages in the event the appeal is held to be well founded.[73] Such request can be granted only if the damage was caused by the order that was annulled by the court. The court has discretion as to whether such a request will be granted. If the appellant's damage was caused in part by acts of the respondent other than the annulled order, the administrative court may reject the request, leaving the damages issue to the civil courts (see below). As the respondent is usually an organ of a legal entity, the court will, if an award is made, identify the entity liable for it. If the damages cannot be fully assessed before the judgment is rendered, the court can decide that its enquiry be reopened in preparation for a further judgment on the amount of the award. A request for an award for damages can also be made with a request to withdraw the appeal where the respondent authority has satisfied the objections of the appellant in whole or in part.

The second way to obtain damages is to request the respondent to issue a new decision with an award for damages. If the damage is directly caused by the order that was annulled by the court, the new decision is regarded as an order and can be subjected to objection proceedings and, if necessary, appeal to the administrative court. If the damage is caused (in whole or in part) by another act of the respondent, the new decision is not an order, so it can only be reviewed by the civil courts.[74]

Thirdly, a successful appellant can sue the respondent authority in a civil court with a claim based in tort. As long as the respondent has not issued a new decision in response to a request for an award of damages, the civil court has jurisdiction.[75] Traditionally, although a civil suit can be rather time consuming and expensive, the civil courts have been the preferred forum for damages claims against administrative authorities as they have more expertise in relation to damages claims than the administrative courts.

4.9 Special Appeal Proceedings

4.9.1 Simplified Proceedings

If, after having reviewed the contents of the notice of appeal and the documents provided by the respondent authority, the court comes to the conclusion that a further investigation is not necessary, the enquiry is closed and the parties are not invited to a hearing.[76] The case will then be handled by means of so-called simplified proceedings (*vereenvoudigde behandeling*). The District Court will render judgment on the basis of the file, making one of the following decisions: (i) the District Court manifestly lacks jurisdiction; or (ii) the appeal is manifestly inadmis-

73. Art. 8:73 Awb.
74. Central Appeals Council 28 July 1994, AB 1995, 133, LJN: ZB0806.
75. Supreme Court 17 Dec.1999, AB 2000, 89, LJN: ZC3059 (*Groningen/Raadgever*),.
76. Art. 8:54 Awb.

sible; or (iii) the appeal is manifestly unfounded; or (iv) the appeal is manifestly well founded.[77]

No higher appeal is available from a judgment in simplified proceedings.[78] However, an interested party or the respondent authority can file an objection (*verzet*) against the decision to apply the simplified proceedings and render judgment without a hearing.[79] Such objection must be filed with the same District Court. Judges other than those who were involved in the primary judgment will rule on the objection. The petitioner in these proceedings can request a hearing, and this request will be granted unless the court considers the objection obviously well founded. If the objections are held well founded, the primary judgment rendered in the simplified proceedings will be annulled and the enquiry will be resumed.

4.9.2 Accelerated Proceedings

It will usually take at least a year for a court to decide on an appeal.[80] Parties cannot always wait that long without running the risk of irreversible adverse consequences arising from the contested order. If a case needs to be decided urgently, any of the parties may request that the proceedings be accelerated (*versnelde behandeling*). This request is typically made when an appeal is filed. It can be made regardless of whether the appellant has also applied for preliminary relief (see § 5). While preliminary relief proceedings will only create a preliminary measure, accelerated proceedings have the advantage of leading to a judgment on the merits, which will become final if not appealed within six weeks.

The court has discretion in respect of a request for accelerated proceedings. If granted, the court may take one or more of the following measures: (i) reduce the time allowed for paying the court fee; (ii) reduce the time allowed for the respondent authority to submit the file with all relevant documents pertaining to the matter and to submit its statement of defence; (iii) exclude (in whole or in part) interested third parties from the right to be heard; (iv) deny the parties their right to submit their views as to what an expert investigation should seek to achieve if such an investigation is required; and (v) reduce the time allowed for the parties to state their views on the report of an expert if an expert investigation has been conducted.[81]

If, during the accelerated proceedings, the court finds that the case is no longer sufficiently urgent to justify the use of accelerated proceedings, the case will be

---

77. Art. 8:54 Awb. In addition, in the case of direct appeal the District Court may instruct the administrative authority to apply the standard procedure for review and to commence pre-proceedings at the government level, if it rules that the case is unsuitable for direct appeal (see § 4.1.3): Art. 8:54a Awb.
78. Art. 47(2) WRvSt; Art. 18(2) Appeals Act; Art. 20(3) Wbbo; Art. 27h(2) General Tax Act (*Algemene wet inzake rijksbelastingen*).
79. Art. 8:55 Awb.
80. The 'new case handling' by the District Courts is designed to shorten the appeal proceedings.
81. Art. 8:52 Awb.

handled in the usual way.[82] This decision cannot be appealed. In practice, many accelerated proceedings result from a 'compromise' offered by the administrative judge in preliminary relief proceedings. In the event the court is uncomfortable with or unwilling to grant preliminary relief (for example in light of the factual complexity of the case at hand), it regularly proposes to accelerate the proceedings on the merits, provided the petition for preliminary relief is withdrawn and the respondent agrees to submit its full statement of response within an agreed brief period of time.

5. PRELIMINARY RELIEF

5.1 General

As with proceedings on the merits, administrative courts have jurisdiction in proceedings for preliminary relief only if the proceedings concern an order by an administrative authority or a judgment by a lower administrative court on such order. Moreover, such order should be subjected to judicial review by the court or administrative review in administrative pre-proceedings before preliminary relief can be provided. Preliminary relief proceedings are, therefore, ancillary to the proceedings (or pre-proceedings) on the merits.

Since the filing of a notice of objection or notice of appeal or higher appeal does not ordinarily suspend the effect of the contested order or judgment,[83] the claimant or appellant who would like this order or judgment suspended until his objections or appeal have been ruled upon must generally initiate preliminary relief proceedings. Such proceedings are quite common and form an essential element of the effective legal protection provided in Dutch administrative litigation. The judgment in these relief proceedings is of a preliminary nature, so that it does not prejudice the judgment on the merits (except if the judge expressly issues a judgment on the merits, as is discussed in more detail below (see § 5.5.2)).

Some administrative courts have been particularly helpful in accommodating the need for immediate access to the courts to provide preliminary relief in a timely manner. The following is an example, albeit an exceptional one. During the auction process for frequencies for mobile telecommunications in the years 1998 and 2000, the Rotterdam District Court was informed that preliminary relief might become necessary within ten minutes, the period between a decision of the auctioneer to disqualify a party and the start of the next round from which that party was excluded. Knowing that huge financial interests might be at stake, the court issued a

82. Art. 8:53 Awb.
83. Art. 6:16 Awb.

mobile telephone number on which the parties could, if necessary, contact the clerk of the preliminary relief judge. The judge would be able to suspend the decision of the auctioneer by telephone until the parties had argued their case in a hearing later the same day, and a judgment on the request would be rendered.

5.2 Requirements

5.2.1 Jurisdiction

The preliminary relief judge has jurisdiction if the court to which he belongs has or will have jurisdiction on the merits. Therefore, if a certain order has been appealed to a District Court, a request for preliminary relief in relation to that order must be directed to the preliminary relief judge of that same District Court. If the order is still the subject of objection proceedings pending before the authority which issued the order, jurisdiction for preliminary relief lies with the court that will have jurisdiction to hear the appeal from the reviewed order that will result from the objection proceedings. If a higher appeal is pending, the preliminary relief judge of the appellate court will have jurisdiction.

5.2.2 Admissibility

A request for preliminary relief is admissible only if proceedings on the merits are pending at the same time, either objection proceedings or appeal or higher appeal.[84] As objection proceedings also lead to a decision by the authority on the merits, references in this chapter to 'proceedings on the merits' will refer to both objection proceedings and appeal proceedings. The requirement of pending proceedings on the merits in relation to preliminary relief proceedings is generally referred to as connectivity (*connexiteit*).[85]

Strictly speaking, proceedings on the merits only need to be pending at the time the court rules on the request for preliminary relief. In practice however, if the proceedings on the merits are not yet pending when the need for preliminary relief arises, they will be initiated immediately prior to the filing of the request for preliminary relief with the court.[86] The court must also receive a copy of the notice

---

84. Where the order in question is subject to pre-proceedings in the form of administrative appeal (see § 3.1), preliminary relief can be granted once the administrative appeal proceedings are pending with the competent authority.
85. More precisely, the requirement described above is referred to as 'procedural connectivity', while the term 'substantive connectivity' is used to describe the requirement that requests for preliminary relief must directly concern the order or judgment that is contested in the proceedings on the merits.
86. If both documents are sent to the same institution (either the authority or the court), this institution must forward the wrongly addressed document to the institution that has jurisdiction: see Art. 6:15 Awb.

of objection in order to be able to verify that it is pending and to understand the case at hand.[87] It is good practice, especially in urgent matters, for the party requesting preliminary relief to send a copy of its request to the respondent authority as well.

If the claimant or appellant withdraws the proceedings on the merits before the request for preliminary relief is ruled upon, the request must generally be declared inadmissible.

A second issue in relation to admissibility concerns who is entitled to request preliminary relief. If an appeal or higher appeal on the merits is pending, any party to such appeal proceedings can file such a request: the appellant, the respondent authority or an interested third party which was admitted to the proceedings. During objection proceedings, only the claimant, i.e. the party which filed a notice of objection against the order in question, can generally file such a request.[88]

Once preliminary relief has been granted, the issue may arise as to who is entitled to request the court to terminate or alter such relief. The preliminary relief judge may do so on his own initiative or, more commonly, pursuant to the request of a party.[89] The circle of parties with a right to file a request to terminate or to alter earlier preliminary relief is larger than those with a right to request the relief in the first place. For instance, an interested party which is directly affected by the preliminary relief, even if it did not itself file a notice of objection against the original order, can also file a request for the termination or alteration. The authority which must still decide on the notice of objection and issue a reviewed order is also entitled to request the termination or alteration of preliminary relief issued against the original order.

Other issues that could lead to the inadmissibility of a request for preliminary relief are the failure to satisfy the basic requirements for the request (compare § 3.2.3) or to pay the court fees.

5.2.3 Substantive Criterion

The substantive criterion which is used to evaluate a request is whether the relief sought is urgently required in view of the interests involved.[90] Case law on the meaning of this criterion is rather case-specific. However, a few rules have become clear in recent case law.

The judge, in forming his preliminary opinion, will have to weigh the interests involved. He will evaluate whether the interest of the petitioner in obtaining preliminary relief urgently warrants an exception to the general rule that the commencement of the proceedings on the merits does not suspend the order's legal effect.

87. Art. 8:81(4) Awb.
88. Arts 8:81(2) and 8.81(3) Awb.
89. Art. 8:87 Awb.
90. Art. 8:81(1) Awb.

Also, he will weigh whether the urgent interest outweighs the general interest that a government decision should stand until a competent court has ruled on the merits, on the basis of full proceedings, that the order is illegal. Whether preliminary relief will be granted is therefore dependent on a balancing of the urgent interest of the petitioner against the judge's preliminary opinion about the legality of the contested order.

At the two ends of the spectrum of possible outcomes, the result of the balancing act is quite clear. If the contested order is likely to be considered illegal in the proceedings on the merits, preliminary relief is likely to be granted, even though the interests of the petitioner may not be very urgent. If, on the other hand, the contested order is likely to lead to very far-reaching and irreversible consequences and therefore the interests are urgent, a little doubt about the legality of the order may be sufficient to obtain the relief sought. Between these two extremes, each case strikes its own balance.

In some cases, judges will examine the urgency of the matter closely. If not convinced of the gravity and irreversible nature of the consequences of the order under review, they will deny the request for preliminary relief. For example, this approach is often found in cases where the interest of the petitioner is primarily of a financial nature. The idea behind these decisions is that if the proceedings on the merits prove successful, the respondent authority shall be liable for all the damage which has resulted from the order which was found to be illegal, so that an interest of a financial nature will be made whole even without preliminary relief. Unless the petitioner shows that his financial distress is likely to threaten the continuity of his business or private life, no urgent interest will therefore be attributed to a request for financial relief. In one case, the preliminary relief judge of the Trade and Industrial Affairs Appeal College took this approach so far as to deny the existence of an urgent interest in any matter in which an award of damages could compensate the petitioner for the allegedly illegal consequences of the contested order.[91]

In other cases, especially when the relief sought is not primarily of a financial nature, the judge will first evaluate the legality of the contested order, while the urgent interest is but one of the factors to be taken into account.

---

91. Trade and Industrial Affairs Appeal College 28 Jan. 2005, AB 2005, 194, LJN: AS5300, in the matter of KPN *versus* OPTA (*in re Iriscadeaubon*). In this case, the contested order prohibited a particular marketing action and damaged (allegedly illegally) the petitioner's market position. If this approach were followed generally, it would substantially reduce the significance of preliminary relief proceedings, as many of the adverse consequences of illegal orders can be redressed by way of financial compensation. In another case (involving the same parties and a comparable order), the same judge granted the preliminary relief requested on the basis that damage to the market position could not (in this case) be fully compensated in the form of an award for damages: judgment of 25 Jul. 2005, LJN: AT9967 in the matter of KPN *versus* OPTA (*in re digital fun camera on keyring*).

5.3 Available Remedies

If the request for preliminary relief is granted, the order is usually suspended (i.e. temporarily stripped of its legal effect). If the preliminary relief is sought during the objection proceedings, the order under review will be the original order. Any relief granted will necessarily pertain to this order. In the event that the proceedings on the merits are pending at the court in an appeal against an order issued after objection proceedings, this reviewed order will be the primary subject of the preliminary relief proceedings. In such a case, the petitioner may have to request specifically that the judge suspend not only the reviewed order, but also the original order. For instance, if the original order imposes an obligation on the claimant and the reviewed order finds that his objections are unfounded, it will affirm the original order. In such a case, a suspension of only the reviewed order would not by itself be a useful form of relief, as the original order and the obligation in it would remain in force.

In addition to or instead of a suspension, another temporary measure may be taken in relation to the contested order. For instance, a temporary licence may be granted. It should be noted, however, that it is significantly easier in practice to convince a judge to have a particular status quo continued (for instance by suspending an order and thereby preventing the change in the legal or factual situation envisaged by the order) than to convince him to change the status quo (for instance by allowing the petitioner to commence an activity which he was not previously allowed to perform).

5.4 The Proceedings

As in civil cases, preliminary relief proceedings are handled by a preliminary relief judge of the relevant court, sitting alone with the help of one clerk. In the administrative division of the District Court and other administrative courts, senior judges who also handle appeals on the merits handle preliminary relief cases.

The procedural rules which apply to appeal proceedings on the merits also apply to preliminary relief proceedings, with a few exceptions. After the request for preliminary relief has been filed, the court invites the parties as soon as possible to appear at a hearing. Usually, this will be held between two and four weeks after the filing of the request. However, such a hearing may not take place if: (i) the court lacks jurisdiction; (ii) the request is manifestly unfounded; (iii) the request is manifestly well founded; or (iv) speed is of the essence and the interests of the parties will not be prejudiced by the omission of a hearing.[92] Absent such circumstances, the respondent authority will submit the file with all relevant documents as

92. Art. 8:83 Awb.

soon as possible. Additional documents may be submitted up to one day before the hearing. Although it is not required that the respondent authority submit a statement of response, in complex matters it sometimes elects to do so (and can do so no later than one day before the hearing).

5.5 Judgment

5.5.1 General

The preliminary relief judge renders his judgment as soon as possible, either orally or in writing. He may declare (i) that he lacks jurisdiction; (ii) that the request is inadmissible; (iii) that the request is unfounded; or (iv) that the request is well founded.[93] If the judge finds (in his preliminary opinion) that the proceedings on the merits are very likely to be inadmissible, this will not affect the admissibility of the request for preliminary relief, but rather its chances of success. For instance, if the preliminary relief judge finds that the decision contested in the proceedings on the merits is not an order issued by an administrative authority or that the claimant or appellant in the proceedings on the merits does not qualify as an interested party, the proceedings on the merits cannot, in his opinion, result in a substantive evaluation of the contested order, as they are likely to be inadmissible. In such a case, the preliminary relief judge must abstain from rendering a preliminary opinion on this evaluation. As a result, he will conclude that the request is unfounded and that it should be denied.

5.5.2 Simultaneous Judgment on the Merits

It is important to note that, in preliminary relief proceedings, the judge may choose to not only rule on the request for preliminary relief, but also to render judgment on the merits at the same time. He can do this if he concludes after the hearing in the preliminary relief proceedings, that a continuation of the enquiry would not contribute to the analysis of the case. The court must advise the parties in the invitation to the hearing that this power can be used in their case.[94] This power, commonly referred to as the power to short-circuit a case (*kortsluiting*), is an important means of expediting the administration of justice, and is exercised quite frequently.

---

93. Art. 8:84(1) Awb.
94. Art. 8:86 Awb.

5.6 No Appeal, Only Alteration or Termination

Appeal against the judgment of the preliminary relief judge is not possible. However, the court may alter or terminate any preliminary relief granted, both on request by an interested party and on its own initiative.

6. JUDICIAL REVIEW BY THE CIVIL COURTS

6.1 Jurisdiction

The Constitution confers the power to adjudicate all disputes related to civil law relationships to the civil courts.[95] Whether a civil court has jurisdiction depends solely on the assertions of the claimant in the writ of summons. If he claims a civil right which entitles him to the relief sought, jurisdiction will be assumed. Because of this wide-ranging jurisdiction, the civil courts function as a 'safety net', providing legal protection where the administrative courts have no jurisdiction.

6.2 Admissibility

The Supreme Court has held that the civil courts may only admit a case against an administrative authority if no adequate legal protection is available to the claimant through administrative litigation.[96] Adequate protection requires that the claimant should have access to independent courts and that they be able to offer comparable legal protection. As administrative courts are, for example, unable to provide declaratory relief, relief not directly linked to an order, or relief linked to an order in relation to which the claimant is not an interested third party, the civil courts offer supplementary legal protection in such instances.

A claimant who has failed to use the administrative litigation remedies that were available to him will generally not be admitted in the civil court. Even in cases of doubt claimants must exhaust the administrative remedies first. In the event that a claim is brought before an administrative court and this court rules that the claim may only be brought before a civil court, this ruling must be included in the judgment, and the civil court will be bound to rule on the claim because of such judgment.[97]

95. Art. 112 Constitution.
96. Supreme Court, 15 Nov. 2002, NJ 2003, 617, LJN: AE8464 (*Staat der Nederlanden/Zevenbergen*).
97. Art. 8:71 Awb.

6.3 Doctrine of Formal Legal Effect

The civil courts assume that an order, or a judgment on an order, which was not subjected to administrative or judicial review, where such means were available, is entirely lawful. This is generally referred to as the doctrine of formal legal effect (*formele rechtskracht*). This doctrine implies that an order that can no longer be challenged before an administrative court can no longer be challenged before a civil court either. Orders that were not subjected to judicial review by the administrative courts will be considered by the civil courts to be lawful with regard to both procedural aspects and contents. With regard to orders that have been challenged before administrative courts, the civil courts will follow the administrative courts' judgment on the legality of such orders.

Generally, the doctrine of formal legal effect will apply even when it is clear that, if judicial review by the administrative courts had been sought, the order would have been annulled.[98] There are a number of reasons for this. First, the legal certainty of administrative acts would be jeopardised if orders could be challenged in civil courts for longer periods than the time period during which administrative review and review by administrative courts can be sought (generally six weeks). In addition, it is believed that claimants should be encouraged to challenge orders by administrative authorities in the specialised courts created for that purpose. This also avoids contradictory case law between civil and administrative courts. However, a few exceptions to this doctrine are made, for instance if the claimant had no way of knowing that an administrative remedy was available to him. In such a case, he may be granted a new time limit to initiate administrative proceedings.[99]

The doctrine of formal legal effect works not only against citizens seeking legal protection against the government, but also in their favour. Once an order has been annulled by an administrative court on the basis of a successful appeal, this judgment is binding on the civil courts. Therefore, the annulment of an order by an administrative court is sufficient to prove in a civil tort action (i) the unlawfulness of the order, and (ii) the error of the legal entity of which the authority forms part.[100]

6.4 Procedure

In civil proceedings against the State of the Netherlands or any other public legal entity or private entity with public powers, the standard rules of civil procedure apply, with a few exceptions. The standard rules are set out in Chapter 1 of this book.

---

98. Supreme Court 18 Jun. 1993, NJ 1993, 642, LJN: ZC1006 (*Sint Oedenrode/Van Aarle*).
99. Supreme Court 16 May 1986, NJ 1986, 723, LJN: AC9347 (*Heesch/Van de Akker*).
100. Supreme Court 31 May 1991, AB 1992, 290, LJN: ZC0261 (*Van Gog/Gemeente Nederweert*); Supreme Court 12 Jun. 1992, NJ 1993, 113, LJN: AN4622 (*Bedrijfsvereniging Bank- en Verzekeringswezen/Boulogne*).

7. COMPLAINTS PROCEEDINGS

7.1 General

In a civilised democratic society, a citizen should be able to file a complaint against a governmental authority if he does not agree with the way he has been treated and this complaint should be handled openly and fairly. This is deemed to be part of the principles of proper administration.

Dutch law provides for two types of complaint proceedings. First, a citizen should be able to file a complaint with the governmental authority against which the complaint is directed. The procedure for such complaints is referred to as internal complaints proceedings (*intern klachtrecht*; described in the GALA as *klachtbehandeling door een bestuursorgaan*).[101] Furthermore, a complaint can be filed with a specially created body, independent of the authority concerned. The proceedings for complaints to such independent bodies are referred to as external complaints proceedings (*extern klachtrecht*; described in the GALA as *klachtbehandeling door een ombudsman*).[102] The GALA provides for a set of minimum requirements for each type of complaint proceedings.

7.2 Internal Complaints Proceedings

Under the rules for internal complaints proceedings, anyone with a grievance against an administrative authority has the right to submit a complaint to that authority. Complaints must be directed against the behaviour of the administrative authority, which can include the issue of orders or other legal acts or behaviour that was not intended to have particular legal consequences (often referred to as factual acts).[103] Even if someone is not affected by the government behaviour, this person may file a complaint. The reasoning behind this approach is that since the government should behave properly, any person should be able to call its behaviour into question.

The rules for internal complaints proceedings contain a general obligation to handle both oral and written complaints in a decent and proper manner. A more elaborate set of rules applies provided (i) the complaint meets some minimal formal requirements,[104] and (ii) the complaint deals with government behaviour by which the complainant is directly and personally affected.

---

101. Title 9.1 Awb.
102. Title 9.2 Awb.
103. Such factual acts (*feitelijk handelen*) include a wide range of behaviour, from a car accident caused by a civil servant driving in the line of duty, to a statement by the Mayor in an interview with the press.
104. It should be dated and filed in writing and contain at least the claimant's name, address and signature and a description of the behaviour against which the complaint is directed: Art. 9:4(2) Awb.

If the more elaborate set of rules applies, the authority must send the complainant a written notice of receipt of his complaint. The complaint must be handled on behalf of the authority by individuals who were not involved in the behaviour that is the subject of the complaint. The authority is not obliged to deal with a complaint if *inter alia* (i) it concerns an order which can be subjected to judicial review by the administrative courts, (ii) it concerns behaviour which has already been the subject of complaints proceedings, (iii) it concerns behaviour which occurred more than a year before the complaint was submitted, or (iv) if the complaint appears to be of negligible importance.[105] If the authority decides to admit the complaint, it is obliged to hear both the complainant and the person(s) of the authority whose behaviour is being questioned. It must deal with the complaint within six weeks, though this period may be extended by four weeks. By this deadline, the authority must notify the complainant in writing of the results of its investigation of the complaint, its opinion on these results, and any conclusions it may draw from these. This notification marks the end of the internal complaints proceedings.

The notification does not constitute an order under the GALA, which means that no further legal protection is available. However, it is possible to file a complaint pursuant to the external complaints proceedings (see § 7.3) or to commence an action in the civil courts.

An administrative authority may elect to appoint an adviser or put in place an advisory committee to advise it on any complaints that meet the minimal formal requirements set out above. In certain circumstances, the law may prescribe the involvement of such an adviser or advisory committee. The GALA provides some basic rules about the procedure when such advisory function forms part of the internal complaints proceedings.[106]

7.3 External Complaints Proceedings

7.3.1 General

The most important external complaints proceedings are those before the National Ombudsman (*Nationale Ombudsman*), an official appointed by the Lower House of Parliament pursuant to the Act on the National Ombudsman.[107] When the National Ombudsman was first appointed in 1982 his organisation had 41 employees and handled some 4,000 requests for investigation and another 2,500 issues by telephone. In 2007, after 25 years of service, some 160 employees, including 70 investigators, handled some 13,000 written requests and another 24,000 phone calls. These requests led to 325 reports (following investigations with an average

105. Art. 9:8 Awb.
106. Division 9.1.3 Awb.
107. *Wet nationale ombudsman*, Stb. 1981, 35, as amended.

duration of 13.5 months), while another nine reports were issued on the National Ombudsman's own initiative.

In addition to the National Ombudsman, decentralised branches of government pursuant to the Municipalities Act (*Gemeentewet*), the Provinces Act (*Provinciewet*), the Water Boards Act (*Waterschapswet*) or the Joint Regulations Act (*Wet gemeenschappelijke regelingen*) may establish rules pertaining to other external complaints proceedings and independent complaints bodies (an *ombudsman* or committees). Since 2005, the GALA has contained a minimum set of procedural rules for all external complaints proceedings.[108] Those will be briefly described below. The term 'ombudsman' refers to both the National Ombudsman and any independent complaints body established pursuant to any of the statutes described above, unless stated otherwise.

7.3.2 Requirements

An external complaint can as a rule be admitted only after a complaint has been filed with the authority in question. This rule was made to encourage administrative authorities to maximise the number of complaints that can be handled internally to the complainant's satisfaction. There are, however, two exceptions to this rule. An externally filed complaint will be admissible without internal proceedings having been completed where (i) the complaint concerns the way in which the authority handled a previous complaint, or (ii) where filing the complaint with the authority cannot reasonably be required under the circumstances of the case at hand. This could arise where the relationship between the complainant and the authority is seriously disrupted, where the complaint concerns a structural issue in respect of the authority in question, which authority has been the subject of previous investigation, or where the authority in question has stated that it will not respond to complaints of this particular type.

7.3.3 Procedure

Within these parameters, anyone has the right to file a complaint about improper behaviour on the part of an administrative authority with the competent ombudsman. These complaints proceedings do not constitute legal proceedings, but legal proceedings may be the subject of a complaint. In fact, many complaints are about delays in the decision-making process of the administrative authorities in the context of administrative review.

---

108. Title 9.2 Awb. The Act on the National Ombudsman sets out his scope of authority and the institutional framework, as well as some supplemental procedural rules.

Any party can request the ombudsman to initiate an investigation into the behaviour of an administrative authority, unless more than a year has passed since the internal complaints proceedings ended (or should have ended). Where there is no prior requirement to complain to the administrative authority (due to one of the two exceptions described above), the term expires a year after the events concerned have taken place. Any pending legal proceedings that relate to the complaint at hand will create an extension of this time limit. The ombudsman is obliged to begin an investigation, unless it is impossible for him to investigate, e.g. when a complaint is made in relation to general government policy or in relation to the general policy of the administrative authority involved. In such a case, he must communicate this fact to the complainant. There are several other grounds on which the Ombudsman should decline jurisdiction or may refuse an investigation.[109]

During the investigation, the ombudsman will give both the complainant and the respondent authority the opportunity to be heard. He may also hear witness testimony, bring in experts, visit any locations of importance with regard to the case, and request documents. Before the investigation is completed, the respondent authority is given the opportunity to present its views on the findings of the ombudsman.

At the end of the investigation, a final report is drawn up in which the ombudsman presents his opinion on the case and makes recommendations. Although these recommendations are not legally enforceable, they generally have significant influence on the administrative authority involved.

8. SUPERVISION AND ENFORCEMENT

8.1 Introduction

An important source of administrative litigation is the enforcement practice of administrative authorities (*handhaving*). In July 2009 Awb-IV entered into force and introduced some important changes to the rules on administrative supervision and enforcement, which will be discussed below. Most administrative authorities have various means at their disposal to enforce the obligations of citizens arising under statutes, regulations or previous orders within their domain. The most common ones are: (i) an instruction under threat of administrative coercion (*last onder bestuursdwang*), (ii) an instruction under threat of penalty payments (*last onder dwangsom*), (iii) an administrative fine (*bestuurlijke boete*), and (iv) withdrawal of a favourable order. Enforcement requires the finding of an infringement, which finding can only be made after supervision (*toezicht op de naleving*).

109. Arts 9:22 and 9:23 Awb.

It is important to note that the flipside of any supervisory or enforcement power of an administration or its designates is the obligation on the part of citizens to allow this power to be exercised, provided of course the conditions for its application are met. Any supervision or enforcement power requires an express statutory basis: the authority in question must be expressly empowered to exercise its supervisory or enforcement function (the legality principle). In order to harmonise the supervisory and enforcement powers created in numerous statutes for specific situations, Chapter 5 of the GALA contains some general provisions which statutes can refer to and build upon when granting further powers.[110] Therefore, the basis of most supervisory and enforcement actions is found in both individual statutes and the GALA.

A distinction is made between enforcement powers of a reparatory nature (reparatory sanctions; *herstelsancties*) and those of a punitive nature (punitive sanctions; *bestraffende sancties*). Both categories of power are referred to as sanctions. It is not always clear in which category a particular sanction should be placed: instruction under threat of administrative coercion and the instruction under threat of penalty payments are clearly reparatory sanctions, whereas an administrative fine is clearly a punitive one. But the withdrawal of a favourable order or the publication of the imposition of an administrative sanction have elements of both.

A related issue is whether an administrative sanction qualifies as a 'criminal charge' within the meaning of Article 6 of the ECHR or Articles 14 and 15 of the ICCPR.[111] The European Court of Human Rights has held that administrative sanctions can qualify as criminal charge,[112] depending on the nature of the offence and the severity of the punishment. As a result, the Dutch administrative courts have taken the case law on due process rules under the said articles into account when reviewing significant administrative fines and other punitive sanctions based on, *inter alia*, tax law, social security laws, competition law and other economic law and regulations.

8.2 General Provisions on Administrative Enforcement

Awb-IV introduced a title with general provisions and definitions of certain important legal concepts with regard to administrative enforcement, provisions on the content of decisions with regard to the imposition of a sanction (*sanctiebeschikking*), the principle of legality (*legaliteitsbeginsel*) and the concurrence of sanctions

---

110. Division 5.1 Awb contains an overview of general provisions on enforcement. Division 5.2 Awb contains an overview of supervisory powers. Division 5.3 deals with the reparatory sanctions: instruction under administrative coercion and instruction under threat of penalty payments. Division 5.4 deals with the administrative fines.
111. International Covenant on Civil and Political Rights of 16 December 1966, Trb., 1966, 99.
112. See, e.g., European Court of Human Rights 8 June 1976, NJ 1978, 223, LJN: AC0386 (*Engel*).

(*samenloop*). An offence (*overtreding*) is defined as a form of conduct in violation of a requirement under or pursuant to any statutory provision.[113] The terminology 'under or pursuant to' implies that not just violations of statutory provisions, but also violations of for example permit provisions will constitute an offence.

An administrative authority can only impose an administrative sanction when this authority is empowered to do so under or pursuant to a statutory provision. The general provisions laid down in Division 5.1 principally apply to the three enforcement instruments laid down in the GALA: instruction under threat of administrative coercion, instruction under threat of a penalty payment and an administrative fine.

8.3 Supervisory Powers

Whereas the power to enforce public law obligations is vested in the competent administrative authority, the power to supervise whether citizens actually observe their obligations is generally vested in the individuals designated by the authority competent to enforce the rules in question. The GALA refers to these individuals as supervisors (*toezichthouders*).[114] They are mostly, but need not be, employed by the authority competent to enforce the relevant obligations.

Administrative authorities are often endowed with the power to supervise such observance with one or more specific sets of regulations. These powers must be expressly conferred by or pursuant to statute. The GALA contains a catalogue of supervisory powers[115] which does not directly empower any supervisor. Rather, supervisors are empowered by specific legislation which refers to all or part of this catalogue in order to grant the relevant powers to the supervisors appointed in or pursuant to this legislation. Not only the applicable legislation, but also the competent authority, may limit the powers of the supervisors whom it has designated. Furthermore, any supervisor may only exercise his powers as far as is reasonably necessary in the performance of his duties (proportionality principle; *evenredigheidsbeginsel*).[116]

The first power mentioned in Division 5.2 of the GALA is the power to enter any place, with the exception of a private dwelling, in which case the consent of the occupant must be obtained.[117] The supervisor may do so alone or with individuals designated by the supervisor for this purpose (e.g. IT experts). If necessary, the police will accompany the supervisor. Furthermore, the supervisor is empowered to request information,[118] to inspect business records and documents,[119] to make copies

113. Art. 5:1 Awb.
114. Art. 5:11 Awb.
115. Title 5.2 Awb.
116. Arts 5:13 and 5:20 Awb.
117. Art. 5:15 Awb.
118. Art. 5:16 Awb.
119. Art. 5:17 Awb.

of relevant information (and take them away briefly for copying and inspection),[120] to inspect and quantify goods, to take samples and to inspect means of transportation.[121] Everyone, not just the addressee of an order, is obliged to render, within the term set by the supervisor, all cooperation reasonably necessary for the exercise of the supervisor's duties.[122] This obligation does not apply to the extent that the cooperation requested cannot be rendered without violating a professional or statutory duty of secrecy. To the extent that the supervisory powers are used in preparation of an administrative fine or other punitive sanction, the limitations imposed by Article 6 of the ECHR apply, including the right of a citizen to remain silent during questioning. After the coming into force of Awb-IV, this right to remain silent and the obligation to caution a person involved (*betrokkene*) before a hearing are laid down in the GALA.[123]

8.4 Instruction under Threat of Administrative Coercion

Most administrative authorities are empowered, by the legislation determining their jurisdiction, to impose an instruction under threat of administrative coercion.[124] Before Awb-IV came into force, the GALA contained a power for an administrative authority to rectify by their own action any infringement of a public law obligation arising under such legislation (administrative coercion). The former wording of the provision dealing with administrative coercion focused on the power of the administrative authority to take action to ensure compliance with the law. However, in practice the order authorising administrative coercion was not actually enforced because its mere publication was sufficient to incite an interested party to undertake the action required to rectify the infringement. To make sure that the wording of the provision corresponds with reality, the provision introduced by Awb-IV focuses on the instruction of the order (*last*) and the possibility to prevent action by the administrative authority by ending the violation itself.[125] According to the legislative history no material change of the law was intended.[126] Local governments and Ministries mostly apply this sanction in matters concerning land planning.

An instruction under threat of administrative coercion requires that the competent authority adopts an order in writing which sets out (i) the infringement itself, (ii) the time scale within which the infringement should be rectified by the offender

120. Art. 5:17 Awb.
121. Art. 5:18 Awb.
122. Art. 5:20 Awb.
123. Art. 5:10a Awb.
124. The general rules concerning the instruction under threat of administrative coercion are contained in part 1 of Division 5.3 Awb.
125. Art. 5:21 Awb.
126. MvT 29 702, No. 3, p. 100-101.

or by any other interested party,[127] and (iii) the fact that the costs for execution of the instruction under threat of administrative coercion will (generally) be recovered from the offender, in case the administrative authority rectifies the infringement by its own action.[128] The order must be addressed to the offender, to those entitled to use the object that may become the subject of the instruction under threat of administrative coercion, and to any third party who has complained about the infringement and requested the administrative authority to impose an instruction under threat of administrative coercion. Although the order does not create an obligation for any of the addressees to perform the actions described therein and merely states that, if the authority needs to take the action, the costs can be recovered from the offender, this should create an incentive for the offender to rectify the situation himself. As explained above, the mere imposition of the instruction is often sufficient to ensure compliance without the administrative authority taking action itself. It must be noted however that he may no longer be able to do so. For instance, if the offender has since sold the object concerned, he may no longer be at liberty to perform the necessary action. In such a case the new owner would be able to perform the necessary action and may have a strong interest in doing so to avoid the administrative coercion.

The instruction under threat of administrative coercion is subject to administrative review and, subsequently, judicial review. This instruction can be followed by two other decisions: a request to execute the administrative coercion (*beschikking tot toepassing van bestuursdwang*) and a decision on the costs of executing the administrative coercion (*kostenbeschikking*). To prevent numerous separate legal proceedings against these decisions, the legal protection against the instruction under threat of administrative coercion is combined with the other two decisions.[129] If rectification of the infringement is so urgent that there is no time to issue and publish an order in writing beforehand, this should be done as soon as possible thereafter.[130] In order to allow the authority's employees or contractors to carry out the necessary corrective action, certain specific powers have been created to enter premises, secure sites, buildings and fixtures on and in them, and to remove objects, if necessary.

8.5 Instruction under Threat of Penalty Payments

If, and only if, an authority is empowered by, or holds powers pursuant to, a statute to apply an instruction under threat of administrative coercion, it is also empowered to issue as an alternative a so-called instruction under threat of penalty payments

127. Art. 5:24 Awb.
128. Art. 5:25 Awb.
129. Art. 5:31c Awb.
130. Art. 5:31 Awb.

(*last onder dwangsom*).[131] The two powers may not be exercised simultaneously.[132] Instructions under threat of penalty payments can be used to deter future violations or to end ongoing violations. They are issued regularly by supervisory and regulatory authorities such as OPTA and AFM in specific economic sectors, as well as increasingly in environmental matters.

The penalty due if an instruction is not fully complied with may be either a lump sum or an amount for each violation or for each specified period in which the violation continues. Instructions issued to undo a past infringement or to prevent future infringement must specify a grace period (*begunstigingstermijn*) during which the instruction can be honoured while no penalty payments become due. The authority that has issued the instruction can, at the request of the offender, withdraw the instruction, suspend its duration for a certain period or mitigate the penalties, in the case of temporary or permanent inability to comply with the instruction in whole or in part. Furthermore, the rules set out above for the instruction under threat of administrative coercion apply likewise to the instruction under threat of a penalty payment.

8.6 Administrative Fine

The power to impose an administrative fine (*bestuurlijke boete*) has been provided for in many areas of administrative enforcement, such as those affecting taxation, social security, traffic violations[133] and in most, if not all, economic regulations, including competition law and financial services regulations. After Abw-IV came into force, Division 5.4 of the GALA contains general rules on enforcement by means of administrative fine. The Awb-IV introduces a set of general rules on the imposition of administrative fines broadly in line with those currently set out for instructions under threat of administrative coercion and for instructions under threat of penalty payments.

Division 5.4 of the GALA basically harmonises the regimes that had already been developed and that used to be set out in the individual statutes authorising specific authorities to impose administrative fines for certain types of violations. Division 5.4 of the GALA is divided into two parts: (1) general provisions, and (2) provisions regarding the procedure for imposing an administrative fine.

131. The general rules concerning the instruction under threat of penalty payments are contained in part 2 of Division 5.3 Awb.

132. Art. 5:6 Awb.

133. The enforcement of traffic violations has been entrusted to a newly created, highly automated division of the Ministry of Justice in order to alleviate the burden on the criminal justice system. The orders by which fines are imposed by this division are subject to administrative appeal (see § 3.1) to the public prosecutor in the district where the offence was (allegedly) committed, whose decision is, in turn, subject to judicial review by the cantonal division of the District Court. The rules governing these procedures are a mixture of criminal and administrative law.

In part 1 an administrative fine is defined as an punitive sanction constituting an unconditional obligation to pay a certain sum of money.[134] Other than in criminal proceedings, there is no requirement for the imposition of an administrative fine to be based on proof of intent or negligence: evidence of the facts constituting the infringement is sufficient, unless the alleged offender is completely blameless.[135] Awb-IV codifies the principle of double jeopardy (*ne bis in idem-beginsel*): an administrative authority is not allowed to impose an administrative fine twice for the same offence.[136] Furthermore, an administrative authority is not allowed to impose an administrative fine if criminal proceedings regarding the same conduct have started or a punishment order has been issued by a public prosecutor (*strafbeschikking*).[137] The maximum amount of an administrative fine has to be laid down in a statute. In case the amount of the administrative fine is not determined in statutory provisions, the administrative authority must take into account the seriousness and duration of the infringement, as well as the degree to which the offender can be blamed for the infringement. The rules on the imposition of administrative fines in specific statutes has been influenced significantly by obligations under Article 6 of the ECHR. The general provisions on administrative enforcement laid down in Division 5.1 of the GALA are also applicable to the imposition of administrative fines. As a result of the requirements of Article 6 of the ECHR, any order imposing an administrative fine can be made subject to administrative review by means of a notice of objection. The order issued after such review can subsequently be made subject to judicial review by the administrative courts in two instances. The courts can exercise a full review of the finding of the infringement and of the amount of the fine.

Part 2 deals with the procedure for the imposition of an administrative fine. There are two regimes for imposing an administrative fine: one for fines up to a maximum of EUR 340 and one for higher fines. The procedure for higher fines requires (i) the supervisors (the individuals so appointed by the competent authority) who have investigated the violation in question to draw up a report, and (ii) the competent authority to hear the offender's comments on the report and on the case in general. The decision imposing an administrative fine should mention the name of the offender and the amount of the fine.

8.7 Withdrawal of a Favourable Order

Some statutes expressly empower the competent authority to withdraw a particular favourable order in the event that the relevant regulations are not complied with. Favourable orders can be withdrawn without an express statutory basis in the case

134. Art. 5:40 Awb.
135. Art. 5:41 Awb.
136. Art. 5:43 Awb.
137. Art. 5:44 Awb.

that an order has been issued on the basis of incorrect information supplied by the party who requested the order or if this party should have reasonably understood the order to be incorrect. Except for the withdrawal of orders in which a subsidy has been granted, the GALA does not yet contain any general rules in this respect. As a withdrawal of a favourable order will only influence the legal situation and will not always have factual consequences, administrative coercion or an instruction under threat of penalty payments may be required to effect these.

8.8 Discretion in Relation to Enforcement

Although Dutch administrative law statutes rarely contain an obligation for the competent authorities to take enforcement action against an infringement that comes to their attention, case law has established that there is an obligation to enforce in principle (*beginselplicht tot handhaving*). Only under special circumstances may the competent authority decide to allow the infringement to continue (*gedogen*), for instance if the illegality of the situation is likely to cease to exist in the foreseeable future or if enforcement would be disproportionate.

A failure to enforce can appear in various forms: a mere inaction, an express refusal to enforce in response to a request for enforcement, an express policy to allow certain illegal situations to continue or even an express decision allowing a particular illegal situation for a certain period and (generally) under specified conditions. For such decision to be upheld, the courts require, *inter alia*, that it is foreseeable that the illegality of the situation is of a temporary nature. If one or more of the conditions set out in the decision to allow are violated, the authority is unable to enforce compliance with these conditions for lack of a statutory basis. However, the authority will be able to exercise its enforcement powers against the illegal situation that it previously allowed.

Glossary English to Dutch

Abuse of a procedural right	Misbruik van procesrecht
Administrative appeal	Administratief beroep
Administrative authority	Bestuursorgaan
Administrative coercion	Bestuursdwang
Administrative division of the District Court	Rechtbank, sector bestuursrecht
Administrative review	Bestuurlijke heroverweging
Advisory committee for objection proceedings	Bezwaarschriftencommissie
Annul (an agreement), to	Vernietigen (van een overeenkomst)
Appeal to the Supreme Court	Cassatie
Appellant	Appellant
Applicant	Verzoeker
Attachment	Beslag
Attorney	Advocaat
Attorney-general	Advocaat-generaal
Autonomous administrative authority	Zelfstandig bestuursorgaan
Binding force	Gezag van gewijsde
Cantonal division of the District Court	Rechtbank, sector kanton
Central Appeals Council	Centrale Raad van Beroep
Civil law notary	Notaris
Claimant	Eiser (burgerlijk procesrecht) / bezwaarmaker (bestuursprocesrecht)
Closing arguments	Pleidooi
Code of conduct (of the Dutch Bar Association)	Gedragsregels (van de Nederlandse Orde van Advocaten)

Complainant	Klager
Complaint	Grief
Complaints proceedings	Klachtenprocedure
Connectivity	Connectiviteit
Consolidation of cases	Voeging van zaken
Council for the judiciary	Raad voor de rechtspraak
Court approved scale of costs	Liquidatietarief
Court of Appeal	Gerechtshof
Court registry fee	Griffierecht
Cross-appeal	Incidenteel appel
Decision (administrative litigation)	Beschikking
Declaration of enforceability	Exequatur
Declaration of law	Verklaring voor recht
Default judgment	Verstekvonnis
Depositary receipt for a share	Certificaat van aandeel
Direct appeal	Rechtstreeks beroep (bestuursprocesrecht)
District Court	Rechtbank
Docket decision	Rolbeschikking
Docket judge	Rolrechter
Docket rules	Rolreglement
Doctrine of formal legal effect	Beginsel van formele rechtskracht
Enquiry proceedings	Enquêteprocedure
Enterprise Court	Ondernemingskamer
Escrow (into account of a state)	Consignatie
Examining magistrate	Raadsheer-commissaris
Executory attachment	Executoriaal beslag
Expert	Bindend adviseur / deskundige
Expert determination	Bindend advies
Expert opinion	Deskundigenbericht
Explanatory Memorandum	Memorie van Toelichting
Extrajudicial collection costs	Buitengerechtelijke incassokosten

Final and conclusive	Kracht van gewijsde, in
Follow-up proceedings for the determination of damages	Schadestaatprocedure
Forced exit proceedings	Geschillenregeling
Formal legal effect (doctrine of)	Formele rechtskracht (beginsel van)
General principles for proper administration	Algemene beginselen van behoorlijk bestuur
Indemnification proceedings	Vrijwaringsprocedure
Interim judgment	Tussenvonnis
Interlocutory application / motion	Incidentele vordering
Intervention	Tussenkomst
Joining of the litigation (in support of one of the parties)	Voeging
Judgment	Vonnis, arrest (burgerlijk procesrecht) / uitspraak (bestuursprocesrecht)
Large company	Structuurvennootschap
Legal entity	Rechtspersoon
Legal personality	Rechtspersoonlijkheid
Legality principle	Legaliteitsbeginsel
Letter of request	Rogatoire commissie
Lis pendens	Litispendentie
Litigation Division of the Council of State	Afdeling Bestuursrechtspraak van de Raad van State
Mandatory injunction	Gebod
Motion	Incident
Notice of objection	Bezwaarschrift
Objection	Verzet (bestuursprocesrecht)
Objection proceedings	Bezwaarschriftprocedure
Opposition	Verzet (burgerlijk procesrecht)
Order	Beschikking (burgerlijk procesrecht) / besluit (bestuursprocesrecht)
Personal appearance (after statement of defence)	Comparitie na antwoord
Petition	Verzoekschrift

Pre-judgment attachment	Conservatoir beslag
Prejudice of the right to take action	Verval van instantie
Preliminary expert's report	Voorlopig deskundigenbericht
Preliminary relief	Voorlopige voorziening
Preliminary relief judge	Voorzieningenrechter
Preliminary relief proceedings	Kort geding
Preliminary witness hearing	Voorlopig getuigenverhoor
(Dutch) private limited liability company	Besloten vennootschap met beperkte aansprakelijkheid
(Dutch) public limited liability company	Naamloze vennootschap
Proceedings on the merits	Bodemprocedure
Procurator-general	Procureur-generaal
Prohibitory injunction	Verbod
Proportionality principle	Evenredigheidsbeginsel
Provisionally enforceable (notwithstanding an appeal)	Uitvoerbaar bij voorraad
Public preparatory procedure	Uniforme openbare voorbereidingsprocedure
Removal from docket list	Royement
Rescind, to	Ontbinden
Respondent	Geïntimeerde / verweerder
Reviewed order	Beslissing op bezwaar
Revocation (of a judgment or an arbitral award)	Herroeping (van een (arbitraal) vonnis)
Right to decline to give evidence	Verschoningsrecht
Service (of process)	Betekening
Set aside (an arbitral award), to	Vernietigen (van een arbitraal vonnis)
Short statement	Akte
Specific performance	Nakoming
(Statement of) defence	Conclusie van antwoord
(Statement of) rejoinder	Conclusie van dupliek
(Statement of) reply	Conclusie van repliek

(Statement of) response	Verweerschrift
Squeeze-out proceedings	Uitkoopprocedure
Strongly connected	Verknocht
Supreme Court	Hoge Raad
Trade and Industrial Affairs Appeal College	College van Beroep voor het bedrijfsleven
Usufruct / holder of a right of usufruct	Vruchtgebruik / vruchtgebruiker
Withdrawal	Afstand van instantie
Writ (of summons)	Dagvaarding

Glossary Dutch to English

Administratief beroep	Administrative appeal
Advocaat	Attorney
Advocaat-generaal	Attorney-general
Afdeling Bestuursrechtspraak van de Raad van State	Litigation Division of the Council of State
Afstand van instantie	Withdrawal
Akte	Short statement
Algemene beginselen van behoorlijk bestuur	General principles for proper administration
Appellant	Appellant
Beginsel van formele rechtskracht	Doctrine of formal legal effect
Beschikking	Order (civil procedure) / decision (administrative litigation)
Beslag	Attachment
Besloten vennootschap met beperkte aansprakelijkheid	(Dutch) private limited liability company
Beslissing op bezwaar	Reviewed order
Besluit	Order (administrative litigation)
Bestuurlijke heroverweging	Administrative review
Bestuursdwang	Administrative coercion
Bestuursorgaan	Administrative authority
Betekening	Service (of process)
Bezwaarmaker	Claimant (administrative litigation)
Bezwaarschrift	Notice of objection
Bezwaarschriftencommissie	Advisory committee for objection proceedings

Bezwaarschriftprocedure	Objection proceedings
Bindend advies	Expert determination
Bindend adviseur	Expert
Bodemprocedure	Proceedings on the merits
Buitengerechtelijke incassokosten	Extrajudicial collection costs
Cassatie	Appeal to the Supreme Court
Centrale Raad van Beroep	Central Appeals Council
Certificaat van aandeel	Depositary receipt for a share
College van Beroep voor het bedrijfsleven	Trade and Industrial Affairs Appeal College
Comparitie na antwoord	Personal appearance (after statement of defence)
Conclusie van antwoord	(Statement of) defence
Conclusie van dupliek	(Statement of) rejoinder
Conclusie van repliek	(Statement of) reply
Connectiviteit	Connectivity
Conservatoir beslag	Pre-judgment attachment
Consignatie	Escrow (into account of a state)
Dagvaarding	Writ (of summons)
Deskundige	Expert
Deskundigenbericht	Expert opinion
Eiser	Claimant (civil procedure)
Enquêteprocedure	Enquiry proceedings
Evenredigheidsbeginsel	Proportionality principle
Executoriaal beslag	Executory attachment
Exequatur	Declaration of enforceability
Formele rechtskracht (beginsel van)	Formal legal effect (doctrine of)
Gedragsregels (van de Nederlandse Orde van Advocaten)	Code of conduct (of the Dutch Bar Association)
Gebod	Mandatory injunction
Geïntimeerde	Respondent
Gerechtshof	Court of Appeal
Geschillenregeling	Forced exit proceedings

Gezag van gewijsde	Binding force
Grief	Complaint
Griffierecht	Court registry fee
Herroeping (van een (arbitraal) vonnis)	Revocation (of a judgment or an arbitral award)
Hoge Raad	Supreme Court
Incident	Motion
Incidenteel appel	Cross-appeal
Incidentele vordering	Interlocutory application / motion
Klachtenprocedure	Complaints proceedings
Klager	Complainant
Kort geding	Preliminary relief proceedings
Kracht van gewijsde, in	Final and conclusive
Legaliteitsbeginsel	Legality principle
Liquidatietarief	Court approved scale of costs
Memorie van Toelichting	Explanatory Memorandum
Misbruik van procesrecht	Abuse of a procedural right
Naamloze vennootschap	(Dutch) public limited liability company
Nakoming	Specific performance
Notaris	Civil law notary
Ondernemingskamer	Enterprise court
Ontbinden	Rescind, to
Pleidooi	Closing arguments
Procureur-generaal	Procurator-general
Raad voor de rechtspraak	Council for the judiciary
Raadsheer-commissaris	Examining magistrate
Rechtbank	District Court
Rechtbank, sector bestuursrecht	Administrative division of the District Court
Rechtbank, sector kanton	Cantonal division of the District Court
Rechtspersoon	Legal entity
Rechtspersoonlijkheid	Legal personality

Rechtstreeks beroep (bestuursprocesrecht)	Direct appeal
Rogatoire commissie	Letter of request
Rolbeschikking	Docket decision
Rolrechter	Docket judge
Rolreglement	Docket rules
Royement	Removal from docket list
Schadestaatprocedure	Follow-up proceedings for the determination of damages
Structuurvennootschap	Large company
Tussenkomst	Intervention
Tussenvonnis	Interim judgment
Uitkoopprocedure	Squeeze-out proceedings
Uitspraak	Judgment
Uitvoerbaar bij voorraad	Provisionally enforceable (notwithstanding an appeal)
Uniforme openbare voorbereidingsprocedure	Public preparatory procedure
Verbod	Prohibitory injunction
Verklaring voor recht	Declaration of law
Verknocht	Strongly connected
Vernietigen (van een overeenkomst)	Annul (an agreement), to
Vernietigen (van een arbitraal vonnis)	Set aside (an arbitral award), to
Verschoningsrecht	Right to decline to give evidence
Verstekvonnis	Default judgment
Verval van instantie	Prejudice of the right to take action
Verweerder	Respondent
Verweerschrift	(Statement of) response
Verzet	Opposition (civil procedure) / objection (administrative litigation)
Verzoeker	Applicant
Verzoekschrift	Petition
Voeging	Joining of the litigation (in support of one of the parties)

Voeging van zaken	Consolidation of cases
Vonnis	Judgment
Voorlopig deskundigenbericht	Preliminary expert's report
Voorlopig getuigenverhoor	Preliminary witness hearing
Voorlopige voorziening	Preliminary relief
Voorzieningenrechter	Preliminary relief judge
Vrijwaringsprocedure	Indemnification proceedings
Vruchtgebruik / vruchtgebruiker	Usufruct / holder of a right of usufruct
Zelfstandig bestuursorgaan	Autonomous administrative authority

List of Abbreviations

ABRvS	*Afdeling Bestuursrechtspraak van de Raad van State* (Litigation Division of the Council of State)
AFM	*Stichting Autoriteit Financiële Markten* (Netherlands Authority for the Financial Markets)
Arbitration Act	Book 4 of the CCP on arbitration (Articles 1020-1076 CCP)
Awb	*Algemene Wet Bestuursrecht* (General Administrative Law Act)
Brussels Convention	EC Convention of 27 September 1968 on jurisdiction and the enforcement of judgments in civil and commercial matters, amended in 1978, 1982, 1989 and 1996
B.V.	*Besloten vennootschap met beperkte aansprakelijkheid* (Dutch private limited liability company)
BW	*Burgerlijk Wetboek* (Civil Code)
CCP	Code of Civil Procedure (see also Rv)
CJEU	Court of Justice of the European Union
EC Evidence Regulation	EC Council Regulation of 28 May 2001 on cooperation between the courts of the Member States in the taking of evidence in civil or commercial matters, No. 1206/2001
EC Regulation	EC Council Regulation of 22 December 2000 on jurisdiction and the recognition and enforcement of judgments in civil and commercial matters, No. 44/2001
EC Service Regulation	EC Council Regulation of 13 November 2007 on the service in the Member States of judicial and extrajudicial documents in civil or commercial matters, No. 1393/2007

ECHR	European Convention for the Protection of Human Rights and Fundamental Freedoms (also called European Convention on Human Rights), Rome, 4 November 1950
EEIG	European Economic Interest Grouping
EFTA	European Free Trade Association
EK	*Eerste Kamer* (Upper House)
EU	European Union
GALA	General Administrative Law Act (see also Awb)
1954 Hague Convention	Hague Convention on Civil Procedure of 1 March 1954
Hague Evidence Convention	Hague Convention on the Taking of Evidence Abroad in Civil or Commercial Matters of 18 March 1970
Hague Service Convention	Hague Convention on the Service Abroad of Judicial and Extrajudicial Documents in Civil or Commercial Matters of 15 November 1965
ICCPR	International Covenant on Civil and Political Rights of 16 December 1966
Lugano Convention	Convention on jurisdiction and the enforcement of judgments in civil and commercial matters of 30 October 2007
Model Law	Model Law of UNCITRAL 1985
MvT	*Memorie van Toelichting* (Explanatory Memorandum)
NAI	*Nederlands Arbitrage Instituut* (Netherlands Arbitration Institute)
New York Convention	Convention on the Recognition and Enforcement of Foreign Arbitral Awards, New York, 10 June 1958
NMa	*Nederlandse Mededingsingsautoriteit* (Netherlands Competition Authority)
NMI	Netherlands Mediation Institute
N.V.	*Naamloze vennootschap* (Dutch public limited liability company)
OJ. EUR.COMM.	Official Journal of the European Union
OPTA	*Onafhankelijke Post en Telecommunicatie Autoriteit* (Independent Telecommunications and Postal Authority)

RO	Wet op de Rechterlijke Organisatie *(Judicial Structure Act)*
Rome Convention	Convention on the Law applicable to Contractual Obligations, Rome, 19 June 1980
Rome I	EC Council Regulation of 17 June 2008 on the law applicable to contractual obligations (Rome I), No. 593/2008
Rome II	EC Council Regulation of 11 July 2007 on the law applicable to non-contractual obligations (Rome II), No. 864/2007
Rv	*Wetboek van Burgerlijke Rechtsvordering* (Code of Civil Procedure or CCP)
Stb.	*Staatsblad* (Official Statute Book)
Stcrt.	*Staatscourant* (Government Gazette)
TFEU	Treaty on the Functioning of the European Union as amended by the Treaty of Lisbon and in force since 1 December 2009
TK	*Tweede Kamer* (Lower House)
Trb.	*Tractatenblad* (Treaty Book)
Wbbo	*Wet bestuursrechtspraak bedrijfsorganisatie* (Act on Administrative Litigation for Trade Organisations)
WCAM	*Wet Collectieve Afwikkeling Massaschade* (Act on the Collective Settlement of Mass Damage)
Wob	*Wet openbaarheid van bestuur* (Public Access Act)
WRvSt	*Wet op de Raad van State* (Council of State Act)
WTFV	*Wet Toezicht Financiële Verslaglegging* (Act on the Supervision of Financial Reporting)

LEGAL JOURNALS

AB	*Administratiefrechtelijke Beslissingen* (Case law)
ARO	*Actuele Rechtspraak Ondernemingspraktijk* (Case law)
ECR	*European Court Reports* (CJEU case law)
JOR	*Jurisprudentie Onderneming & Recht* (Case law)
JBPr	*Jurisprudentie Burgerlijk Procesrecht* (Case law)

KG	*Kort Geding* (Case law, until 2004)
LJN	*Landelijk Jurisprudentie Nummer* (number given to all judicial decisions published in the Netherlands, most of them to be found on <www.rechtspraak.nl>), as from 1 January 2013 to be substituted by the ECLI (European Case Law Identifier)
NJ	*Nederlandse Jurisprudentie* (Case law)
NJF	*Nederlandse Jurisprudentie Feitenrechtspraak* (Case law)
NV, de	*Maandblad De Naamloze Vennootschap* (Journal on company law, until 1998)
Prg	*De Praktijkgids* (Case law)
RvdW	*Rechtspraak van de Week* (Case law)
TvA	*Tijdschrift voor Arbitrage* (Journal on arbitration)
TVVS	*Tijdschrift voor vennootschappen, verenigingen en stichtingen* (Journal on company law, until 1998)

International Litigation Contacts Allen & Overy LLP

AUSTRALIA
General Disputes
Anti-trust Litigation
White Collar and Regulatory Defence

• John Samaha
john.samaha@allenovery.com

BELGIUM
General Disputes
International Arbitration
Anti-trust Litigation
White Collar and Regulatory Defence
Employment Litigation
Intellectual Property Litigation

• Koen Van den Broeck
koen.vandenbroeck@allenovery.com

CZECH REPUBLIC
General Disputes
International Arbitration
Anti-trust Litigation
Securities Litigation
Employment Litigation

• Mikulas Touska
mikulas.touska@allenovery.com

CHINA
International Arbitration
Anti-trust Litigation
Employment Litigation
Intellectual Property Litigation
Local law restrictions apply

• Fai Hung Cheung
fai.hung.cheung@allenovery.com

FRANCE
General Disputes
International Arbitration
Anti-trust Litigation
White Collar and Regulatory Defence
Employment Litigation
Intellectual Property Litigation

• Dennis Chemla
dennis.chemla@allenovery.com

GERMANY
General Disputes
International Arbitration
Anti-trust Litigation
Employment Litigation
Intellectual Property Litigation

• Daniel Busse
daniel.busse@allenovery.com

HONG KONG
General Disputes
International Arbitration
Anti-trust Litigation
White Collar and Regulatory Defence
Employment Litigation

• Simon Clarke
simon.clarke@allenovery.com

HUNGARY
General Disputes
International Arbitration
Anti-trust Litigation
Employment Litigation

• Balázs Sahin-Tóth
balazs.sahin-toth@allenovery.com

ITALY
General Disputes
International Arbitration
Anti-trust Litigation
White Collar and Regulatory Defence
Employment Litigation
Intellectual Property Litigation

• Massimo Greco
massimo.greco@allenovery.com

LUXEMBOURG
General Disputes
Anti-trust Litigation
Employment Litigation
Intellectual Property Litigation

• Donata Grasso
donata.grasso@allenovery.com

• Vincent Naveaux
vincent.naveaux@allenovery.com

MOROCCO
General Disputes

• Yassir Ghorbal
yassir.ghorbal@allenovery.com

NETHERLANDS
General Disputes
International Arbitration
Anti-trust Litigation
White Collar and Regulatory Defence
Employment Litigation
Intellectual Property Litigation

• Marieke van Hooijdonk
marieke.vanhooijdonk@allenovery.com

• Peter Eijsvoogel
peter.eijsvoogel@allenovery.com

POLAND
General Disputes
International Arbitration
Anti-trust Litigation
Employment Litigation
Intellectual Property Litigation

• Jaroslaw Iwanicki
jaroslaw.iwanicki@allenovery.com

ROMANIA
General Disputes
International Arbitration

• Jane Townsend
jane.townsend@allenovery.com

SAUDI ARABIA
General Disputes

• Julian Johansen
julian.johansen@allenovery.com

SINGAPORE
International Arbitration
Employment Litigation
Local law restrictions apply

• Andrew Pullen
andrew.pullen@allenovery.com

SLOVAKIA
General Disputes
International Arbitration
Anti-trust Litigation
Employment Litigation
Intellectual Property Litigation

• Martin Magal
martin.magal@allenovery.com

SPAIN
General Disputes
International Arbitration
Anti-trust Litigation
White Collar and Regulatory Defence
Employment Litigation

• Antonio Vazquez-Guillen
antonio.vazquez-guillen@allenovery.com

THAILAND
General Disputes
International Arbitration
Anti-trust Litigation
Employment Litigation

• Dumnern Subpaisarn
dumnern.subpaisarn@allenovery.com

UNITED ARAB EMIRATES
International Arbitration
Employment Litigation
Local law restrictions apply

• Chris Mainwaring-Taylor
chris.mainwaring-taylor@allenovery.com

UNITED KINGDOM
General Disputes
International Arbitration
Anti-trust Litigation
White Collar and Regulatory Defence
Employment Litigation
Intellectual Property Litigation

• Tim House
tim.house@allenovery.com

UNITED STATES OF AMERICA
Commercial Litigation
International Arbitration
Anti-trust Litigation
White Collar and Regulatory Defence
Securities Litigation
Intellectual Property Litigation

• Michael Feldberg
michael.feldberg@allenovery.com

DUTCH BUSINESS LAW SERIES

1. Marieke van Hooijdonk and Peter Eijsvoogel, *Litigation in the Netherlands: Civil Procedure, Arbitration and Administrative Litigation*, 2012, 2nd edition (ISBN 978-90-411-4143-9)

2. Ferdinand B.J. Grapperhaus and Leonard G. Verburg, *Employment Law and Works Councils of the Netherlands*, 2009 (ISBN 978-90-411-2858-4)

3. Bas Jennen and Niels van de Vijver, *Banking and Securities Regulation in the Netherlands*, 2010 (ISBN 978-90-411-2863-8)